Resolution of Prison Riots

RESOLUTION OF PRISON RIOTS
Strategies and Policies

Bert Useem
Camille Graham Camp
George M. Camp

New York   Oxford
OXFORD UNIVERSITY PRESS
1996

Oxford University Press

Oxford   New York
Athens   Auckland   Bangkok   Bogota   Bombay
Buenos Aires   Calcutta   Cape Town   Dar es Salaam   Delhi
Florence   Hong Kong   Istanbul   Karachi
Kuala Lumpur   Madras   Madrid   Melbourne
Mexico City   Nairobi   Paris   Singapore
Taipei   Tokyo   Toronto

and associated companies in
Berlin   Ibadan

Copyright © 1996 by Oxford University Press, Inc.

Published by Oxford University Press, Inc.
198 Madison Avenue, New York, New York 10016

Library of Congress Cataloging-in-Publication Data
Useem, Bert.
   Resolution of Prison Riots / Bert Useem, Camille Graham
Camp, George M. Camp.
      p.   cm.
   Includes index.
   ISBN 0-19-509324-0
   1. Prison riots—United States—Case studies.   2. Prison
administration—United States—Case studies.   3. Prison riots—
Prevention.   I. Camp, Camille Graham.   II. Camp, George M.
III. Title.
   HV9469.U84   1996   95-32607
365'.641—dc20

1 3 5 7 9 8 6 4 2

Printed in the United States of America
on acid-free paper

Acknowledgments

This project was made possible by the financial support of the National Institute of Justice (Project Number 90–IJ-CX-0026) and the Federal Bureau of Prisons. Ms. Voncile Gowdy of the National Institute of Justice helpfully saw the project through.

The project was also made possible by the on-site corrections practitioners who opened many doors, and security gates, for us. Their commentary was forthright, insightful, and generous. Our every request for assistance and information was fulfilled. We would like to thank each by name but can not.

One group we do wish to thank by name is the directors of the agencies in which we conducted the research. They were unreservedly helpful in providing information, both written and from memory. We gratefully thank

Former Director J. Michael Quinlan, Federal Bureau of Prisons
Former Commissioner Thomas A. Coughlin, New York State Department of Correctional Services
Former Director Gary Maynard, Oklahoma Department of Corrections
Former Director Samuel Lewis, Arizona Department of Corrections
Former Commissioner Parker Evatt, South Carolina Department of Corrections
Former Commissioner Joseph Lehman, Pennsylvania Department of Corrections
Former Director Richard Vernon, Idaho Department of Corrections

Also, a number of individuals at the interview sites went above and beyond the call of duty in their assistance. Special gratitude goes to Warden Kenneth McKellar, South Carolina Department of Corrections; Superintendent Gary Filion and Crisis Intervention Unit Director Richard Roy, New York State Department of Correctional Services; Mr. George Miller, Idaho Department of Corrections; Superintendent Jeffrey Beard, Pennsylvania Department of Corrections; Director Dave Miller, Oklahoma Department of Corrections; Regional Director Sam Samples, Bureau of Prisons, Atlanta, Georgia; and Warden Roger Scott, Federal Corrections Institute, Talladega, Alabama.

We also thank the directors of each correctional agency in the United States who answered a survey at the start of this study. Their responses provided a sample of disturbances from which to choose. Professor Matthew Silberman, Bucknell University, helped make available transcripts of testimony given to two state legislative committees inquiring into the Camp Hill, Pennsylvania, riot. We very much appreciate his effort. Mr. Jeffrey Dupont helped prepare the figures.

The manuscript benefited greatly from comments by John DiIulio, Renie Dugan, Patrick O'Day, John Roberts, Patricia Useem, and especially Peter A. Kimball. David Gascon (LAPD) contributed indirectly but significantly to the final product. At Oxford University Press, editors David Roll and then Gioia Stevens helped see the project through. To all, a deep note of appreciation.

Albuquerque, New Mexico   *B.U.*
South Salem, New York   *C.G.C.*
                                                                 G.M.C.

September 1995

Contents

Authors' Note

We wish to express our special appreciation to Renie Dugan, Research Associate at the Criminal Justice Institute, for her commitment to the publication of this book. Involved in the project from beginning to end, she contributed significantly to the quality of the final product and we are deeply indebted to her for her persistence and thoroughness.

Resolution of Prison Riots

1

Introduction

It would seem that a prison should be less subject to riots than any other sort of place. Elsewhere—on the public streets, in the city squares, in shopping centers, at sporting events—people are free to discuss, initiate, and (to an extent) organize riots. Masses of people not previously known to the authorities may congregate and move about as they please; the police are constitutionally barred from taking many actions that might impede riots from developing.

In prison, the situation is different. The very purpose of the institution is to restrict and regulate the behavior of its inhabitants. The courts respect the authorities' comparatively broad powers to restrain movement and restrict speech. Authorities are permitted to know and to regulate the inmates' locations, associates, and activities at all times. The inmates' personal histories are known to the authorities. They are free to classify inmates, disperse them, group them together—in short, place each in the setting in which his or her behavior can most easily and most certainly be controlled, whether it be a work camp in a remote forest or a fortress of stone and steel. The greater the inmate's inclination to defiance, the more intense the regulation can be.

And yet prison riots are chronic. Two dozen or more times every year inmates seize and hold territory within prisons. In the course of the riot they may capture hostages, make demands, destroy property, or attack one another. Some of these disturbances last no more than an hour or two, some 10 days or more. These riots occur even, indeed especially, in those units where regulation is tightest and physical constraints are supposed to make riots impossible.

Prison riots are also costly to all involved. The tab for a single riot can exceed $100 million. The suffering imposed on the hostages can not be measured in money. Inmate perpetrators may have years of prison time added to their existing sentence. Inmate nonparticipants may lose work and program opportunities, or themselves be victimized during the riot.

This book is about reducing those costs, by avoiding violent disturbances; preparing to meet them; taking action to prevent the small incident from expanding into a full scale riot; limiting the extent or damage of riots in progress; and terminating riot situations in the least costly fashion.

Before the Riot

The importance of advance preparation in all its guises can not be overstated. The superior force that the state can muster after the riot has begun is no substitute for effort made in advance to maintain the institution's physical setting and the morale of its staff. It is the preexisting situation within the prison that is likely to determine whether a disturbance is easily contained, or whether it spreads to involve and endanger the entire institution. When "locked" gates have not stayed locked, safety precautions have not been carried out, or "unbreakable" glass has given way when clubbed by angry inmates, the cost of a riot in money and lives has mushroomed.

Rapid response in executing a riot-control plan can be crucial in minimizing harm to staff and inmates. If key places can be occupied in force shortly after the beginning of a disturbance, it can often be kept small and brief. When no quick response is available (likely in the absence of preparation), buildings, areas, housing units, and correctional staff may be engulfed in rapid succession.

Resolution strategies may fall short because the state's efforts become disorganized or its strategy unclear to those who must take action. Clausewitz's comment on the conduct of war applies equally to the control of prison riots: "Everything in war is very simple, but the simplest thing is difficult. The difficulties accumulate and end by producing a kind of friction that is inconceivable unless one has experienced war."[1]

As in war, the friction of prison riots often stems from the same sort of garden-variety snags that we experience in ordinary life, only multiplied by the pressures of the event: vehicles that break down, spent batteries in communication equipment, lost keys to doors or gates, unplanned delays in arrival, and messages that are garbled or not transmitted. Officers stationed in towers may, at the moment of truth, aim their weapons with far less precision than they did throughout qualification training. Some officers may freeze altogether. Command officers must handle these unpredictable problems as they arise, but their own mistakes may only add to confusion. Command may have a clear idea of what it wants done but issue orders that seem ambiguous or confusing to line officers.

The efforts at resolution often include both a negotiating component and the tactical means to retake the institution, whole or in part, by force. The tactical squad and negotiating team may each be well practiced. If, however, their training was conducted separately, the two units may find it difficult to coordinate their operations during a disturbance. Who, in any case, will direct the resolution efforts in the field and who has final authority over the resolution strategy: the warden, the director of the department, (in some jurisdictions) the regional director, or a higher political authority? This issue should be settled in advance, but sometimes it is not.

Successful resolutions require a controlled, measured response. Important are an orderly command post, clear lines of authority, effective communication, appreciation of the consequences of alternative lines of actions, and a sense among correctional officers that their skills and training are adequate to meet the challenge at hand.

During the Riot

Prison officials have three options to end a riot. They may order the forcible retaking of the prison (the tactical solution). They may end the riot through talking (the negotiation solution). Or they may let the riot die of its own accord (the waiting solution).

In actual riots, however, the boundaries between these strategies may break down and the options become indistinct. Negotiations can be used to collect information for a tactical assault or to tire and demoralize the inmates so they will surrender. A policy of waiting can be used to strengthen the administration's tactical capabilities or, if used in conjunction with deprivation of food, water, or electricity, to force inmates to bargain seriously. A visible tactical mobilization may permit inmates to see more clearly the consequence of failed negotiations or to tire and wear down their mental faculties. Still, at any given time, prison officials must commit themselves to one course or another, based on a calculation of its costs and benefits against the costs and benefits of other options.

However, in a prison riot of serious magnitude, these choices must be made in a complex and uncertain environment. Prison officials must assemble material and human resources from within the prison facility, from within the broader corrections agency, and (sometimes) from outside the agency. The viability and outcome of any particular course of action can be in serious doubt even (or especially) for a tactical course of action.

Furthermore, prison riots are public events. They are resolved under the eye of the media and top state officials. Officials' careers can be advanced or shattered by their choices, by the post hoc evaluation of their choices, or, indeed, by luck. One senior-level state official told us that those outside of command often make intemperate demands "to get it over with." Those who make such demands, he explained, fail to appreciate not only the potential costs of a tactical solution but also the practical difficulties in achieving it. One can not merely order a tactical solution that stays within reasonable costs any more than a general can order a military victory. Between the order and the desired results are formidable tasks, not the least of which is assembling the necessary resources and preparing the tactical teams.

Perhaps those who dogmatically demand an immediate assault (keeping in mind that a recommendation for immediate tactical assault is not always dogmatic) see resolving a prison riot as similar in principle (say) to removing a recalcitrant inmate from his cell. One simply brings overwhelming force to bear. But the two are not comparable. The force that can be brought to bear will undoubtedly be sufficient to retake the institution militarily, but if one intends in addition to prevent the deaths of staff, hostages, or inmates, then the task is much more difficult. (This is one of the lessons of the Attica riot that retains its force today.)

After the Riot

This period encompasses short-term problems associated with returning the prison to order, medium-term problems with repairing the damage and reestablishing work schedules, and long-term problems related to restoration and change.

By "short term" we mean the first 6–12 hours after resolution of the riot.[2] Injured or ill staff and inmates must be treated. The prisoner count must be cleared, and inmates must be searched for contraband and moved to secure areas. A failure to attend to these tasks can set the stage for another riot.

Another important task is to attend to the needs of hostages, providing the necessary medical attention and moral and psychological support. We shall see that some agencies are better prepared to handle the trauma of hostage taking than others. Not only are professional services, such as psychological counseling, required, but also the corrections leadership must demonstrate that they recognize the sacrifice required by hazardous duty. The moral and human elements of leadership are crucial to overcoming the personal suffering of hostages.

Finally, action during this period may be crucial to the state's determining what actually happened, either for purposes of an internal investigation or for the prosecution of the rioters. The processes of cleanup, dispersion of the inmates, and restoration of order may destroy evidence and taint the recollections of eyewitnesses and participants.

The medium-term problems include repairing damage to the physical plant, administrative follow-up associated with the disturbance, and returning employees to their normal work routines. The severity of these problems will depend, of course, on the duration and intensity of the riot. Inmates may destroy some or most of the prison's buildings. But, for their own reasons, they may choose to do otherwise, in which case reoccupancy may be possible soon after the riot is over.

The term "administrative follow-up" understates the substantive problems that officials may face. If employees file for disability, claiming to have been traumatized by the disturbance, what criteria will be used to grant it? Will disciplinary hearings be held for employees whose mistakes may have contributed to the takeover? Will the department initiate an investigation of the disturbance and, if so, with what resources and for what purpose?

The impact of the riot on staff morale is crucial. By staff morale we mean identification with the agency, respect for leadership, and commitment to the goals of the agency. Prison riots may undermine these attachments, or they may strengthen them. Much depends on how well prepared the department was and the effectiveness of the actions taken during the riot. After the riot, staff will ask, "Did management act to take control of the situation, or was it indecisive? Were the staff adequately trained, or were they allowed to drift into the situation unprepared?"

When handled properly, prison riots can bolster morale. Hours of preparation will have paid off. A new sense of unity may emerge, both within particular units and within the department as a whole, based not on mere speeches and symbolic gestures but on a shared crucial experience.

When handled improperly, a riot can damage a department's internal integrity. Staff may feel that lack of riot preparation was evidence of indifference to their safety. Poor judgment by management during the riot may be taken as evidence of lack of competence. Lack of support by the central office to the institution's superintendent during the riot may raise doubts about its concern for those outside the central office. If morale plummets, absenteeism and turnover can be expected to increase. There may be a flood of employees filing disability claims, even those who only witnessed the events and were not taken hostage.

There is also the question of what is to be done with the inmate participants. Can they be identified? Will participants be punished administratively or tried in the courts? In the latter case, has evidence and testimony been secured that will result in their being convicted? How will the institution deal with the stress of the trials? Will agreements made during negotiations be adhered to, or will they be ignored as "made under duress"?

While riots can be tragic events, they also challenge policy makers to rethink policies, procedures, structures, and commitments. After a riot, the organization may become more adaptable, allowing for innovation that otherwise would not be initiated. Those who want change can point to the riot as evidence of its necessity. Additional funds may be made available. Changes may be made to improve the agency's normal operations or to improve its riot response plans.

These opportunities may not be recognized, of course. A department may respond defensively, arguing that it did nothing materially wrong before the riot and that the occurrence is nothing more than can be expected from a population of hardened criminals. Alternatively, the riot, or its poor resolution, may be attributed to the blunders of a few. Funds may be more difficult to secure after the expenses of the riot are settled.

Approach to Research

To gain a greater understanding about how prison riots are resolved, we selected eight disturbances for in-depth study.[3] We then went directly to the scene of the disturbances to interview staff who had been involved in the resolution of the disturbance, to observe the areas in which the disturbance occurred, and to study relevant documents and reports. In most cases, we were able to view videotapes of the disturbance and its aftermath.

The individuals we interviewed on site were from all ranks of the institution and agency. We did not interview inmates who were in the facilities during the riots, but we gained their perspective through other reports in which their statements and opinions were presented, as well as through (in several cases) the transcripts of interviews on which those reports were based.

We talked at some length with a number of persons who had been taken hostage during the riots. These interviews gave us valuable insight into how the disturbances began and what happened in the inmate-controlled areas. Their moving recollections of their own personal experiences, nightmares that many of them live with to this day, attest to the tragic consequences when an institution is temporarily out of control.

The riots under study break naturally into two groups: protracted riots, those lasting more than a day (chapters 2 through 5); and contracted riots, those a day or less in length (chapters 6 through 9). The Camp Hill, Pennsylvania, riot was actually two riots, each less than a day in length, but we consider it a protracted riot because the riot situation lasted for three days.

In the final section, we present conclusions about the course of prison disturbances and strategies for their limitation and resolution.

I

PROTRACTED RIOTS

2

United States Penitentiary, Atlanta

November 23–December 4, 1987

This uprising by Cuban nationals lasted 11 days, involved more than 100 hostages, and required protracted negotiations to resolve. It occurred concurrently with a nine-day disturbance, also by Cuban nationals, at the Federal Detention Center, Oakdale, Louisiana. The combined cost of the two riots to the federal government was over $100 million. (Both the Atlanta and Oakdale facilities are part of the Bureau of Prisons [BOP], U.S. Department of Justice.)

Like the Attica riot of 15 years earlier, the Atlanta and Oakdale incidents became benchmarks against which to compare other prison disturbances and strategies to resolve them. The BOP itself undertook the task of redesigning its emergency response strategy based on what it learned from Atlanta and Oakdale. Those changes were put to the test in the summer of 1991 when Cuban detainees rioted at Talladega, Alabama (see chapter 3).

The account of the Atlanta disturbance begins with an incident that took place in 1980 at the Peruvian embassy in Havana, Cuba.[1]

History of Boatlift and Attorney General's Review Program

On April 1, 1980, a group seeking asylum crashed a bus through the gates of the Peruvian embassy in Cuba.[2] In an exchange of gunfire, a Cuban policeman was killed. Three days later, after the Cuban government removed its security force from around the embassy, 11,000 Cubans entered the tiny compound. Embarrassed by the international press coverage of thousands of citizens yearning to leave Cuba, the Cuban government announced that the port of Mariel would be open to anyone who wanted to leave the country. Over the next six months, 125,000 Cubans boarded small boats for the United States.[3]

A small portion of the exiles were mentally ill or had committed serious crimes in Cuba. The exact number was never known. According to one estimate, 16 percent of the Mariel refugees had spent time in Cuban jails, but their crimes ranged from minor infractions, such as petty theft or vagrancy, to politically motivated ones, such as opposition to the regime, to violent offenses, including murder.[4] In any case, allegations that Castro had used the flotilla to empty Cuba's jails and mental hospitals, though denied by the Cuban government, alarmed U.S. immigration officials and residents of Florida.

The Immigration and Naturalization Service (INS) set up a half-dozen processing centers in several states. By August 1981, the INS had released the vast majority of the Mariels (as the would-be immigrants came to be called) on "immigration parole." This allows aliens to be released into the community without formal admission into the United States. Immigration parole can be revoked for several reasons, most commonly for a criminal conviction.

The INS continued to detain about 1,800 Mariels as unfit to release in the United States. These "excludables" were moved to fourteen BOP prisons, including the facilities in Talladega, Alabama; Leavenworth, Kansas; Oxford, Wisconsin; Lewisburg, Pennsylvania; McNeil Island, Washington; and Atlanta, Georgia. In each facility, the unsentenced detainees were segregated from the general population of convicted felons. The detainees were provided separate living quarters, recreation, and meal service.

This arrangement proved unsatisfactory. The numerous small pockets of segregated Mariels were absorbing a disproportionate amount of staff time. More important, the detainees were very hard to manage, at least in this kind of arrangement. They assaulted one another and staff, engaged in self-mutilation, and committed or tried to commit suicide at very high rates compared to the BOP's other prisoners. Prison officials theorized that this was in part a carryover from their experience in Cuban prisons, now magnified by the detainees' uncertainty over their status in the United States.[5] It was also believed that their restricted environment was contributing to their failure to adjust.

The proposed remedy was to consolidate the detainees in one facility. The burden on the other BOP facilities would be eliminated, and the BOP could offer the Mariels a prison routine closer to what it provided most of its other inmates. Educational, work, and recreational programs could be increased and tailored to the special cultural needs and interests of the Mariels. Meals could be provided on a normal schedule. As another benefit, consolidation would allow the INS to process the Mariels more efficiently. In March 1981, the BOP relocated the Mariels to the U.S. Penitentiary at Atlanta.

Immigration judges began to hold hearings for the detainees at Atlanta, anticipating that those denied admission would be returned to Cuba. As it developed, however, the Cuban government refused to accept them. This response raised the question of whether the government should continue to imprison those slated for deportation and, if not, how they should be released. With the large number of cases to be handled, the attorney general established a review program in August 1981: Four two-member panels reviewed a detainee's file, interviewed him or her if the file did not support a finding of parole, and made a recommendation to the commissioner of the INS for a final decision. A detainee approved for parole would not be released until a suitable sponsor on the outside could be found.

In December 1984, the review program was interrupted. The U.S. State Department negotiated an immigration agreement with Cuba. Cuba would repatriate 2,746 detainees and, in return, the United States would issue up to 20,000 visas to Cubans. However, in May 1985, after only 200 detainees had been returned, Cuba suspended the agreement in a dispute over the start of Voice of America radio broadcasts to Cuba.

Meanwhile, the Atlanta penitentiary was becoming increasingly crowded. The review program resumed releasing those detained, eventually reducing to 210 the number who had remained in custody since first setting foot on U.S. soil. But the incoming Mariels exceeded in number those paroled. Most of the newly arriving detainees had been convicted of a crime, had served out their sentence in a state or local facility, and then had been turned over to the BOP.

A second development contributed to a short-term crowding problem at Atlanta. In 1984, the BOP entered into a consent order ending a protracted conditions-of-confinement suit. (The suit had been filed by U.S. citizen inmates in 1979 and was joined by Mariel detainees in 1981.) While the warden explained that the decree "was essentially a restatement of the Bureau's own internal policies,"[6] two large blocks had to be temporarily closed for renovation. In November 1986, the Oakdale Federal Detention Center was converted to a Cuban-only facility to absorb the spillover from Atlanta. Oakdale was considered a low–medium-security facility, because of its open, dormitory-style housing units and the absence of a segregation unit for disruptive detainees.

In the first part of November 1987, representatives from the Department of State and the Cuban government met in Mexico City to negotiate a reinstatement of the 1984 repatriation agreement. The Department of State kept the negotiations secret to all but a handful in its own agency. This was because negotiations a year earlier had broken down when their terms, leaked by a U.S. official, had appeared on the front page of the *New York Times*. If the new round of negotiations were to succeed, a State Department spokeswoman would later explain, they had to be conducted with the "utmost discretion."[7]

Although the Department of Justice was not the suspected source of the leak, the State Department did not inform its sister agency. The State Department assumed that, because the 1984 negotiations had not led to disturbances by the detainees, there was no reason to suppose the new negotiations would do so either: "The linkage . . . didn't seem to be there, just based on history."[8]

This position, however, assumed that the situations at Atlanta in 1984 and 1987 were roughly the same. They were not. In 1984, Atlanta was under a lockdown; that was not the case in 1987. In fact, through good behavior, the detainees had earned more freedom of movement than ever before. Also, even with improving prison conditions, detainees' hostility toward their legal situation may have festered in the three years between 1984 and 1987. With the State Department operating on a "strict need-to-know basis,"[9] the BOP did not have an opportunity to make its own evaluation of the danger of disturbance.

A treaty was signed on the evening of November 19, 1987. The Cuban negotiators told their American counterparts that Havana would announce the treaty at noon the next day. At about 8:00 A.M. on November 20, Assistant Secretary of State Elliot Abrams called Attorney General Edwin Meese to inform him of the agreement. Bureau of Prisons Director J. Michael Quinlan received a call a little after 10:00 A.M. A Miami television station broke the story by 11:00 A.M., an hour before the Department of State had scheduled its announcement (and an hour after the BOP had heard the news for the first time). Oakdale detainees seized control of their facility the next day, November 21, after a mass-escape attempt failed. Taking 36 hostages, the Oakdale inmates held the facility until November 29.

The Prison and Its Detainees

The U.S. Penitentiary, Atlanta, is located a few miles from downtown Atlanta. Residential neighborhoods border three sides and a factory is on the fourth. Opened in 1902, Atlanta had traditionally held inmates with long federal sentences, mostly from the Southeast. The prison was scheduled to close in 1980, but, with the influx of the Mariels and the growth of the federal prison population, those plans were canceled. In 1981, the prison began housing primarily Cuban detainees and a small number of U.S. citizen inmates. On the eve of the riot, there were 1,400 Cuban detainees and 200 citizen inmates.[10]

Prison Compound

A massive wall enclosed the 28-acre main compound. On the grounds were an administration building, a dining room/kitchen, a hospital, a recreation building, a large prison industry building, and 11 housing units (see Figure 2-1). On the eve of the disturbance, three cellhouses, A, C, and E (a segregation unit), housed the vast majority of Cuban detainees. In Cellhouse A, the cells were designed for four inmates but held eight at the time of the riot.[11] Detainees in Cellhouse C lived in cells of two. Another 170 Cuban detainees were housed in two dormitory units (Dormitories 1 and 2). One hundred eighty-one U.S.-born inmates lived in two other dormitory units (Dormitories 3 and 4). Cellhouses B and D were closed for renovation. On adjacent land was the BOP's southeast regional office. (The BOP manages its facilities through six regional offices.)

Conditions of Confinement

The history of the Atlanta penitentiary from 1981 to 1987 is primarily a history of improving conditions. During 1981, the first year that the de-

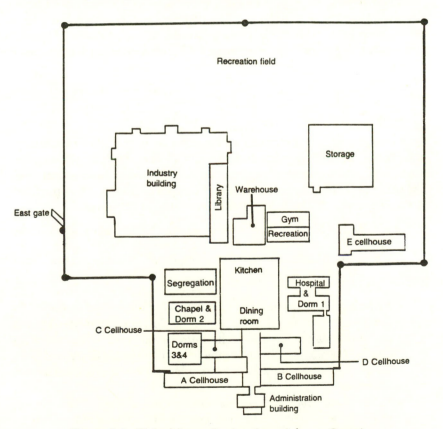

Figure 2-1   United States Penitentiary, Atlanta, Georgia.

tainees were housed at Atlanta, the prison was noisy and dangerous. The
initial high rates of assault, suicide, and self-mutilation among the inmates
did not abate, as had been hoped, with consolidation. In the cellhouses,
detainees dismantled the light fixtures in nearly every cell and used the
components to fashion weapons. Mattresses, sheets, and blankets were
routinely destroyed.[12] Gradually, however, the detainees began to adjust.
By 1982, the numbers of stabbings, suicides, and mutilations were lower.
In response, the detainees were given more freedom of movement and
increased work opportunities.[13]

In November 1984, detainees seized a cellhouse and held it for nine
hours. Large quantities of tear gas were used to end the disturbance.
Damage to the cellhouse and overtime salaries amounted to $1 million.
(This disturbance is further described below.) The prison was locked down
and remained so until the spring of 1986. Hostilities escalated during this
18-month period. Again, there were numerous assaults, self-mutilations,
staff and inmate injuries, and small disturbances.

Evidence of Atlanta's problems was heard by a congressional subcommittee in 1986. Mariels accounted for a third of the assaults against BOP
staff and half of those against inmates, even though they were only a small
fraction of total BOP population. The turnover rate for the Atlanta staff
was 20 percent, well above the average for the Bureau as a whole.[14] Based
on the tour of the facility, Committee Chairman Robert Kastenmeier
observed:

> the conditions under which these persons live are worse than those which
> exist for the most dangerous convicted felons. The conditions of confine-
> ment at Atlanta do not appear to meet minimum correctional standards.[15]

Then, during the year and a half leading up to the 1987 riot, conditions at the facility improved dramatically. A new warden upgraded the
prison's overall appearance. Recreation was expanded, new educational
and vocational training programs were introduced, and work opportunities were increased. The BOP's 1987 investigation of Atlanta

> [did] not find a litany of complaints concerning food, housing, medical care
> or other factors related to conditions of confinement. On the contrary, con-
> ditions prior to the disturbances were very good at Atlanta and at Oakdale.[16]

Additional data support this assertion:

- *Reduction in the number of assaults and other serious incidents*. In
  the 17-month period leading up to the riot, when compared to the
  previous 17-month period, the number of inmates assaulted decreased from 85 to 48, the number of staff assaulted decreased from
  73 to 43, and the number of homicides and suicides dropped from
  six to three.
- *Reduced turnover rate among correctional officers*. The turnover
  rate among correctional officers at the facility was reduced to 16
  percent, no longer significantly above the average rate for the BOP.

• *Security audit suggested few deficiencies.* In October 1987 the BOP regional office conducted a security audit of the prison. Several deficiencies were found, but overall, the prison met the BOP's standards for security.

Thus, on the eve of the disturbance, the prison appears to have been well managed, the conditions of confinement were far better than they had been in recent history, and the detainees were responding favorably to the improved conditions.

From this set of facts, the BOP's *Report* draws the conclusion that the underlying causes of the Atlanta/Oakdale riots are unique. The Atlanta disturbance, in particular,

> did not result from issues related to the conditions of confinement which, historically, have been responsible for most mass disturbances in American prisons. Rather, the disturbance was precipitated by events [the repatriation agreement] over which the Bureau of Prisons had no control.[17]

While we think the BOP's conclusions are factually correct, we do not think that these causes are unique, as they conclude. Their position overlooks two important continuities between the events leading up to Atlanta and the causes of other mass disturbances in U.S. prisons.

History of Collective Violence among Detainee Population

During the six years leading up to the 1987 riots, the Cuban detainees engaged in numerous episodes of collective protest and violence. This is important because, in general, the willingness of inmates to engage in collective violence is not (in our view) a direct function of "bad" conditions. Some inmates rebel against perceived poor conditions or injustices, but others do not. For example, inmates in the early 1970s were far more likely to resort to riotous means than those in the early 1960s; inmates in some regions of the country were more disposed to violence than those in other regions. This variation cannot be explained by differences in prison conditions alone.

Soon after their initial detention, the Mariels began what would be a sustained history of collective violence. Some detailing of these disorders will be useful in conveying their persistence and seriousness. By April 1980, there were mass escape attempts at the INS processing center at Eglin Air Force Base, Florida, and hunger strikes at Atlanta.[18] In June, 1,000 Cuban detainees rioted at the INS processing center at Fort Chaffee, Arkansas. They burned five buildings and attempted to storm the front gates. This riot lasted two hours, with one detainee killed and 40 detainees and 15 state troopers injured.[19]

Later, in the summer of 1980, there was a major riot at the INS processing center at Fort Indiantown Gap, Pennsylvania.[20] The 82nd Airborne Division was flown in from Fort Bragg, North Carolina, to control the disturbance. Demonstrations by Cubans occurred at federal prisons at

Leavenworth, Oxford, and Atlanta. These were followed by a riot at the federal prison at Fort McCoy, Wisconsin, in which four staff members and 20 Cubans were injured. A disturbance occurred at the federal prison at Terre Haute, Indiana, and a second riot occurred at Fort Indiantown Gap, Pennsylvania. In November 1983, a group of about 15 detainees at Atlanta began a hunger strike to protest their continued detention. Two of them persisted for more than 50 days.[21]

Collective protest and violence erupted again in 1984. In October of that year, 75 detainees were grouped in the recreation yard at Atlanta. They unfurled a banner with the slogan "Liberty or Death" and waved other prison-made signs calling for a prisoners' strike. Correctional officers cordoned off the protestors from the other inmates on the yard and then escorted them into a building to be searched. Some inmates scuffled with correctional officers.[22]

The prison was locked down after the incident. Over the next two weeks, the lockdown was gradually lifted and activities returned to normal. On November 1, a detainee who had emerged as a protest leader was ordered into segregation. Along the way, he was allowed to retrieve some personal property from his cell in Cellhouse B. As he entered the block, the detainee pulled away from his staff escorts, leaped over the railing to the next level, and yelled for other detainees to join him. They did and, carrying pipes, advanced on correctional officers. The officers were able to avoid injury, but only by evacuating the block.

Inmates controlled the unit for the next nine hours. They burned sheets and towels, shattered windows, shouted slogans, and hung banners from windows demanding their freedom. Finally, at about 3:00 A.M., large quantities of tear gas were used to force the inmates out of the unit.[23] As noted above, the entire facility was locked down for the next 18 months.

Finally, in July 1985, detainees in temporary custody at the Brooklyn Correctional Facility rioted, resulting in injuries to 14 correctional officers and 12 detainees.[24] A month later, 65 Cuban detainees in a federal detention center in Florence, Arizona, rioted.[25] They held three of the prison's four cellblocks for 14 hours, destroying much of the prison.

In sum, the Cuban detainees had engaged in collective violence relatively often over a number of years; they had become experienced at it. In this respect, there is continuity between Atlanta and other prisons that have had major disturbances.[26]

Breakdown of Legitimacy of Imprisoning Criteria

A second similarity between the situation of the detainees and that existing before some other major prison riots is that the detainees did not see their confinement as legitimate.

Most inmates most of the time accept as legitimate the imprisonment of their fellow inmates.[27] They may protest their own convictions, but, at the same time, they believe that the other inmates are guilty of crimes, deserve prison sentences, and ought not to be discharged en masse. In uncommon periods, however, these beliefs may be challenged. When this occurs, it is a short step from the claim that imprisonment is arbitrary to the belief that rebellion is justified. This chain of reasoning became prevalent in some prisons in the early 1970s, contributing to the most serious wave of prison riots in U.S. history.[28] It also developed at Atlanta.

Throughout the period under consideration, critics charged that the review program was neither rational nor fair. It was not rational (they said) because, contrary to government claims, many detainees were not a threat to public safety, having been convicted of only minor crimes. In fact, they should be viewed as refugees from tyranny and lovers of freedom. It was not fair because the review program was said to lack the due process safeguards that would allow detainees to rebut the charges against them.

Along these lines, judicial scholars wrote articles in law journals,[29] advocacy groups tried to sway public opinion, and congressmen gave speeches on the floor of the House.[30] In July 1987, 13 congressmen (most with strong civil-rights credentials) wrote the commissioner of the INS to complain about the "indefinite detention" of the Mariels, suggesting that they would introduce legislation unless something were done.[31] (The riot occurred before a response from the INS was received.)

INS and Department of Justice officials defended their position, arguing that INS had both the authority and duty to detain dangerous aliens who cannot be deported. The review program, they asserted, had reasonable due process safeguards. To rebut the charge that the government was indefinitely detaining excludables, the government pointed to diplomatic efforts underway to reinstate the 1984 agreement.[32]

The debate was played out in litigation extending over a number of years. The federal judiciary was not united on the issues. A federal district judge in Atlanta ruled time and again that detainees have limited due process rights, and ordered that the detainees be given case-by-case judicial hearings. These rulings were just as consistently vacated by the 11th Circuit Court of Appeals, with those reversals later upheld by the Supreme Court.

The higher courts ruled that the detainees have no constitutionally protected rights because, technically, they had not entered the country. From this it followed that immigration hearings were an administrative, not a judicial, matter. The critics saw irony in this. Mariels charged with a crime had the same constitutional rights as any citizen to defend themselves against those charges. Yet once convicted and having served their sentences, they could be held for deportation without further recourse to the courts.

The practical force of this discord is illustrated by the outcome of the jury trial of two leaders of the 1984 riot. During the trial, several correctional officers testified that they had witnessed the defendants carrying homemade knives and exhorting their fellow prisoners to riot. The presiding federal judge would later say that, in his view, there was ample evidence to authorize a guilty verdict.[33] Yet the jury voted to acquit. Jurors explained both to the judge and to the press that they had, in effect, pardoned the two defendants because they were "incensed that people would be incarcerated for years on end without a meaningful hearing."[34]

It seems likely that the lessons of the trial, as well as the wider controversy, were not lost on the Atlanta detainees. Detainees seeking to justify their rebellious impulses could lean on supportive statements, not merely from political outsiders and dissidents but also from respected officeholders, including federal judges and some congressmen. If a jury of Atlanta citizens found the 1984 riot excusable, detainees might have reasoned, would not an additional three years of incarceration provide additional justification for direct action? A riot would not be the detainees' fault, in a moral sense, but rather the inevitable outcome of misguided government policy.

Preriot Situation

At about 10:30 A.M. on Friday, November 20, 1987, BOP Director Quinlan called the regional director in charge of Atlanta to tell him that the United States and Cuba were reinstating the 1984 treaty. The treaty would permit the repatriation of 2,500 Cubans. Still undetermined was the number of Atlanta detainees who would be among them. The regional director called the warden, who in turn assembled his management staff, consisting of associate wardens, department heads, and unit managers. This began a 72-hour period in which the entire chain of command, from Director Quinlan to line staff, exchanged information and worked intensely to avoid a disturbance.

The key issue, as viewed throughout the three-day period and in postriot analyses, was whether to lock down the facility. As the *Report* points out, this was not a single decision made at one time, but an option reassessed time and again throughout the three-day period.[35] The decisions were made by the warden with the advice of his closest advisors and the concurrence of the director and regional director. The *Report* also cautions that "hindsight is 20/20 vision."[36] In fact, hindsight provides somewhat less than perfect vision. Even with its unfair advantage, one is hard-pressed to identify a strategy that would, with some measure of certainty, have avoided the disturbance that was to come. Still, as we shall see, the process of collecting information and making decisions was flawed.

Decision makers in the situation had to weigh several competing considerations. First, prison officials felt that there was a reasonably good chance that they could talk their way out of the situation.[37] Staff could rely on the positive relationships they had developed with the detainees to calm fears and soothe tempers. This was the strategy taken to contain the situation from Friday afternoon, November 20, until about an hour before the disturbance. On Friday afternoon, the superintendent of industries was told that talking to the 1,000 detainees under his supervision should take precedence over production. Over the weekend, extra staff were called in with instructions to talk to inmates in an attempt to avoid a disturbance.

However, the effectiveness of a talking solution depends not only on preexisting trust but also on what can be said. Here prison officials were in a weak position. Based on information provided by the INS, the staff told the detainees that only 95 Atlanta detainees would be returned to Cuba. Apparently, few detainees believed this. The door for speculation had been opened, not closed, by the reassurance that only a "handful" of Atlanta detainees would be among the 2,500 slated for deportation. (After the riot began, the INS changed the number to 350.[38])

Second, even if detainees accepted the figure of 95, this would not necessarily preclude a disturbance. If 95 angry detainees started a disturbance (either those actually slated for deportation or others with a mistaken belief that they were among them), additional detainees might be willing to join an ongoing disturbance. The riot would expand geometrically.

Third, the warden thought that a lockdown might provoke a riot.[39] On one hand, the detainees might see a lockdown as the last straw, prompting them to rebel. On the other, there was no guarantee that a lockdown would physically prevent a riot. More than 170 detainees were housed in dormitory units in which inmates could not be confined to cells. While it might be pointed out that these detainees were the prison's lowest security risks, the risks posed by Oakdale's inmates (who began their riot on Saturday, November 21) were considered to be even lower, so this was no guarantee. Further, because two of the prison's four cellhouses were closed for renovation, the remaining two cellhouses were far over capacity. Finally, 123 detainees in Cellhouse E (segregation) were already locked down. Their cell doors, however, were in disrepair and might be knocked out during a disturbance.[40] In short, the warden believed that a lockdown did not foreclose the possibility of a riot and might provoke one.

Fourth, prison officials were keenly aware of the potential long-term costs of a lockdown. The lockdown imposed after the November 1984 riot took 18 months to lift, a costly period for detainees and staff alike. Much progress had been made since the lockdown had been lifted. Education programs had been introduced and work opportunities expanded. Prison officials were concerned that a lockdown would reverse those gains.[41]

Finally, in meetings with his executive staff and department heads throughout the weekend, the warden received reassuring reports.[42] The detainees, he was told, were not unusually hostile or uncooperative toward staff. Weekend recreation and meals were normal and without incident. Only one inmate requested to be locked in segregation over the weekend and there was no increase in commissary purchases. Surprisingly, on Saturday night, detainees seemed indifferent to the television news of the Oakdale riot.[43] The warden would later comment that it did not make sense to lock down the prison when "the atmosphere and attitude were so good."[44]

However, while the reports to the warden gave no hint of a riot, the information being collected by and disseminated among line staff and first- and second-level supervisors was that a riot was likely, imminent, and probably planned. Several events occurred during the weekend:

- A correctional officer overheard several detainees talking about taking hostages and helping their brothers in Oakdale. The officer prepared a memorandum on the conversation for the shift lieutenant (the senior officer in charge of the shift).[45]
- The outgoing mail was much heavier than normal.
- Several Spanish-speaking officers were advised by detainees not to come to work on Monday and that the factory might be burned and hostages taken; this, too, was transmitted to the lieutenant's office.
- Several detainees sent notes to the lieutenant's office warning of trouble.
- A correctional officer was told by a U.S.-born inmate that the Cuban detainees planned to seize the factory building on Monday morning; this information was recorded on a confidential report form and forwarded to the lieutenant's office.

In fact, many prison inmates were whispering warnings to correctional officers. "It was in the air," one correctional officer later explained. "We had a pretty good idea that something was going on."[46]

Apparently, much, if not all, of this information did not reach the warden. The *Report* describes this as a result of an "unexplained communication problem." The *Report* goes on to speculate that

> one possible explanation could be that the Atlanta Administration had become desensitized to detainees' threat to riot. During numerous occasions throughout the past seven years . . . Atlanta staff had received information or intelligence that the Cuban detainees were going to take over the Building [industry] the next day, only to have normal operations.[47]

That warnings had become fairly commonplace might explain a tendency to dismiss them as without foundation. More difficult to explain, however, is why those warnings and supporting information were not *transmitted* to the warden, who could then make his own assessment of the detainees' disposition (angry or accepting), organization (unified behind leaders, splintered, or leaderless), and, if possible, intentions (planning a riot or not). Too many features of the situation suggested that the warnings were anything but routine: the signing of the repatriation agreement, the riot at Oakdale by inmates considered less dangerous than those at Atlanta, and the sheer volume and consistency of the threats.

It may be that the warden did not receive the warning signs because they were filtered out of reports as they moved up the chain of command. Over an 18-month period, he and his associates had worked hard to lift the 1984 lockdown and develop programs for the detainees. Their management strategy was one of "openness," as BOP researcher Peter Nacci characterizes it, and it had achieved success.[48] A lockdown might reverse the hard-won gains. Subordinates may have been tempted to provide only that information they felt the warden and his immediate staff wished to hear. Any coloring of reports would not have been a deliberate effort to distort information—that was in no one's interest—but, rather, would have stemmed from the perceived priorities of the warden. Since the warden was relying predominantly on second-hand reports, he was not in a position to catch this, although one could argue that he could have inquired more or observed firsthand the situation in the cellblocks.

In any case, the warden later told BOP investigators that he would have locked down the facility if he had known that a riot was developing, but he did not.[49]

On Sunday night, November 22, the warden and his executive staff left the prison at about 8:00 P.M. with the understanding that the prison would begin its normal operations at 5:45 A.M. for breakfast, unless indications of serious problems surfaced that night. In fact, during the night several officers stated their alarm in confidential report forms.[50] One officer reported that, in conducting the 3:00 A.M. count, he observed that over half the detainees had remained dressed. Another officer reported that a work detail of U.S. inmates initially refused to go to work as scheduled at 4:30 A.M.

Having received these and other alarming reports, the lieutenant in charge of the midnight to 8:00 A.M. shift was reluctant to unlock the housing units for breakfast. If the inmates were released for breakfast and their work details, any lockdown ordered would have to wait until later in the day. He phoned the associate warden to express his concern.[51] The associate warden came to the facility, according to the lieutenant, and gave the order to open the units for breakfast at 5:45 A.M. In postriot interviews, however, the associate warden denied that he received a call from the lieutenant, discussed the lieutenant's concern once he arrived at the prison, or even ordered the prison to begin its normal operations.[52] Regardless of who authorized it, the detainees were released from their cells for breakfast.

The warden met with his top staff at 6:00 A.M.[53] He explained that, during the day, prison staff were to circulate among detainees to reassure them as best they could. According to the warden, no information surfaced at this meeting that would suggest a riot might begin soon.

At 7:30 A.M., the warden held over the 30 officers from the midnight shift, assigning them the task of talking to inmates. Yet by 8:30 A.M., new warning signs began to appear. The detainees were slow reporting for breakfast, and most were wearing tennis shoes rather than the normal work shoes.[54] A correctional counselor received a note stating "there is going to be a riot at 10:30 today with hostages, with people getting hurt, and Industries burning."[55] In the kitchen, an inmate clerk told the food service administrator that he should not have come to work that day.[56] Another detainee told his work supervisor that the female staff should be kept out of the building that day.

About 9:00 A.M., the warden apparently reached the conclusion that the prison was on the brink of a disturbance. At 9:15, he ordered the evacuation of female employees from the main compound, which was completed by 9:45. In addition, 30–40 off-duty staff were called in to be available for deployment in a riot control squad. As they began to arrive, the riot broke out.

Riot Initiation and Expansion

The riot began in three locations—in the industry building, in the dining room, and on the yard—all at about the same time, roughly 10:30 A.M. Emergency alarms were sounded in all three locations. Correctional officers rushed to respond, but they were unable to control the hundreds of detainees joining the rebellion. One supervising officer on the scene later stated that "99 percent" of the detainees were participating.[57]

Detainees took hostages wherever they could. The largest number were seized in the industry building (25 staff) and dining hall (19 staff). On the yard, hundreds of detainees chased and tried to grab staff before they could escape. Fleeing staff were afforded some protection by officers in towers. A tower officer shot and killed a detainee as he was pursuing an officer with a large knife. Five other detainees were shot and wounded as they threatened to assault officers. One group of detainees charged the prison's east gate (one of the prison's two operating exits) but was stopped by warning shots from a tower.

About seven minutes into the incident, the detainees positioned a correctional officer on the yard where he could be seen by officers in the towers. He was forced to yell to the towers that hostages would be killed if the shooting continued. The officers stopped firing.[58]

Twenty minutes into the disturbance, a group of detainees passed through a sally port (a small antechamber with steel grilles at both ends) to a locked grill that led onto the main corridor from the administration building. They used makeshift machetes to jab at officers on the other side of the grille, while one used a key taken from an officer to try to unlock the grille. The officers fought back, first with riot batons and then with tear gas, and the detainees retreated.[59]

This confrontation marked the farthest expansion of the riot. Officials retained control of the main corridor, Cellhouse A, and the administration building. Everything else inside the perimeter wall was in the detainees' hands. Cellhouse E and the hospital were the exceptions; for a time they were in limbo (see Figure 2-2).

Figure 2-2 The United States Penitentiary in 1993, six years after the 1987 disturbance. The Administration Building is at the front of the institution, and behind it are the main cellblocks (Cellhouse A on the left and Cellhouse B on the right of the longest building, and Cellhouses C and D at the right and left, respectively, of the shorter building in back of that). The square building with the cupola behind Cellhouse C and D is the institution's kitchen and dining room; to the right of that are the hospital, hospital annex, and Dorm 1. During the disturbance, the hospital continued to function as a medical facility, though the staff considered themselves the hostages of the inmates in the building. Cellhouse E, the institution's segregation unit, was located at the lower right corner of the perimeter wall; the building has since been demolished. The UNICOR (industry) building, at the back left of the compound, was seriously damaged in the riot and has been replaced with the new whiteroofed structure. Media were able to situate themselves on the private property across the street from the institution (by 1987, the area had become more developed and commercial), which became a complicating factor during the incident. *Source*: Federal Bureau of Prisons, U.S. Department of Justice.

Sixteen staff members were trapped in Cellhouse E, the segregation unit. While staff maintained control within the unit, rioters on the yard prevented them from escaping. Detainees approached the cellhouse several times, threatening to kill hostages unless they were given entrance. Officers in the tower responded that they would use lethal force if the rioters tried to gain entrance into the block, and, in fact, the rioters made no such attempt.

Another 26 staff were trapped in the hospital, including physicians, medical assistants, correctional staff, several contract employees, and about a dozen detainees who worked as orderlies. Whether, or when, the staff in the hospital became hostages later became a matter of dispute. For the first several days, the command center did not include the hospital staff in its list of hostages, even though they were not free to leave. In postriot interviews, some staff stated that they considered themselves to be the hostages of the orderlies from the outset. Still, staff outnumbered the orderlies more than two to one and maintained control of the key to the exterior door.

In any case, throughout the 11 days, staff continued to operate the hospital as a medical facility. Only detainees needing treatment were admitted. The pharmacy was not looted, and all medications were dispensed by a pharmacist under a doctor's orders. In essence, the building was held hostage, but the staff inside it continued to provide medical treatment unimpeded.

State of Siege

The detainees controlled the prison from midday on Monday, November 23, until early morning on Friday, December 4. This 11-day period can be divided into three phases. In the first phase, Monday afternoon through Thursday (Thanksgiving) evening (November 23–26), detainees and officials negotiated agreements to end the disturbance, only to have the agreements collapse. In the second phase, from Friday through the following Wednesday (November 27–December 2), government negotiators took a "harder" position in their negotiations. This stance yielded an effective settlement on Thursday afternoon, December 3, marking the start of the third phase. The remainder of Thursday and early morning on Friday, December 4 were taken up by putting the final touches on the agreement and arranging a surrender.

Phase 1: Monday through Thanksgiving Thursday (November 23–26)

The BOP regional director for the Southeast region arrived at the prison within 10 minutes of the onset of the riot and immediately contacted the director in Washington, D.C., by telephone. Other prison officials began to collect information about the hostages' condition and location. From everything they could learn, the hostages were unhurt. Damage to the physical plant mounted, however. Fires were started at about 11:00 A.M. and burned until late evening. Several fire companies responded with equipment, and later a National Guard helicopter dropped water using forest fire buckets, but all to no avail. The industry building, a warehouse, and the recreation center were destroyed by fire.

At 5:30 P.M., the director, regional director, warden, and FBI officials concluded that the 16 BOP employees trapped in Cellhouse E could be safely rescued. An FBI Special Weapons and Tactics (SWAT) team threw rope ladders over the compound's wall and positioned themselves to provide cover for the employees who then escaped.

A plan to rescue hospital staff was under continual consideration both in Atlanta and in Washington throughout the 11 days of siege but was never carried out because of its risks. The hospital, unlike Cellhouse E, was located in an area where detainees congregated. The concern was that if force had to be used during a rescue effort, the detainees would retaliate against the other hostages. Further, the element of surprise in any rescue effort might be compromised. Television crews were broadcasting live pictures of the prison's perimeter. Throughout the siege, detainees (and hostages) watched this coverage almost continually. Finally, the hospital was maintaining its integrity as a medical facility, serving the needs of those inside the compound. This lessened the necessity (perhaps even desirability) of a rescue.

NEGOTIATIONS START

The situation at Atlanta was materially influenced by the government–detainee negotiations that had already begun at Oakdale. On Sunday night, November 22, U.S. Attorney General Edwin Meese sent Oakdale detainees a letter responding to their verbal demands.[60] The letter offered to impose a moratorium on the deportation of Mariel detainees at Oakdale and at "all other" detention centers.[61] The moratorium would permit a "full, fair, and equitable review" of each detainee's eligibility to stay in the country. In return, it was expected that the hostages would continue to be treated "fairly and safely" and released without delay. On late Monday afternoon, the attorney general held a news conference in which he reiterated his offer to the Oakdale detainees and extended it to those at Atlanta. He added that the rioters' "best course is to accept this offer and the fair treatment it guarantees."[62]

Meanwhile, at Atlanta, on-site negotiations began at about 1:00 P.M. A BOP lieutenant contacted several detainees over the radio, one of whom claimed that he had the authority to negotiate for the detainees. He and three other detainees were permitted to pass through the dining room door and enter an office off the main corridor. About an hour later, trained FBI negotiators joined the lieutenant. The attorney general's offer of a moratorium was conveyed to the inmate negotiators, who said they would take it back to the other detainees for discussion.[63] Officials were optimistic that the disturbance could be settled by the day's end.

It soon became apparent, however, that the negotiations would be much tougher and longer. Numerous other detainees, in groups or individually, contacted officials by telephone, all claiming that they spoke for the detainees.[64] The warden commented the next day in a news conference:

> Last night, quite frankly, I thought we had agreement and this would be
> settled by 7:45. We found out quickly that as soon as we had agreement
> and it was brought back to them they had a new leader taking over and we
> had a new set of demands.[65]

The demands made, and the priorities given to them, varied from one
spokesman to the next. In aggregate, the demands included the immediate release of all detainees; a meeting with Attorney General Meese, the
congressman representing the prison's district, and a legal-aid lawyer who
had worked on the detainees' behalf; the right to remain in the United
States and to become citizens; a supply of food and water; a personal
guarantee from the warden that they would not be returned to Cuba; total
amnesty; and a guarantee that correctional officers would not retaliate
against detainees.[66]

When the Monday negotiations failed to produce a settlement, officials began to plan for the possibility of a protracted incident. The warden and his executive staff stayed at the prison most of the first night,
thinking that a resolution might be at hand at any moment. By the second day, however, they needed relief.

OVERALL MANAGEMENT OF CRISIS

The resolution of the riot was given extraordinary attention at the top
levels of the federal government. Attorney General Meese personally
directed the overall strategy, canceling a long-planned trip to Europe.[67]
He chaired daily meetings of all top Department of Justice officials. In
the negotiation process, all written agreements required word-by-word
approval from the attorney general.

The Justice Command Center, a round-the-clock facility opened in
1986 for the management of major national crises, was activated. In addition, each of the Department of Justice components involved (the BOP,
the FBI, the U.S. Marshal's Service, and the INS/Border Patrol) established
their own round-the-clock command posts.

In Atlanta, the BOP and the FBI were the lead agencies, establishing
local command centers in adjacent offices in the penitentiary's administration building. The southeast regional director assumed overall control
of the operation at Atlanta. It was agreed that the decision whether to
retake the institution by force would rest with the BOP, after consulta-
tion with the attorney general. If a decision to use force was made, the
FBI would take charge of the operation.

Continuity in the command post at Atlanta was maintained by bringing
in regional directors from the north central and western regions and wardens from two other federal prisons. Once there, tandem teams of a regional
director and a warden rotated duties in the prison's command center.

RESOURCES MOBILIZED: PERSONNEL AND MATERIAL

Arriving from the outside were 406 BOP staff members, dispatched from
42 prisons, the central office, regional offices, and the staff training acad-

emy. Over the course of the riot, 623 FBI agents were assigned to Atlanta, plus hundreds of agents from the U.S. Marshal's Service, the INS, and the Border Patrol.[68] The Pentagon sent 100 specialists in hostage rescue to provide advice.

Tactical Component. The tactical forces, under the command of the FBI, included several of the BOP's Special Operations Response Team (SORT), dozens of FBI SWAT teams, and the FBI's Hostage Rescue Team (HRT), which had originally been sent to Oakdale.[69] The SORTs and SWATs are units of specially trained staff who, when released from their normal duties, can operate as a team in high-risk situations. The HRT, formed in 1983, is the FBI's unit dedicated to training for counterterrorist and other high-threat tactical operations. If a tactical assault or rescue operation had become necessary, the HRT would have taken the primary role.

Negotiations Component. The FBI took the lead in the negotiations because of its extensive experience. Teams, each composed of two FBI negotiators and one from the BOP, were assigned to rotating 12-hour shifts.[70] To maintain continuity, each team wrote a summary of events that occurred on its shift, including a synopsis of conversations with detainees and comments on the psychological profile and disposition of the detainee negotiators. In addition, a log and tapes were made of the negotiations, and a "critical incident board" on the wall of the command center provided a quick overview of transpiring events. A psychological consultant, who had trained with the FBI, served as a member of the negotiating team. His role was both to help interpret the behavior of the detainees and to watch government negotiators for signs of stress, fatigue, and overinvolvement.[71]

Equipment. There was an initial shortage of equipment, especially communication equipment. During the takeover, numerous staff radios were taken from hostages, leaving officials with no secure channels. Prison officials initially were forced to rely on telephones and runners to coordinate their operations. The FBI and the Department of Defense provided the necessary communications equipment. Over the course of the 11 days, a vast array of other equipment was assembled, ranging from armored personnel carriers and helicopters, to emergency crash saws and sledge hammers, to automatic weapons and body armor.[72]

Services for Hostage Families. Soon after the riot started, family members of the hostages began to gather in front of the prison. Around midnight on Tuesday, November 24, the Washington BOP command post decided to establish a special team to assist the hostages' families. This was the first time the BOP had ever done this. Reflecting the importance given to the project, a warden from another federal prison was flown to

Atlanta to organize the effort. The Hostage Family Services Center took advantage of the facilities of the nearby regional office. Later in the incident, trailers and tents were added. Open 24 hours a day, the center provided the families with medical, psychological, and pastoral services, sleeping accommodations, hot meals, child care, and briefings. At its peak, the staff included 15 psychologists and psychiatrists, 11 chaplains, and 10 support staff.

While the center's services were clearly beneficial, tensions between the families and BOP officials began to rise after the first few days. The point of contention was the information that BOP officials would or would not provide the families. Regularly scheduled briefings were held the first few days, but they became less frequent as the incident wore on and there was less new information to report. A decision was made that only confirmed information would be passed to the hostage families. With speculation and rumors flowing from many sources, some family members came to believe that prison officials were withholding information.[73]

HANDLING THE MEDIA

Within a day of the takeover, 300 media personnel crowded the residential and business properties across the two-lane street in front of the penitentiary. One local television station put its camera on the roof of an auto repair shop. Next door, Cable News Network (CNN) set up two tents in the parking lot.[74] From the point of view of federal officials, the media presented three problems, beyond the normal difficulties of mobilizing a staff with the necessary background and skill to handle a flood of national media. (The Department of Justice sent experienced media relations experts to both Atlanta and Oakdale.)

First, television broadcasts transmitted from the front of the prison gave detainees information, sometimes false, that they would not otherwise have received. As previously noted, media coverage was one consideration in the decision not to rescue the hospital staff. Later in the week, a local reporter mistakenly reported that a tactical assault was under way when in fact he was only observing a routine change of shift.[75] Detainees bound the hostages and threatened them with knives, and several anxious hours followed. Prison officials did not know if they had the authority to restrict the media from access to strategic but public areas in the event of an assault.

Second, as the days wore on, the media intruded into the privacy of hostage family members. To protect the families, the media were barred from the Hostage Family Services Center, but even this was less than foolproof. One reporter, posing as a hostage's wife, entered the center feigning crying and distress.[76] Another reporter offered to allow a hostage's wife to hear a tape of a recorded message from her husband in exchange for an interview. Many of the hostage families became incensed over the media's intrusiveness.

Finally, the detainees attempted to "negotiate" directly through the media, or at least communicate with outsiders. A rooftop loudspeaker system (dubbed "Radio Mariel," apparently after the Voice of America's Radio Marti) was used to broadcast messages directly to the media. Inside the compound, detainees watched almost continuously the dozen television sets they had available. The *Report* states that "the detainees tried to use their access to the press as a means of circumventing the negotiating process."[77]

The *Report* makes the point that this direct communication with the media was negative because it "impaired" the negotiations process.[78] This assessment, however, should be tempered by the observation, made elsewhere by three of the FBI negotiators, that providing the detainees an opportunity to air their grievances was crucial to the eventual resolution.[79] Direct communication with the media may have helped meet this need, even as it made the official negotiations more difficult in the short run.

NEGOTIATIONS CONTINUE

As of Tuesday morning, the detainees held 102 hostages. (This includes the hospital staff, but not the employees who had been trapped in Cellhouse E, who by then had been rescued.) Prison officials provided the detainees with a Polaroid camera, and they in turn provided pictures of all of the hostages but two.[80] From time to time over the next 10 days, detainees released hostages, mostly for medical reasons or as gestures of good will. Eighty-nine hostages were held for the duration of the riot.

Almost without exception, the hostages received reasonably good care. They were not physically abused, were allowed to keep their watches and billfolds, and were given three meals a day, opportunities to shower, and reading material. Late in the week, detainees turned over to authorities a dangerous U.S.-born inmate because they feared he would kill a hostage. Still, the hostages were told repeatedly that they would die if the government tried to rescue them. To the hostages, the threats seemed credible.[81]

On Tuesday, the government established its overall negotiation strategy. Officials were convinced that an armed assault would result in the deaths of many of the 100 hostages. Because hostages were being held in a number of locations behind fortified barricades, no quick rescue would be possible. Given this situation, on Tuesday afternoon Director Quinlan held a news conference in which he said that no assault would be made as long as the hostages were not hurt. "The safety of the hostages is paramount," he stated, adding, "my patience is endless."[82] The hostages would later report that this improved their treatment and calmed the detainees.[83]

At the same time, prison officials sought to keep the pressure on detainees. Water to the compound was cut off and there was no heat.[84] Helicopter flights over the prison were meant to prevent the detainees from coming to believe that they were really in control.

Negotiations proceeded intermittently from Tuesday, November 24, through Thursday, November 26, Thanksgiving Day. When prison officials began to feel they were making progress, the terms of negotiation would shift. By Thursday evening, negotiations appeared to be stalled.

THANKSGIVING DAY

At the start of the day, Attorney General Meese sent a message to hostage families, telling them, "The safety of your loved ones is our paramount goal."[85] A few hours later, the attorney general and Director Quinlan made conference calls to family members.

The involvement of third-party volunteers was important to Thursday's negotiations and to the ultimate resolution of the riot. Selection of the volunteers was planned carefully. In general, they had to agree that they would neither serve as advocates for the detainees nor add items to the negotiations. The inmates repeatedly asked that the prison's congressman be included in the negotiations and, by his own account, he was eager to accept the role. However, the Justice Department declined his offer.[86]

Shortly after 4:00 P.M., three prominent Cuban-Americans were escorted into the prison to assist with the negotiations. One was a well-known poet who had spent 22 years in a Cuban prison; another was the chairman of the public affairs organization for Cuban-Americans; and the third had spent 28 years in a Cuban prison.[87] They met with three detainees and, over a three-hour period, reached an agreement that would allow the release of 50 of the 94 hostages then being held. In return, the detainees would be permitted to have a press conference. An Atlanta television news team was escorted into the prison. At 9:30 P.M., an FBI spokesman told the press that he was "cautiously optimistic" that some hostages would be freed and that a fragile agreement had been reached.[88]

At the appointed time, however, the detainee negotiators produced only three hostages, having apparently had trouble convincing the other rioters to accept the deal. The government negotiators offered a limited news conference in exchange for the three, but the detainee representatives abruptly left the scene, taking the hostages with them.

Phase 2: Friday through Wednesday (November 27–December 2)

Following the Thanksgiving negotiations, prison officials and government negotiators rethought their strategy. Officials had thus far avoided telling the detainees that their central demand, no deportations to Cuba, would not be met, fearing retaliation against the hostages. But with the failure of the Thanksgiving agreement, the government shifted toward a more hard-line approach.

At 10:20 P.M. on Friday, the detainees presented government negotiators with a new list of seven demands. In a preamble, the detainees explained they had "been unfairly and arbitrarily incarcerated by the Immigration and Naturalization Service for over seven years of suffering at Atlanta prison."[89] They thus felt "compelled to do what we have started here."[90] The demands, paraphrased, were as follows:

- the suspension of all treaties between Cuba and the United States that concerned Mariels;
- a ban on deportation of Mariels to Cuba;
- the immediate release of all detainees who were not serving criminal sentences or who are not under criminal investigation, and [an apparent contradiction] a detainee would be released when he proved that he had family members or some other sponsor to return to;
- the government would, within six months, find halfway houses for those detainees without family members or sponsors on the outside;
- detainees would be given constitutional protection, including the right to speedy decisions and hearings by impartial courts;
- mentally ill detainees would be sent to hospitals for treatment;
- a guarantee of no physical reprisals against the detainees or punishment for participation in the riot.[91]

Further, the detainees asked that an agreement to these demands be signed in front of live television cameras, whereupon the hostages would be released.[92] The detainees also warned that they were prepared to die "before we give up our hopes and demands for deserved freedom and liberty." They also stated that no other hostages "under any circumstances" would be released, except for medical reasons.[93]

The government's response did not come until Sunday evening. Over the weekend, Washington focused on the Oakdale situation, which was nearing resolution. It was thought that if Oakdale's detainees would agree to end their riot, Atlanta's would soon follow. The Oakdale riot ended Sunday afternoon, November 29.

That same afternoon at Atlanta, about 1:00 P.M., the detainees released four hostages as a gesture of good faith. All four reported that they and the other hostages had been treated well and had been protected from the more dangerous detainees. In response to the release, the government gave the detainees their mail, which had been accumulating since the start of the disturbance. The water system was turned on.

At about 6:30 P.M. on Sunday, negotiations resumed between FBI negotiators and three Atlanta detainees. Also in attendance were the three Cuban-American advisors. Government negotiators explained the terms of the agreement that ended the siege at Oakdale. They then responded to the seven demands issued by the detainees on Friday, point by point. The government stood fast on some and remained flexible on others.

On the first two points raised by the detainees, government negotiators gave a flat no. The United States would not reverse its position that some detainees would be deported to Cuba, nor would it abrogate its treaty with Cuba. The negotiators were instructed to point out that a cancellation of the treaty between the two countries would prevent further migration from Cuba to the United States.

On the third, fourth, and fifth points, the BOP negotiators offered a middle ground. Using the Oakdale agreement as a framework, the government was willing to provide each detainee a "full, fair, and equitable" hearing to determine whether he could be released.[94] These would be administrative hearings, however, and detainees would not be extended formal protection under the Constitution. Consensus was reached on the sixth point. Detainees with a medical need or mental illness would be moved to a medical or psychiatric facility.

Finally, on the issue of amnesty, the government was unsure where to draw the line. The instructions to the government negotiators were to promise the detainees that there would be no "unlawful physical reprisals against any of the detainees." Anticipating that this might not be enough, the negotiators were authorized to add that they would be prosecuted only for "incidents of physical violence or major misconduct." It was not specified what was meant by physical violence or major misconduct. There was in fact room for further negotiation on this point, since the Oakdale detainees had been additionally promised no criminal liability for damage to the prison that occurred during the riot.

The negotiation session ended at 8:00 P.M. with two issues unresolved. First, the detainees were under the impression that, if they held out long enough, the attorney general might reverse himself on their primary demand—no deportations. This hope was expressed by detainees in negotiations as late as Wednesday, December 2.

A second obstacle had to do with the terms of the promise that detainees would receive "fair" hearings. Actually, from a technical standpoint, the broadly worded pledge of case-by-case review did not go beyond existing procedures. What the detainees wanted was some sort of guarantee that the process would be more favorable and expeditious.

On Monday, November 30, the three Cuban-American leaders brought in to assist the BOP negotiators returned home. They and government officials agreed that the detainees had lost confidence in them and that they could no longer play a useful role. There was no shortage of volunteers to take their place. On their own initiative, an 18-member delegation of Miami dignitaries, including the city's mayor, had flown to Atlanta to offer their assistance. Several went as far as to say that they would exchange themselves for hostages.

Instead, the government decided to draw on the services of Bishop Agustin Roman (auxiliary bishop of the Archdiocese of Miami) and an Atlanta legal-aid attorney, Gary Leshaw. The Cuban-born Bishop Roman, widely revered in the Cuban-American community, had helped resolve the Oakdale disturbance,[95] a fact known to the Atlanta detainees through the media coverage.[96] The Atlanta attorney had represented the detainees in their conditions suit against the penitentiary and many of them individually concerning their immigration status.

On Tuesday and Wednesday, December 1 and 2, the attorney met with the detainees and was allowed to answer legal questions that they raised. Afterward, he wrote a memo to the attorney general reporting that the inmates found "acceptable" the attorney general's response on retaliation. He asked for clarification on whether participation in the riot, in itself, would be punishable, and on what the Department of Justice meant by a "full, fair, and equitable" hearing and how such hearings would go beyond those previously provided.[97]

On the crucial demand of no deportations, the memo seemed to accept that the government would not yield to the detainees' demand but, at the same time, sought to soften the impact of this stance. The attorney suggested that before a detainee was deported to Cuba, he or she should be allowed to apply to emigrate to another country. He explained that such a provision would not challenge the right of the government to deport the detainees to Cuba, but it would make the government's position "more palatable" to the detainees.

The attorney general responded in a memo accepting each of the suggestions and clarifying uncertainties where asked. There would be no prosecutions for participation in the riot or destruction of government property. Prosecution would be reserved to "assaultive violence against persons or major misconducts." Detainees would be given the opportunity to apply for emigration to a third country before deportation to Cuba. Finally, to ensure that hearings were full, fair, and equitable, a new review process would be developed by a panel appointed by the attorney general. Both the Atlanta attorney and Bishop Roman would have input into the development of that process.

Phase 3: Thursday and Early Friday Morning (December 3 and 4)

A turning point occurred in the afternoon of Thursday, December 3. During an emotionally taut two-and-a-half-hour negotiation session, eight detainees met with four government negotiators. One of the FBI negotiators told the detainees in no uncertain terms that their primary demand would never be met, that it was nonnegotiable. Adding to the emotional force of the moment, he said, "You cannot and will not bring the U.S. government to its knees"[98] and stated that the detainees, not the government, would have to change their position if a peaceful solution was to be achieved. Further, the negotiator urged the detainees to concentrate on those issues that could be negotiated, rather than continue to wage a lost battle over the demand for no deportations.

Apparently, the strategy worked. The feared retaliation against the hostages did not materialize. The detainees told government negotiators that they were ready to sign the seven-point agreement, and that they recognized that the agreement did not ban deportations to Cuba.[99] The signing would wait, however, until Bishop Roman could be present.

While Bishop Roman had offered to help several days earlier, it was decided that his assistance would be most useful when an agreement was being finalized rather than in the negotiation process itself. He would give the agreement legitimacy, reassuring the detainees that it was fair or at least the best they could achieve. He arrived at the penitentiary by helicopter at 9:45 P.M.

An obstacle emerged at the last moment. At about 11:00 P.M., the detainees insisted that the attorney general sign the agreement and that more witnesses observe the signing. At 12:00 A.M., the associate attorney general talked to a detainee negotiator over the phone from Washington, assuring him that the regional director had authority to sign for the government. About the same time, officials escorted into the prison three of the eight observers that the detainees had requested to witness the signing. One was a Cuban-American leader; two others were active in detainee advocacy groups. At 1:00 A.M., the agreement was signed by the regional director and detainee representatives and witnessed by Bishop Roman and the three other observers. The signing was broadcast live over CNN.

Ten minutes later, the first hostages began to walk out of the facility. By 1:30 A.M., all of the hostages had been released and accounted for. Over the next 24 hours, detainees were searched, had their property boxed, and were then placed on buses for transportation to other facilities.

At 6:00 P.M., December 4, Director Quinlan and Attorney General Meese toured the facility and met with some of the hostages.

Aftermath

After the riot had ended, Congress, other politicians, and the media offered extensive commentary on the incident, but the farthest reaching response was from the BOP itself.

A primary target of criticism was the short notice given by the State Department to the Department of Justice of the immigration treaty between the United States and Cuba. Some also criticized the BOP for not taking more forceful measures to avert a riot at Atlanta, especially after the riot began at Oakdale.[100] Mostly, however, the BOP and other agencies involved in the resolution were praised for their professional handling of the riots.[101]

One point of controversy was whether the government had gone too far in granting amnesty to the detainees. The congressman who represents Oakdale, Louisiana, told his colleagues in hearings:

> There is no place for these terrorists in America. What exactly is the difference between giving in to the demands of a foreign terrorist and capitulating to the edict of angry detainees?[102]

The attorney general saw it differently: "I don't think we yielded to the demands of hostage takers. I don't think we violated any of our principles."[103]

Study and Implementation

The BOP took seriously the job of finding out what happened, why it happened, and what lessons could be learned. A study team was assembled with members from the BOP, the Public Health Service, and the INS. Its report includes an hour-by-hour account of the events at Atlanta and Oakdale, an analysis of those events, and 107 recommendations. In the main, the recommendations called for new training programs that would allow staff to better predict and respond to disturbances, the acquisition of additional emergency response equipment, and the development of new crisis management strategies, such as in the areas of media relations and hostage negotiations.

After the *Report* was issued in February 1988, various divisions and offices reviewed those recommendations that affected their units. Each unit determined the cost of implementing the recommendations and suggested a course of action. These appraisals were then sent to the BOP's executive staff. In four meetings held between May 1988 and September 1989, the BOP's executive staff approved 103 of the 107 recommendations.

Primary responsibility for implementing the recommendations was given to an office established for that purpose. When the Office of Emergency Preparedness (OEP) opened on March 1, 1990, it was given two main tasks. One was to keep track of the progress made in achieving the 103 recommendations. OEP developed a questionnaire to be given to all BOP facilities, asking whether the recommendations relevant to their facility had been put into practice. The results, and other data collected from on-site observation, were issued in regular reports.

Second, OEP was to improve the emergency response training of both command and line staff. This involved developing a new training program for captains and lieutenants in emergency preparedness, as well as on-site observation and critique of existing exercises and mock emergency drills at institutions and at national training seminars.

Another aspect of training was to develop a program for Hostage Negotiation Teams (HNTs). In writing a plan for this, it was noted that the BOP's SORT (tactical) teams had traditionally been given the resources, training, and status to develop their teams. A similar level of support and opportunity was needed for the HNT cadre to develop a distinctive identity and expertise.

On a broader plane, the Atlanta and Oakdale riots turned on the issue of the government's obligations to the detainees. Before the riot, there were some—in Congress, in the judiciary, and among the public—who believed that the government had not lived up to those obligations. The fact that the attorney general was willing to enter into genuine negotiations with detainees suggests that the administration saw the rioting detainees as more than mere criminal kidnappers or terrorists. The merits of the detainees' case were taken seriously.

The attorney general, however, was unwilling to concede that the government owes constitutional protection to foreign nationals who have entered the United States illegally. Four years later, detainees at Talladega would attempt to reopen the question, but with much less success.

3

Federal Correctional Institution, Talladega, Alabama

August 21–30, 1991

Although the underlying issue in the Talladega riot in 1991 was the same as at Atlanta—the unwillingness of Cuban detainees to be deported—it was in no way a replay of the earlier incident. The preriot situation and the political context were much different.

In settling the 1987 Atlanta and Oakdale riots, Bureau of Prison (BOP) officials had pursued a strategy of "endless patience": negotiate a peaceful resolution without concern for time. Ten days into the Talladega disturbance, officials concluded that time was no longer on their side. Negotiations had stalled, and the health and safety of the hostages were becoming increasingly worrisome. A carefully planned and rehearsed assault, maximizing the element of surprise, ended the incident without serious injuries to the hostages or to the detainees.[1]

The Period between the Atlanta/Oakdale and Talladega Incidents

In the first half of the 1980s, the BOP had consolidated the Cuban detainee population in one facility, the Atlanta penitentiary, with the over-

39

flow going to Oakdale. After the November 1987 disturbances, the detainees were dispersed among BOP's more secure facilities.

Then, gradually, the detainees were reconsolidated, this time in a half-dozen specialized units around the country. One unit housed detainees requiring intensive supervision (U.S. Penitentiary [USP] at Lewisburg, Pennsylvania); two operated as general management units (USPs at Leavenworth, Kansas, and Lompoc, California); and another served as the reception and classification center (USP at Terre Haute, Indiana).[2]

Under the review procedures established in the settlement of the 1987 disturbances, detainees were guaranteed advance notification of a hearing, were permitted counsel, and could appeal an adverse decision to several independent fact-finding review boards. If a detainee felt that the administrative process had been unfair, he or she could file a petition in the U.S. district court.[3] Flights to repatriate excludable detainees, which had been suspended in May 1985, were resumed in December 1988. By August 21, 1991, 458 detainees had been returned to Cuba. Fewer than 12 of the 125,000 original Mariels had been detained continuously since 1980.[4]

In July 1988, the BOP's Talladega, Alabama, facility was designated as a final holding point for detainees being deported. Detainees were transferred to Talladega only after they had exhausted all appeals and their return to Cuba was a near certainty. However, from time to time, the repatriation process was interrupted. A flight to Cuba for 51 detainees was canceled by the Cuban government in mid-August 1991 because of the Pan American games being held in Havana.[5] Flights were planned for August 22, August 27, and September 6. On the morning of the disturbance (August 21, 1991), 67 detainees were within two weeks of deportation.

Federal Correctional Institution, Talladega

Federal Correctional Institution, Talladega, is situated in rural central Alabama. It opened in 1979 primarily as a medium-security prison. On the day of the disturbance, there were 845 medium-custody inmates housed in five adjacent buildings. Each building was designated by a Greek letter.

On the eve of the riot, Alpha Unit held 119 Cuban detainees and 18 U.S.-born citizens serving sentences.[6] The unit was operating at 117 percent of its design capacity.[7] The U.S.-born inmates in Alpha Unit were an overflow from the prison's segregation unit.[8] Thirty-one of the Cuban detainees in Alpha Unit had been at Atlanta or Oakdale during the 1987 disturbances.[9]

Alpha Unit had been upgraded to maximum security at the time of its conversion to detainee housing. The BOP operated on the principle that the detainees were dangerous, could not be trusted, and had to be denied all opportunity for violence. At the time of the riot, 71 percent of the detainees had been previously imprisoned for serious offenses, such as murder, rape, arson, or a significant drug offense. Forty percent had been disciplined while in the BOP's custody for at least one of five infractions defined as "most serious": murder, attempted murder, assault, attempted escape, or major contraband violation.[10] Most feared reimprisonment in Cuba and were desperate to avoid deportation.[11]

In the course of the upgrade, steel plates were installed on the cell walls. Inmates' personal property was limited to toiletries, nonperishable food, legal documents, and educational material. Bedding and other materials in the cells were fire resistant, and detainees were not allowed matches. Unless they needed medical treatment, detainees remained in their cells around the clock except for three showers and seven hours of recreation per week. Television sets were placed in each cell.

Alpha Unit was staffed at a higher level than typical BOP high-security units.[12] Under a unit manager were a lieutenant, 37 correctional officers spread over three shifts, two correctional counselors, a case manager, an education specialist, a unit secretary, and a physician's assistant.[13] The Immigration and Naturalization Service (INS) also assigned four staff to the unit.

Alpha Unit was divided into four sections: two living areas (A wing and B wing), an administrative area between them, and a recreation area (see Figure 3-1). Each wing had two levels of cells arranged in semicircles facing a dayroom space. The offices in the administrative area opened either into a corridor connecting the two wings or into a dayroom space. From the main compound, three entrances led to the unit, one to each of the wings and one to the administrative area. A sally port had been constructed at each of the three entrances.

The recreation yard was an area about 100 feet long and 44 feet deep, located 25 feet to the rear of the building. The area was divided into five miniyards, each enclosed on four sides and above by chain-link fence. Three to five detainees at a time exercised in each miniyard. Since deportation flights were sometimes canceled by the Cuban government on short notice, recreation was provided to detainees even the day before a scheduled flight.

Detainees were moved from cells to the recreation yard one at a time. A detainee's hands would be cuffed behind him while he was still locked in his cell. Two officers would then escort the detainee to a door at the rear of the housing unit, where he was inspected with a hand-held metal detector. The door to the yard was kept locked and bolted, and the walkway leading to the yard was enclosed by a chain-link fence. Once a detainee was inside the miniyard, a four-foot dead bolt was moved across the gate and secured by a padlock. Only then were a detainee's restraints removed.

Once a group of detainees was secured in their miniyards, one officer remained outside to supervise. The officer's time was divided between moving from one recreation unit to the next (lighting cigarettes, providing water) and sitting at a point where he could observe the detainees. The walkway between the rear of the building and the recreation yard

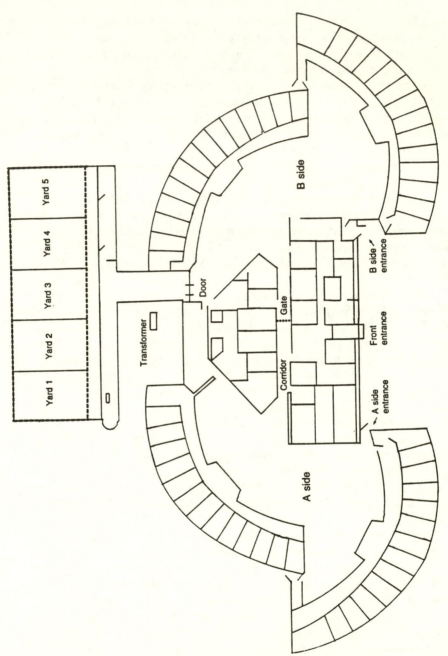

Figure 3-1 Federal Correctional Institution, Talladega, Alabama.

curved past an electrical transformer that serviced the building. The transformer obscured the line of sight between the rear door of the building and the place where the officer would normally sit.

Takeover

On the morning of Wednesday, August 21, 1991, 23 detainees were in the five recreation yards.[14] At around 10:00 A.M., the supervising officer moved a water container from just outside yard 4 to just outside yard 5.[15] Just then, the three detainees in yard 5 removed the locking bar from the gate. BOP investigators later had several theories about how this might have happened (the lock may have been picked by inmates or accidentally left unlocked by officers), but the physical evidence was destroyed in the riot. In any case, the detainees opened the gate, grabbed the officer, and put a prison-made knife to his neck. The officer tried to use his radio to call for help but was stopped. One of the three exchanged his detainee clothes for the officer's uniform.

Inside the block, the unit manager was off duty and a case manager was filling in. A non-Cuban inmate orderly approached the case manager and told him that there was a Cuban in the yard dressed in an officer's uniform. The case manager initially discounted this as unbelievable, but took another officer and went to check for himself. He looked out the window of the door to the yard, but he could not see the yard officer's usual post because the transformer was in the way, so he had the door unlocked and stepped outside with the other officer. The door was not relocked behind them.

Suddenly, the detainee dressed in the uniform sprang from his hiding place. The officer who had accompanied the case manager yelled, "Hey, that's [detainee's name]!" The two ran back into the unit with two detainees in pursuit, one armed with a knife and the other with the four-foot bolt taken from the locking mechanism. The case manager and officer were able to get inside the building before the detainees reached the door, but they could not secure the door in time. A pneumatic device slowed the door's closing. Also, the door opened out and there was a handle on the outside of the door but none on the inside. Once the door reached its frame, only the edging around the panes of the door's window could be used to pull on the door. With the leverage in their favor, the detainees pulled open the door and then entered the unit. One of the detainees yelled, as the case manager remembers it, "Everyone get down on the ground. I'm the sonabitch running the place now."

In the A wing were the case manager, four officers, and an INS staff member. One of the detainees yelled, "If you hit the body alarm, I'm going to kill you," but several officers did anyway. The case manager dialed an emergency number on the telephone; one of the detainees attacked him, and both fell tussling to the floor. The detainee won the advantage, producing a sharpened mop stick that, apparently, had been hidden inside the unit in advance, and threatened to kill the case manager. Just then, an INS officer grabbed the mop stick from the detainee, and he and the case manager ran into an administrative office. The door of this office did not lock from the inside, but they barricaded it with a filing cabinet. The four other officers left on A wing locked themselves in a hearing room and waited for help to arrive.

Meanwhile, the third detainee involved in the initial takeover was unlocking the other miniyards with the keys taken from the officer. The freed detainees began to enter the building. The secretary to Alpha Unit, hearing the commotion, entered the wing from administrative offices, but she was momentarily fooled by the stolen uniform and was quickly taken hostage, along with an INS officer who entered the unit. Detainees took these two hostages into the recreation yard and handcuffed them from behind.

The detainees' numbers had now grown to between 10 and 15, enough to take hostage all staff in the wing. Several rioters ordered the case manager and INS officer to come out of the room they were hiding in; the two decided that resistance would be futile, moved the filing cabinet, and were taken hostage. They were seated in chairs and handcuffed to them. The case manager was kicked several times and hit in the head from behind with the mop stick.[16] He passed in and out of consciousness, finding it difficult to breathe and thinking that he might soon be dead. (As it turned out, he suffered no lasting injuries.)

Meanwhile, other detainees, after attempting to break in a window, found a key to open the hearing room where the other four officers had fled. Outnumbered, the officers surrendered without resistance. Another INS employee and a B-wing officer entered A wing to assist and were taken hostage in their turn. In the incident's first 15 minutes, the detainees had taken 11 hostages, three of whom were female staff members.

Initial Response

Responding to the alarms, the acting captain and several lieutenants entered the B side of the unit and began to walk through the corridor to the A side. They then saw two detainees guarding the doorway to the A side with their makeshift weapons. The captain sent a lieutenant to have riot control equipment brought from the control center in order to confine the riot to the A wing. Two lieutenants charged the inmates and tried to close the A-wing door, but the detainees drove them back with the mop stick and a fire extinguisher used as a club.

Meanwhile, the lieutenant who had been sent for riot control gear reported the situation to the acting warden, who, on the basis of his information, decided to evacuate the building to prevent the taking of additional hostages.[17] The lieutenant carried the order back, and the patrol left the building. By 10:20 A.M., the detainees were in control of all of Alpha Unit.

Counterriot Mobilization: The Prison and the System

Prison officials immediately locked down the remainder of the prison and deployed the prison's Special Operations Response Team (SORT) around the building. The warden arrived a few minutes later and assumed control. Bureau employees, assisted by the Talladega Police Department, began patrols around the prison's perimeter. The central office, the BOP southeast regional office in Atlanta, and the FBI were notified.

Two hours after the riot started, the assistant director for correctional programs established a command center at the BOP headquarters in Washington. The command center staff ultimately comprised two BOP assistant directors, a representative from the Office of Emergency Preparedness, a recorder, a representative of the intelligence staff, and personnel from the FBI, U.S. Marshal's Service, and INS. One of the key tasks of the center was to coordinate the efforts of the various agencies involved. The acting attorney general, William Barr, approved all major decisions and was in frequent contact with the directors of the BOP and FBI. The BOP staff members provided regular briefings to the staff of Congressional committees with oversight responsibility for the BOP.

One of the immediate concerns in the central office was that the Talladega disturbance would prompt riots in other prisons. All BOP facilities were informed that they should watch closely for signs of unrest, especially among Cuban detainees, and take preventive measures when necessary. The BOP also contacted INS facilities and 31 state and local facilities that held sizable numbers of detainees.[18]

A large number of BOP and FBI personnel, both line officers and administrators, were deployed to Talladega from other locations. Twelve SORT teams, each with 12–15 members, were sent to Talladega from other federal prisons.[19] The FBI sent 184 agents and other specialized personnel including the agency's Hostage Rescue Team (HRT) and the Special Weapons and Tactics (SWAT) teams from Atlanta and Birmingham.[20] In addition, 12 U.S. marshals and nine INS employees were sent to the site.[21] Dozens of BOP staff members from nearby facilities were brought to the prison to help maintain its normal operations.[22]

The regional director arrived at 2:30 P.M. on the first day to assume local command of the crisis. Over the next 10 days he would remain the senior BOP official in charge on site and would discuss important decisions with the BOP director. During the course of the incident, a second regional director, two assistant directors of the BOP, and three wardens of other facilities would also be brought to the scene.

Meanwhile, the Talladega facility staff began working 12-hour shifts. They acquired equipment and constructed temporary facilities, such as showers, quarters for negotiators, and shakedown rooms. The warden's office was converted into the prime command area, an executive assistant's office was used as the communication room, and the business office was set up as the local FBI command center. The negotiating team, after it was assembled, operated from a room on the first floor of the same building.

Throughout the disturbance, those in command at Talladega worked intensely gathering and assessing information, developing contingency plans, and assembling resources. This effort continued nearly around the clock, often with the only lull in activity occurring between 3:00 A.M. and 4:00 A.M.

The families of the hostages were notified and a facility was arranged for them at the prison's training center. The family center operated with a staff of 30 at its height.[23] Some family members stayed at the prison nearly around the clock until the hostages were released. During the first evening, the BOP's director spoke by telephone to the families of the hostages and later sent a videotaped message. In the course of the incident, senior prison staff briefed the families as often as every two hours. Psychologists and chaplains were available for counseling. Materials were developed for the families predicting what to expect when the hostages were released and advising how to manage children's stress.

Negotiations Begin and Hostages Wait

When the disturbance began, a counselor assigned to Alpha Unit was at a warehouse just outside the perimeter. Hearing over his radio that a disturbance had begun, he entered the compound on his own initiative and found the detainee leader at the sally-port entrance to Alpha Unit's administrative area. The detainee leader told the counselor that the hostages would not be harmed as long as no effort was made to rescue them. The detainees were demanding, he said, that the deportations be canceled and that all the Talladega inmates be released. He promised to release the case manager because of his injuries (and he was in fact soon released).

Throughout the afternoon and evening of the first day, the inmates insisted that they would speak only with this particular counselor, apparently because of their high regard for him. BOP officials permitted this, even though the counselor was not trained in negotiations. Their decision was based in part on the fact that the detainees were at this point too disorganized to negotiate.

Some of the conversations between the counselor and detainees took place at the Alpha Unit sally port, but most occurred over officers' radios that had been captured by the detainees. The radio conversation was initially chaotic. Five or six detainees were speaking simultaneously on different radios, concealing their names and identifying themselves only as "number three," for example. A physician's assistant who had worked in the unit listened to the conversations and helped the counselor identify voices. Eventually, at the counselor's request, the detainees rounded up all but one radio and limited the conversation thereafter to one at a time.

Over the 10-day period, the hostages were not physically abused. They were allowed to shower and wash their clothes. Female hostages were fed small rations of cereal and candy; male hostages received less. The detainees did not disperse the hostages to make an assault more difficult, as had been done at Atlanta. Instead, the hostages were kept, most of the time, in one room. The warden would later comment that the detainees "acted like they were totally secure."[24]

Still, the detainees made it clear that they were prepared to kill the hostages if an assault were made. Several days into the disturbance, the detainees required the hostages to place their identification cards in a pillowcase.[25] One was drawn, its owner then told that he would be the first to die if an assault were made. During the course of the disturbance, several of the hostages wrote letters to their families in the event of their death.

In the first hours of the disturbance, prison officials had allowed the detainees to make telephone calls to the outside. Many contacted family and friends. Others called the Cable News Network (CNN), and the Atlanta-based legal-aid attorney who had helped settle the 1987 riot. Efforts to contact the *Washington Post* and officials at the United Nations were not successful. On Wednesday evening, a BOP spokesman explained to the press, "We kept the phone lines open because the inmates have threatened the hostages' lives if we don't."[26]

As this illustrates, officials were initially unwilling to defy the detainees' threats against their hostages. Officials had also ordered a temporary fence constructed around Alpha Unit and brought in a tractor to dig post holes. But when the detainees threatened to kill a hostage, the work was stopped.

The detainees were also cautious in their dealings with the authorities. There was little food in the unit, mostly small amounts of commissary items stored in cells. Late Wednesday afternoon, detainees and prison officials agreed to exchange three hostages for sandwiches. The sandwiches, the inmates insisted, had to be commercially produced and in sealed envelopes to ensure that they would not be "laced with drugs." One hundred fifty sandwiches were in fact brought to the prison, but the detainees called off the exchange at the last minute.

About 11:00 P.M. Wednesday night, the counselor who had been acting as a negotiator told the detainees that he had been there all day, was exhausted, and was going home. He left the prison and did not participate further in the negotiations. Two trained negotiators from the prison staff and an FBI special agent from Birmingham took over the task. In subsequent days, they were joined by other specially trained BOP and FBI negotiators and negotiation coordinators, raising the total to 21.[27]

The negotiators worked in three eight-hour shifts. The day and evening shifts each had three FBI and two BOP negotiators, and the overnight shift had two FBI and two BOP negotiators. Negotiating coordinators, two each from the FBI and BOP, worked in 12-hour shifts. They supervised the work of the negotiators, developed negotiation strategies, and reported to on the on-site commanders.[28] The negotiators and coordinators developed a strong rapport among themselves, dubbing their group the "brain trust."

Nine More Days

The subsequent nine days can be divided into four periods: (1) a day and a half during which prison officials worked intensely to develop a resolution strategy and organize resources, but detainees more or less refused to talk to prison officials; (2) four days of stalemated talks; (3) two days in which negotiations seemed to show some promise, but then deteriorated; and (4) the final day, during which the decision to assault was made and then carried out.

The First Two Days: Thursday, August 22, through Friday, August 23

On Thursday, the first full day of the riot, a direct phone line to the detainees was established that would be the main avenue of communications between the BOP and the detainees. Asked about the possibility of using force to retake the unit, a BOP spokesman declared, as they had at Atlanta and Oakdale, "There is no need to go in. We have patience."[29]

However, there was little immediate progress. The detainees apparently remained disorganized; leadership groups would emerge and then apparently decompose. From time to time one detainee or another would raise substantive issues, such as demands to speak with "an authority higher than BOP," for a commitment not to use tear gas, and for the provision of food.[30] These conversations lacked continuity, as demands made by one detainee were not raised by the next. Fistfights among the detainees were frequent.

An exception was the issue of medical treatment for the hostages and detainees, which figured prominently in the early discussions and was repeatedly raised throughout the incident. The detainees were told that one hostage had hypertension; one detainee suffered from diabetes, and another from epilepsy. Late Thursday afternoon an agreement was reached that allowed medical staff to provide medication to three hostages, and in return, three detainees were to receive medication. Officials then permitted the detainees to call the Atlanta attorney involved in settling the 1987 disturbance. The detainees later asked for a second call to the attorney, but that request was denied.

Also on Thursday, detainees twice brought female hostages into the fenced recreation area, apparently to gauge the level of staff readiness or just to see what would happen. On the first occasion, 25 detainees entered the yard with the hostage and began to tamper with the fence. Bureau SORT teams closed in and the detainees retreated. In the second occurrence, seven detainees entered the yard and had their hostage yell to staff that the detainees should be allowed to contact CNN and "international authorities."[31] The authorities were unfazed; in fact, at 1:00 P.M., they disconnected the inmates' outside phone lines that they had previously left open because of the inmates' threats.[32]

Meanwhile, at the prison entrance, media representatives began to assemble, eventually reaching about 50 in number (the coup in the Soviet Union had just occurred, diverting some of the press's attention away from the incident). Prison officials discovered that media personnel equipped with scanning receivers were able to listen to some of the conversations between detainees and prison officials.[33]

The warden explained to reporters that they were hearing only one side of the conversation, missing the response of the prison negotiators, who often asked the detainee to continue the conversation over a secure telephone line. The warden cautioned the reporters that the "possibility of misinterpretation could seriously detract from our efforts to resolve this peacefully."[34] Prison officials jammed the channels to prevent further monitoring.[35] By the next day, the press found the conversation on their scanners inaudible.[36]

An Intransigent Posture: Friday Afternoon, August 23, until Tuesday Afternoon, August 27

On Friday, as there was still no progress toward meaningful negotiations, prison officials felt that something had to be done to engage the detainees' attention. At 2:20 P.M., prison officials moved a large barbecue grill to an area near the entrance of the Alpha Unit, nominally to cook a meal for the general-population inmates. The real purpose was to stimulate conversation with the detainees. The detainees, however, perceived the grill as some sort of tactical weapon, perhaps a huge bomb to breach the entrance or a remotely operated minitank. The detainees told prison officials that they wanted the device removed immediately. Several of the hostages, themselves confused about the grill's purpose, yelled the same thing. The detainees threatened two hostages with weapons and some of the hostages felt they might be killed on the spot.

One of the detainees demanding the grill's removal was considered by BOP officials as someone who might play a constructive role in the negotiations. Officials believed that if he could be seen by other detainees as gaining concessions, he would gain stature among fellow detainees. Partly for this reason, and partly just to ease tensions, they ordered the grill pulled back five feet from the entrance. This led to a long conversation between the two sides that lasted until 4:00 A.M. the next morning, Saturday, August 24. But tangible progress was achieved in only one area: the detainees agreed to allow medical staff to examine 6 of the 10 hostages.

On Saturday morning, medical staff examined the six hostages. The examination was cursory; it was conducted through the entryway grille and physical contact was not allowed. Most of the hostages were in good health, but the medical staff were afraid for the safety of the hypertensive hostage and the diabetic detainee, although they had shown no ill effects so far. But the detainees refused the negotiators' request to release them and later that evening refused permission for another medical examination.

At about 1:40 P.M. the next day, Sunday, August 25, detainees sent out a bottle with two notes. One, purportedly from a hostage, reported that the hostages and detainees were tiring and getting weak. It asked for food and medication and urged the government to "get going" on negotiations.[37] A note from detainees requested a number of medications and listed several detainees wanting to be seen by medical staff. In response to a later telephone request made by a hostage, a transparent bag containing hygienic items, but not the requested medicine, was hung on the entryway grille. The detainees did not retrieve it.

At about 2:30 A.M., on Monday, August 26, the detainees called prison officials to renew their request for medications. They were told that no medications would be provided unless detainees removed the blankets they had placed over the unit's windows. (Auxiliary lighting had been set up around the building.) The detainees refused and made a point of keeping the lights turned off inside the unit to further reduce visibility.

At about 8:45 A.M., medical staff approached the sally port but were refused access. The detainees told them they would stop medicating the hypertensive hostage unless all of the medication they requested was provided. Later that day, they threw the bag with hygienic items away from the building. Bureau staff retrieved the bag and returned it to the grille door. Officials told the detainees that afternoon that the hostage with hypertension needed treatment by a doctor and that his health was of great concern to them.

Early Monday evening, medical staff again approached the unit. The detainees, who apparently now were primarily concerned with getting medical attention for their own number, reciprocated by removing the blankets from the windows. The detainees allowed the staff to examine a number of detainees, but no hostages were brought forward. Midmorning on Tuesday, August 27, the detainees said that they would allow the hypertensive hostage to be examined, but then recanted without explanation.

Beyond these exchanges over medical treatment, conversations between detainees and the government were minimal. There was little discussion of any substantive issues that might lead to a resolution.

Serious Negotiations Begin: Tuesday Afternoon, August 27, through Thursday Afternoon, August 29

On Tuesday morning, it appeared that the inmates had decided to ask for serious negotiations. Detainees cleared the sally port of debris, moved a table out in front of it, and requested a face-to-face negotiation session. This began around 2:00 P.M. The four detainee negotiators remained behind the grille. Three FBI and two BOP negotiators were seated at the table; 20 feet to their rear were two BOP SORT teams.

The detainees stated that they did not want to be repatriated to Cuba. They said they had more specific written demands, which, however, they would give only to individuals of their choosing and not to the BOP negotiators, whom they did not trust. The detainees named a reporter from *El Nuevo Herald* (a Spanish-language newspaper affiliated with the *Miami Herald*), a reporter for CNN, and the Atlanta-based attorney. The detainees also complained about having little food but vowed that neither hunger nor the threat of force would bring their surrender.

The government negotiators argued for the release of at least three hostages, in particular the hostage with hypertension. They insisted that, at a minimum, medical staff be allowed to examine the hypertensive hostage. The detainees denied all of these requests. The conversation lasted about 15 minutes.

At about 6:00 P.M., 20–30 detainees climbed on to the roof of Alpha Unit. They displayed banners reading "Please media, justice or death"; "We haven't had food for a week. The hostages are dying due to lack of food"; and "We love you, pray please."[38]

Several detainees then began to hook up a fire hose, apparently to use against staff. Officers approached the building to turn off the water to the unit. Detainees on the roof threw pieces of concrete and other debris at them. Bureau SORT teams countered with stinger grenades, nonlethal devices that expel a mass of small rubber pellets in a 50-foot spread. This drove all but about a dozen detainees from the roof, with whom the staff then began to talk. They left the roof about 10:30 P.M., in exchange for which staff turned the water back on. The SORT teams did not, however, pull back to their original position, but rather used the incident as an opportunity to tighten the perimeter around Alpha Unit.

The following morning, Wednesday, August 28, the *El Nuevo Herald* reporter was brought to the prison after she agreed to abide by the conditions established by prison officials. She was taken to an area about 20 yards in front of Alpha Unit. Over a bullhorn, the reporter told the detainees that she would discuss with them their situation and report on it. She explained that she would be allowed to remain at the prison one hour, during which time the detainees had to release all hostages in need of medical treatment. If this were done, she would be able to return to the unit to discuss the detainees' situation with them.

About 15 minutes before the deadline, a group of detainees brought one of the female BOP hostages, the unit secretary, to the grille on a stretcher. The detainees allowed medical staff to examine her but would not release her. At this point, additional detainees began to crowd into the area near the grille door, asking for medical attention. They became disorderly, which forced the medical staff to leave. The one-hour deadline passed with no hostage released, and the reporter was escorted from the prison.

Bargaining and maneuvering concerning the ailing female hostage and the reporter continued for the rest of the day. At about 2:45 P.M., a hostage talked to staff by phone, reporting that the unit secretary was still "doing poorly."[39] Three hours later, at about 5:45 P.M., the detainees said that they would release one of the female hostages if the *El Nuevo Herald* reporter was brought back to the unit. She was in fact brought back, whereupon the detainees said they wanted to speak with a CNN reporter as well. Officials countered by escorting the reporter back out again.

At about 6:30 P.M., the detainees gave in: They released the unit secretary in return for the reporter being allowed back in for a third time. In fact, she had feigned her illness to secure her release. After greeting her family, she provided BOP officials with information about the location of the hostages and other details of the situation within the housing unit.

The detainees gave the reporter a two-page typewritten document with five demands. In paraphrased form, the demands were as follows:

- The United Nations immediately pass a resolution condemning the deportation of Mariel Cuban refugees as a violation of United Nations' convention on the status of refugees. The resolution would also call for the abrogation of the 1984 deportation agreement between Cuba and the United States. The U.S. government must agree to abide by this resolution and make this agreement public.
- All Mariel Cubans at Talladega be released directly to their families, sponsors, or representatives of the Cuban community in Miami or another city.
- The U.S. Congress immediately pass a law that would prohibit the U.S. government from repatriating any Talladega detainees and order their immediate release.
- Two representatives from the International Red Cross be brought immediately to the prison to provide medical attention to the detainees and hostages.
- A commission be created that would negotiate with the Department of Justice and INS on behalf of the detainees under conditions established by the detainees. Members of the commission would include the U.N. commissioner for refugees, a U.S. congressman, a U.S. district judge, Coretta Scott King, the Atlanta legal-aid attorney, the *El Nuevo Herald* reporter, and a reporter from CNN.

The document's final, underscored line was "JUSTICE, FREEDOM, or DEATH."[40]

Government officials were disappointed. The government was unwilling to offer anything that would come close to the five demands and was determined to return the detainees to Cuba. There appeared to be little basis for compromise.

The overall situation can be summarized by comparing it to the one at Atlanta. At Atlanta, the detainees had achieved a strong tactical position. The physical layout of the prison and the dispersal of the 100 hostages made a quick tactical strike difficult, if not impossible. In the event of an assault, detainees would have an opportunity to fulfill their pledge to kill at least some of the hostages. Also at Atlanta, there were issues around which negotiations could take place and both sides were willing to make concessions.

At Talladega, however, the detainees' demands exceeded anything the government could accept. From the government's perspective, deportation was a closed matter. The Talladega detainees had already had their cases reviewed under the terms of the Atlanta settlement, and the government had found no grounds to allow them to remain in the country. Further, the Talladega detainees, confident that the government would not launch an assault, kept the hostages in one room. This gave the government a tactical advantage they did not have at Atlanta.

Government officials also feared that making concessions at Talladega might inspire detainees in other BOP facilities to rebel.[41] In fact, later that evening, Cuban detainees in USP Terre Haute created a minor disturbance, flooding a portion of their housing unit. Fifty-seven detainees were placed in detention as a preventive measure.

Preparing the Assault: Thursday, August 29, through Friday, August 30

On Thursday morning, staff provided Alpha Unit a meal of rice, ground meat, bread, and coffee. The purpose was to nourish the hostages, some of whom appeared to be growing ill after a week of meager rations. In return, the detainees allowed medical staff to examine all of the remaining nine hostages at the entry grille. During the examinations, several of the hostages used hand signals to communicate that the situation inside the unit was deteriorating, and that now, more than ever, they feared for their lives.[42] The hostage with hypertension had a markedly elevated blood pressure reading, and his medication was increased.

Through the morning, negotiators for the detainees and the government continued to talk over the telephone, mainly about the provision of food. The detainees asserted that the government had reneged on a promise for additional food. Government negotiators stated that this was not the case. Around noon, the detainees requested a face-to-face negotiation session for 1:30 P.M. Around this time, the detainees held a meeting among themselves; from what staff could observe, the meeting turned into a hostile confrontation.

Before the sessions took place, the BOP and FBI on-site commanders discussed whether the strategy of negotiation should be abandoned in favor of a tactical assault. Several factors pointed in that direction.

First, negotiations had achieved little headway, and the positions of the two sides seemed irreconcilable.[43] Second, hostilities among the detainee factions were flaring up. Officials feared that those detainees who had been safeguarding the hostages would lose their grip on the situation.

Third, the health of the hostages, especially the officer with hypertension, was of growing concern.

Fourth, a tactical rescue looked feasible. An assault team had been trained, using an empty housing unit similar to Alpha Unit for practice runs. To conceal this from the detainees, plastic sheets were used to surround the unit, and the practice runs were conducted at night while the detainees were blinded by floodlights aimed at Alpha Unit.

Fifth, officials were concerned that if they didn't execute a planned assault, the situation might flare up somehow and force them to carry out an unscheduled emergency assault.[44] Maximizing the element of surprise by attacking at night would give the government a crucial edge.

Finally, several facilities around the country had been experiencing disruptions, which seemed related to the prolongation of the Talladega riot. Lockdowns of detainees were necessary at three facilities, and other preventive measures were taken at nine others.

The recommendation of the BOP and FBI on-site commanders for an assault was forwarded to their respective directors.

A passing thunderstorm delayed the face-to-face negotiation session scheduled for 1:30 P.M. until 4:40 P.M. In a drizzle, government negotiators and detainees began to talk, once again at a table placed in front of the unit's entryway grille, with SORT personnel standing behind the government negotiators. Bureau negotiators informed the detainees that the government was unable to meet any of their demands. The government offered to provide detainees an evening meal in return for an opportunity to examine the hostages again.

On Thursday evening, Acting Attorney General William Barr met with BOP Director J. Michael Quinlan, FBI Director William Sessions, and FBI Deputy Director Floyd Clark. He then approved the on-site commanders' recommendations and gave the order to free the hostages forthwith. The decision was not shared with the government negotiators, to avoid the possibility that the detainees might detect a change in their voice inflections.

At about 10:00 P.M., a full meal was taken to Alpha Unit. In providing the meal, officials had three purposes in mind. First, prison officials wanted to be able to see all of the hostages. This was achieved, as the hostages were allowed to eat at a table set up in the sally port. Second, prison officials wanted the detainees to feel that they were the ones gaining ground, having won a victory in obtaining a meal. This perception might lower the detainees' vigilance against an assault. In fact, that evening the detainees did appear to be more relaxed and less concerned. Finally, a full meal might cause the detainees to rest more deeply during the night.

At about 1:30 A.M., Acting Attorney General Barr reconfirmed his order to retake the unit, after having conferred with BOP Director Quinlan, FBI Director Sessions, and tactical and negotiation staff in Talladega.

At 3:40 A.M., FBI HRT personnel used explosives to blow open the two entryways. The HRT stormed into the building with FBI SWAT personnel behind them and BOP SORT deployed on the rooftop. Several flashbang grenades, deafening explosives that create a blinding light, were detonated inside the unit. The detainees, taken by surprise, put up little resistance. The hostages, who had prepared themselves for this moment, barricaded the doorway to their room with mattresses. Several detainees tried to enter the room but were unable to do so before rescuers arrived. An FBI agent described the scene as "loud, confused, and smoky."[45] Within two minutes, all of the hostages were taken out of the unit and identified by Talladega staff. They were taken to a hospital, where all were found to be in relatively good health. One detainee had suffered a minor laceration in the initial explosion.

Once the hostages were removed, the HRT secured the rest of the building. Bureau SORTs entered the unit to apply restraints to the detainees and move them to a grassy area near the building. By 5:00 A.M., all of the detainees had been accounted for and were being temporarily held in a nearby housing unit that had been emptied for this purpose.

Aftermath

Acting Attorney General Barr, BOP Director Quinlan, and FBI Director Sessions flew to Talladega early Friday morning. Acting Attorney General Barr told reporters that "I am grateful beyond words and proud beyond measure."[46] Within the next several days, 63 detainees were flown to Havana.

Damage to Alpha Unit was relatively light. Within 30 hours, the unit was reopened and the detainees returned to it. Over the next year, a new, more secure exercise yard was constructed for Alpha Unit. A video observation system was installed and new, more secure locking procedures were developed.

4

Pennsylvania State Correctional Institution at Camp Hill

October 25–27, 1989

On October 26, 1989, the Governor of Pennsylvania telephoned the authorities at Camp Hill to congratulate them for a job well done. The previous night, they had successfully terminated a brief but serious riot by negotiating the release of hostages. The institution had been peacefully secured, and the situation was calm.

A few hours after this call, inmates seized more hostages and took control of most of the facility. By early the following morning, much of the prison was in ruin. The disappointment and shock produced by this second riot proved to be the catalyst for important changes in the Pennsylvania correctional system.

State Correctional Institution at Camp Hill

Camp Hill is located in rural central Pennsylvania, across the Susquehanna River from Harrisburg. The facility opened in 1941 as a minimum-security reformatory for juvenile offenders.[1] In 1975, it was converted into a facility for minimum- and medium-security adult inmates. At the time of the riot, Camp Hill also served as the Pennsylvania Department of Correction's diagnostic and classification center for new inmates.

The inmates were housed in 10 cellblocks (built in the original construction) and 8 dormitory units (added after 1984) (see Figure 4-1). The cellblocks were divided into three groups. In Group I were Cellblocks A, B, and C, used for inmates undergoing classification, and Cellblock D, the restricted housing unit (RHU) for inmates in punitive segregation. Both Group II (Cellblocks E, F, and G) and Group III (Cellblocks H, J, and K) housed general-population inmates.

The cellblocks had an "outside-cellblock" design: Two galleries of cells, separated by a long corridor, extended the length of each building along the outside walls. The cells had barred, sliding doors. By pushing levers located in the "switchbox," a small room at the front of the galleries, an officer could open and close individual doors or groups of doors. The levers moved rods that ran the length of the galleries in a chase outside and above the cells doors. To prevent inmates from opening doors by manipulating the rods, heavy metal plates were secured over the chases.

Dormitory units 1 through 4 were for general-population inmates with sentences of two years or less, or those with longer sentences as they approached their release date. Units 5 through 8 housed inmates enrolled in a drug treatment program.

In general, Group II and Group III inmates tended to have higher custody classifications. A chain-link fence enclosed the Group II and III cellblocks and the immediately adjacent grounds. An inmate moving from this enclosed area to another part of the facility, such as the recreation field, had to pass through E Gate, normally kept locked with a chain. Also on the prison grounds were program and service buildings, a control center, and industrial shops. The prison's administration building and the department's central office were located on the grounds but outside the perimeter.

There were nine observation towers located on the perimeter, but the area's frequent fog often curtailed visibility.[2] In 1986, after several escapes, a second chain-link fence was added around the perimeter. Both fences were topped with razor ribbon. In 1989, an electronic sensor system was installed that could detect movement between and on the fences. Two mobile units patrolled around the fence 24 hours a day with a direct link to the fence sensor system.[3] The new system met corrections standards as a high-security barrier against escapes.

Preriot Conditions at Camp Hill

In postriot interviews, staff repeatedly described Camp Hill as "a prison with a maximum security perimeter but a minimum security interior."[4] The structures of the prison—physical, human, and organizational—were under severe strain and were ultimately not strong enough or appropriate to the demands placed on them.

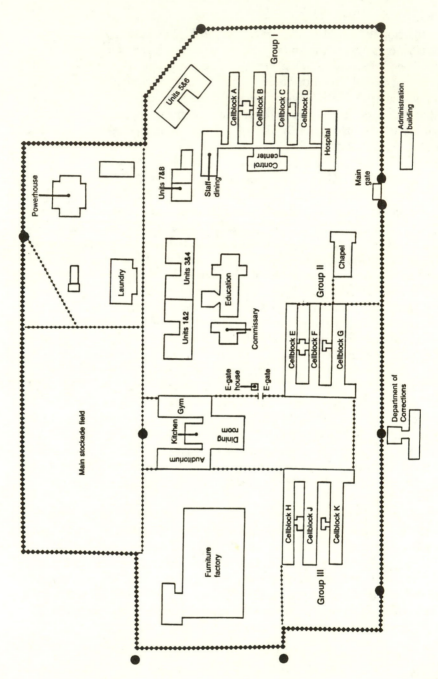

Figure 4-1 State Correctional Institution at Camp Hill.

Physical Plant

Camp Hill was originally designed to house juvenile offenders in need of rehabilitation, not for higher custody adult inmates. The plant had deteriorated with age, posing a number of security problems.

Weak Cellblock Walls

While the cellblocks' exterior walls were of solid masonry material, the interior walls were constructed of hollow blocks with an overlay of ceramic tile. Inmates could break through their cell walls more or less at will.

The walls could have been retrofitted with steel rods or mesh, but this would have been costly. Furthermore, the overcrowding problem (see below) prohibited authorities from taking cellblocks out of service for renovation.

Cell-Locking Mechanisms

The locking mechanisms were old and needed frequent repair, and inmate crews, supervised by staff, repaired them. This practice was apparently a vestige of the period when Camp Hill was a juvenile facility and offered training in the crafts,[5] and there was also a shortage of maintenance personnel. As a result, details of the locking system and its vulnerabilities were apparently common knowledge among inmates.[6] And the system actually was vulnerable. For example, the steel plates that had been installed to shield the locking mechanisms were not attached with security screws and were not difficult to remove.

Installation of Air Conditioners

Over the years, window-unit air conditioners had been installed in most of the buildings, excluding the cellblocks but including the control center. The installation normally required the removal of iron bars from a window. Windows that had been protected by heavy bars were now only as secure as the fastenings holding the air conditioners in place.

Internal Fencing

There were few internal fences. During recreation, inmates could congregate in large numbers sometimes exceeding one thousand. In a disturbance, bands of inmates would be able to spread throughout the facility relatively unimpeded.

The superintendent recognized that additional internal fencing was needed, had requested funds for it, and had labeled this request his top funding priority. The funds, however, were not allocated because of revenue shortfalls.[7]

Chronic Maintenance

As a routine matter, water leaked from the plumbing system, taps would jam, and the heating and lighting systems performed poorly.[8] The facility was under constant repair; for maintenance crews, one major project followed another. Security procedures had become slack with regard to those projects. Vehicles and tools were left unprotected on the grounds without sufficient security, and maintenance workers, as they went about their work, carried with them keys that would open all the internal gates.

Crowding

In 1982, sentence guidelines were enacted in Pennsylvania.[9] The charge to the commission that wrote the guidelines had been to reduce sentence disparities and reverse the perceived leniency of the courts. When the guidelines were first discussed, prison crowding was not an issue: The state held 8,000 inmates in a facilities with a total capacity of 10,000.

It was anticipated that sentencing guidelines would raise the prison population by about 3,000, which it did in the first several years.[10] But other changes in this period contributed to a growing inmate population. Outside the system, the cocaine epidemic raged; within the system, fewer paroles were granted and more of them were revoked. By decade's end, the population reached 23,000, leaving a shortfall of 7,000 beds despite a rapid building program.

Camp Hill, like every other state prison, became crowded; the inmate population rose from 1,600 to 2,600 between 1982 and 1989. The addition of modular units after 1984 increased the prison's capacity by 400, but even with this, the prison was 45 percent over capacity on the eve of the riot.

Furthermore, because of systemwide crowding, inmates were increasingly assigned to facilities based on the available space rather than on their own custody classification. The state's maximum-security facilities were even more crowded than Camp Hill was. Camp Hill therefore ended up holding dangerous and disruptive inmates who ideally should not have been retained there, and it was increasingly difficult to transfer problem inmates elsewhere.[11]

The growth of the inmate population was not matched by a proportional increase in staff support. The superintendent estimated that, on the eve of the riot, the prison was short 88 officers and 60 treatment staff.[12] From this, two consequences followed.

IDLE INMATES

About a third of the inmates had no structured activities.[13] Inmates waiting to participate in programs (basic and postsecondary education, vocational education, literacy training, special education, chemical abuse) numbered in the hundreds. (Some 200 of the idle inmates were parole violators who were particularly unhappy because they could not be assigned to programs until they were classified by an overloaded, slow-moving classification committee.)

DIMINISHED SUPERVISION IN THE BLOCKS

Traditionally each cellblock had been assigned its own sergeant. The block sergeant had had the opportunity to develop a tightly knit management team within the block, to develop a knowledge of and rapport with the inmates under his supervision, and to work closely with the counselors assigned to the block.

As the inmate count rose, sergeants were each given responsibility for two cellblocks, each block now having a higher count. One sergeant reported that his inmate load had increased from 200 to nearly 500.[14] The higher load made the relationship between sergeant and inmates much more tenuous.

Camp Hill's staffing situation was further complicated by a union-negotiated contract that permitted correctional officers to bid for the shift assignments on a seniority basis. Experienced staff tended to prefer the morning and night shifts, leaving the 2 P.M. to 10 P.M. shift with a complement of junior, inexperienced officers.[15] Both riots began on this shift.

Elsewhere it has been argued that administrative strategies can be developed to meet the challenge of a crowded prison.[16] Yet, at Camp Hill, this was difficult to do. The prison was not only overcrowded but was also physically deteriorating and undersupervised as well, and the department of corrections was unable to obtain the resources it needed to remedy the deficiencies (much less build new facilities).

Furthermore, the system's ability to face the crisis was deeply compromised by a crisis of loyalty and authority within its own ranks.

Divided Authority

Camp Hill before the riot was a house divided. Antagonism between administration and staff is not rare in corrections, but at Camp Hill the division was unusually deep.

On December 27, 1987 (about two years before the riot), 11 inmates had refused to return from an exercise yard to their administrative segregation unit (restricted housing unit, RHU). Two inmates who resisted being returned by force were "roughed up"; a third inmate then attacked the captain in charge.

What happened next was disputed. According to the inmate, the captain, using handcuffs wrapped around his fists, battered his face so severely that he required nine days of outside hospitalization and was unable to open his eyes for four days.[17] In the staff's version, the inmate, a brown belt in karate, assaulted the captain with a barrage of snap kicks and punches. The inmate's facial injuries occurred when he was subdued and landed on concrete.[18]

The superintendent of the prison ultimately sided with the inmate. After four months of hearings, the administration concluded that "inmate abuse had taken place under the direction and authority of commissioned officers."[19] The superintendent terminated a captain, two lieutenants, and one correctional officer, demoted another captain, and gave a lieutenant a 30-day suspension. The terminations were upheld in administrative appeal.

This incident was doubly unusual. First, the number of correctional staff disciplined was exceptionally high. Second, those disciplined included *commissioned* officers, those who carried a special responsibility of trust.

Many officers, commissioned and noncommissioned alike, concluded that the punishment was excessive, meted out vindictively, and symptomatic of an administration that was more interested in making inmates happy than in the safety of officers. According to one captain, an 18-year veteran of Camp Hill, "that incident just gave the entire inmate population the message that officers cannot touch inmates."[20] As a result, he explained, officer morale plummeted and remained low in the period leading up to the riot.[21] The deputy for operations defended the administration's actions as necessary, but concurred that "morale slipped in the institution quite a bit after the incident."[22]

The administration and staff also collided over the operation of the RHU. According to the superintendent's account, when he assumed office in 1984, RHU was being run far too loosely, leading to the abuse of inmates:

> There were inmates in there that were drinking out of commodes because officers had shut their water off. We found inmates who had mattresses taken for lengthy periods of time with no authority by the administrative body. We found that inmates were being locked up at will by the commissioned officers and released at their own discretion.[23]

The superintendent reformed RHU procedures, based on the principle that "we had to run it in a humane manner, and we had to run it according to departmental policy and procedure."[24] A program review committee (PRC) was established that periodically reviewed the status of each RHU inmate. The PRC was authorized to release an inmate from RHU after he had served half of his term. In part, the PRC was driven by necessity: there was not enough room in the RHU for inmates to serve their full terms.[25] Still, staff perceived the PRC as undermining their authority to discipline. Inmates, they claimed, saw the shortened RHU sentences as slaps on the wrist rather than serious punishment.[26]

Several points can be made about the division between staff and the administration. One is related to Philip Selznick's observation that an organizational culture—a common understanding of the organization's critical tasks and how to accomplish them—is important to its successful operation.[27] But Camp Hill had not one but two organizational cultures. Each side believed that its own approach represented good corrections and that the other side's approach was unwise and unjust.

Second, where this kind of cultural division exists between employees and administrators, it is tempting for the administrators to ignore it "on principle." After all, the employees are clearly in the wrong; wouldn't it be wrong to negotiate with them, compromise with them, or allow the employees to hold up the wheels of progress? Isn't it better to proceed inflexibly forward and make them fit in?

Current management theory generally recommends a different course, however. This kind of cultural schism poses too many dangers to be ignored. Managers are encouraged to patiently explain their vision of the organization's mission, to try to win employees to that vision, and (at the very least) to recognize that cultural change can not be ordered into existence overnight. Change should be made patiently where possible; where policy change must be rapid, it must be carefully explained.

In retrospect, however, Camp Hill's administration was neither aggressive in efforts to cultivate a shared vision nor appropriately mindful of the dangers posed by the low morale of the staff. The prison's superintendent was rarely seen on the yard, and he was described by numerous staff as aloof and distant.[28] In this climate of distrust, where the staff had in large measure ceased to view the prison administrators as legitimate authority, any policy change could be given the worst interpretation and serve as a lightning rod for discontent.

Policy Changes as Precipitants

On October 16, 1989, nine days before the first riot, the administration issued two policy changes.[29] Traditionally, the families of inmates had been permitted to bring food baskets into the prison on special family days, but these baskets were frequently used to smuggle in contraband. Management now decided to disallow the baskets. The superintendent also planned to give inmates another family day to temper their discontent over the change, but apparently this was never communicated to the inmates.[30]

The second measure affected inmates' access to medical treatment. The practice had been that an inmate could sign up for sick line five days a week.[31] However, the system had become overloaded and cumbersome, and the nurses were putting pressure on the superintendent to streamline the process.[32] The new policy would allow inmates to see a nurse two days a week, on a block-by-block basis.[33] Still, an inmate could request medical attention on any other day by notifying an officer.

The rationale behind the family day change was straightforward: to prevent drugs, money, and weapons from being smuggled in. Inmates complained about the change, but, most likely, it made sense to them. The rationale for the change in the sick-line procedures was far less apparent. The goal of the policy change, in the administration's mind, was to provide better medical services to the inmates. If the new arrangement did not work, the old policy would be restored at the end of a 90-day period.

The problem was that there was little patience for any such experiment. Inmates complained that the new policy violated their right to medical treatment. What made this situation unusual was that many of the correctional staff, both commissioned and noncommissioned, were closer to the inmates on this issue than they were to the administration.

In part, this was because they believed the new policy would be burdensome to them. Officers would now have to judge whether an inmate making a special request to see a nurse was doing so legitimately. They would in effect be the nurses' gatekeepers five days a week, a dubious position in which they might face recrimination, abuse, and maybe even lawsuits from disgruntled inmates.

Aside from the additional burdens the new medical policy would place on officers, some officers knew, or at least believed they knew, that the policy violated department regulations.[34] Furthermore, in an odd reversal in which staff were now complaining that the administration was being too harsh on inmates, officers argued that the new policy was unjust. A captain recalled expressing his objections to the superintendent about the new policy.

> I said [to the superintendent] we're in the United States of America. If I or any other person, even an indigent, a street person, has a medical problem and they go to the hospital, they have to be treated there at that hospital or taken to a facility to be treated. If they don't, they're in violation of the law. I said, how can we do this?[35]

In the nine-day period after the policy changes were issued, Camp Hill became increasingly unsettled.

Protest over Policy Changes

On October 17, the day after the two policy changes were announced, inmates signed up for the sick day in large numbers as a protest. One sergeant reported that in his block, while 30–40 inmates would normally request sick days, 175–200 inmates signed up.[36] In another block, inmates in unison lit the slips of paper that announced the two policy changes and threw them burning onto the tiers.[37]

From the administration's point of view, the most serious problem was that they were receiving reports that officers were condoning, if not encouraging, inmate protest. The deputy for operations later reflected:

> what they [the officers] actually were doing was threatening me and telling me, if you don't back off these policies, we're going to get [inmates] to sign up en masse and we'll make sure that you back off.[38]

Fruit of Islam

For over a year, prison staff had been concerned about the growing influence of a Muslim inmate group called the Fruit of Islam (FOI). In postriot accounts, the administration described the FOI as a "very well organized, very radical group of inmates who preached racial hatred and felt they had a right to take down the institution."[39] According to the deputy for operations, a track meet scheduled for September 23, 1989, had to be canceled because the FOI was planning to disrupt the event.[40] The Adams commission states that it received evidence (staff and inmate interviews, internal reports) that the FOI had been attempting to organize a disturbance among the inmate population over a period of time.[41]

The prison-appointed Muslim Imam (chaplain) later claimed that the FOI was being made the scapegoat for the riot, and that the FOI had no agenda other than a religious one.[42] The Imam himself, however, came under fire for his purportedly antiadministration activities. (For example, the Imam was alleged to have told inmates that the Koran should be used as an "Uzi" against Camp Hill's administration and, immediately prior to the second riot, to have gone from cell to cell fomenting discontent. He strongly denied both charges.[43])

In any event, the FOI does appear to have exercised a significant measure of influence among inmates. The Adams commission states that the FOI used the controversy over family day and sick-line policies to advance their own agenda.[44] The superintendent agreed:

> We were in the process of working through all of this [the problems related to the policy changes] . . . We ran out of time is what happened. And we ran out of time because of the Fruit of Islam being powerful enough to be the nucleus to keep fermenting problems.[45]

Warning Signs

According to the Adams commission, there were numerous signs of an impending riot in the two-week period leading up to the October 25 disturbance. They included both direct warnings from inmates and indirect indicators, such as RHU inmates being unusually quiet.[46] A sergeant described the situation this way:

> You hear rumblings, but you hear rumblings all the time. But things, like at the main line [for eating], weren't right. There were less people coming down eating. It was a lot quieter. People that normally come and talk with you, they walk by and didn't say anything . . . You could almost cut the tension.[47]

On October 23, a major disturbance occurred at the state's maximum-security prison at Huntingdon. Twenty-nine officers and 19 inmates were injured.[48] Apparently, this event further unsettled Camp Hill.

Two Days of Rioting

First Riot Begins at E Gate

About 2:45 P.M. on October 25, 1989, a group of 500 inmates was being moved from the main stockade field to their cells in Groups II and III.[49]

They began to pass through E Gate, whose narrow width invariably acted as a bottle neck. A crowd of inmates were waiting their turn when an officer stationed at E Gate asked an inmate for a pass. Instead of producing the pass, the inmate struck the officer. A sergeant, an officer, and a tradesman came to the aid of the officer.[50] About 50 inmates standing nearby attacked all three. The commissioner saw the event from the central office administration building, which overlooks the area, and notified the Camp Hill superintendent.[51]

On the yard between Groups II and III, a group of three officers, two captains, and a sergeant ordered the inmates to return to their cells.[52] Some but not all of the inmates complied. Between 150 and 300 inmates remained in the area, milling without visible leadership.[53] Officers continued to attempt to move the inmates toward their blocks, but many refused.

Inside the Group II and III blocks, officers were notified over their radios that a disturbance had begun on the yard and they were to lock the doors to the blocks.[54] Inside E Block, inmates (largely parole violators) began to destroy furniture and fashion makeshift weapons. According to at least one account (the details on this are not clear), a commissioned officer on the yard ordered the block's front door opened so that more inmates from the yard could be taken inside and locked down.[55] But once the door was opened, the inmates inside E Block rushed the officers and took their keys. About the same time, the officers still on the yard were assaulted by some of the milling inmates.[56]

Using keys taken from officers, inmates opened the front doors of each cellblock in Groups II and III. Several officers were able to delay their capture by locking themselves in the switchboxes at the front of the blocks. But inmates broke through the walls (made of hollow blocks) and pulled the officers out.[57] Eight correctional officers were taken hostage. They were handcuffed, robbed of their personal possessions, beaten, and then taken to the area in front of H Block. At 3:05 P.M., an officer in a tower near the department administration building observed an officer being beaten by a group of inmates on the yard below him. He fired a warning shot, forcing the inmates to disperse.[58] By this time, the riot had expanded to 600–700 participants, involving all the blocks in Groups II and III and the area within the chain-link fence.[59]

Meanwhile, the officer who had been initially assaulted at E Gate had called the control center to explain the situation. The control center ordered a lockdown of the rest of the institution. Once Group I was secured, the officers thereby made available were ordered to E Gate. In addition, the control center notified the state police and the municipal police.

Loss of E Gate and Consequent Spread of the Riot

About 3:12 P.M., a half hour after the initial incident, a large number of inmates moved to an area near E Gate, apparently intent on breaking through the locked gate to gain access to the rest of the institution. A few minutes later, about 12 unarmed officers arrived on the other side of E Gate.[60] Near the officers were three vehicles that could have been used to barricade E Gate. The officers did not take advantage of the vehicles, nor did they remove them from the yard.[61] About 3:20 P.M., inmates sprayed a fire extinguisher at the officers on the other side of E Gate. This kept the officers at bay, while inmates tried to break the E Gate lock.

In the control center, the deputy for operations ordered a lieutenant to take three officers then at the E Gate to the armory to obtain shotguns and then return to E Gate.[62] However, before this could be done, an inmate produced a key to the E Gate and unlocked it. (Most likely, the key had been taken from a tradesman assaulted at the beginning of the disturbance.) The inmates poured through E Gate in large numbers.

The officers at E Gate retreated to the control center. The officers who had been dispatched to the armory returned with shotguns, but, with E Gate having already been breached, they were redeployed to the main gate, rear gate, and a tower at the front of the institution.

Riot's Spread, Looting, and Destruction

The inmates spread through much of the institution, looting and destroying buildings as they encountered them. An inmate hot-wired one of the vehicles that had been left on the grounds and drove it through the doors of the commissary. A crowd of inmates rushed in, assaulted an officer, looted the building, and set the building on fire.

The commandeered vehicle was then driven through an internal fence, past the main stockade recreation yard, and into the perimeter fences. The vehicle successfully penetrated the first fence but became hung up on the concrete footing of the second fence and could not move further. About the same time, another truck was used to break the fence separating the furniture factory from the rest of the complex. Inmates looted the area for tools and set an office on fire.

The fire in the commissary destroyed the building. Other fires destroyed E Gate house, the basement in B Block, an equipment shed, two vehicles, and a maintenance cart. Small fires caused minor damage in the cellblocks and two modular units.

From about 3:45 to 4:15 P.M., inmates brought hostages out to the Group II and III yard and displayed and beat them in sight of corrections staff and state police. Inmates also assaulted each other in grudge attacks and stole other inmates' property. Some inmates formed groups for self-protection.[63]

Arrival of Emergency Services

The Pennsylvania State Police began arriving at the prison at 3:26 P.M. and were fully assembled by 3:40 P.M., about an hour after the disturbance had begun. Local police, arriving about the same time, were stationed around the perimeter. Local fire companies began to arrive to extinguish fires.[64] The Pennsylvania Emergency Management Agency—a state office responsible for major emergencies—was notified at 3:48 P.M. Correctional officers manned the towers. Off-duty Camp Hill Correctional Emergency Response Team (CERT) members were also arriving, and a captain was dispatched to the rear gate to organize them.

When the state police arrived, Camp Hill management initially denied them permission to enter the facility until instructions could be obtained from the commissioner of corrections. Corrections department policy permitted emergency personnel to carry only shotguns loaded with birdshot rather than the more lethal 00 buckshot. The state police were carrying buckshot. When contacted, the commissioner at first declined to allow the state police onto the grounds, but then reconsidered. The exchange delayed the arrival of the police for about 15 or 20 minutes.[65]

At approximately 4:30 P.M., Camp Hill's CERT and the Pennsylvania State Police entered the institution through the rear gate. They moved the modular-unit inmates who were cooperative to the main stockade field. This covered their backs. Rioting inmates retreated through the E Gate onto the yard between Groups II and III. The state police and CERT forces then formed a skirmish line outside of E Gate, thereby confining the inmates to one area.

Negotiations with Inmates by Deputy Superintendent

Almost immediately after the riot began, inmates tried to contact the control center using both telephones and radios they had obtained from officers. The deputy for treatment answered one of these early calls and found himself speaking with an inmate leader of the FOI.[66] The deputy asked the inmate if any staff had been injured; being told that some had been, he said that it was in no one's interest to have the situation get worse and asked the FOI inmate if he would release the injured officers. To the deputy's amazement, the inmate responded "no problem." Within a few minutes, two injured officers were brought to E Gate and released.[67]

The deputy then asked the superintendent whether he should continue to negotiate with the inmates. The superintendent decided that since he seemed to be getting good results the deputy should continue. It seemed to him that having a high prison official involved in the negotiations "brought us some credibility." The superintendent told his deputy that he would be relieved of all decision-making authority while he was acting as a negotiator, as is the common practice in hostage situations.[68]

In fact, several times during negotiations, the deputy broke off his conversation with the inmates, telling them, "I have to go talk to the superintendent about this." According to the superintendent, "they [the inmates] understood that he [the deputy] was not making the decisions, that I was making the decisions."[69]

The deputy talked to several inmates, but an FOI inmate leader took clear charge. About an hour into negotiations, the inmate told the deputy that he wanted to get the incident over, and that he wanted to have a face-to-face meeting.[70] The deputy agreed.

At approximately 6:45 P.M. the deputy and several other staff members met the six inmate negotiators at a table set up in front of the education building. The FOI leader maintained his leading role. Inmates complained about the policy changes in family day and sick line. They also voiced objections about access to the law library, showering procedures, and lack of out-of-cell time.

The inmate negotiators, however, did not have control of the inmates in the Group II and III area. Hostages were being threatened and beaten in the yard as talks were going on. One of the inmate negotiators went back to the yard to try to control the situation.

Negotiations were concluded when the deputy for treatment promised the inmates that the superintendent would meet with them at 1:00 P.M. the next day to discuss the issues they had raised. The deputy also promised that the superintendent would issue a press release announcing the meeting.[71] The chief inmate negotiator went to the area of Groups II and III and spoke with inmates there for roughly 45 minutes. He then returned to E Gate, informing staff there that the inmates would release the hostages and return to their cells to be locked down.

Release of Hostages and Return of Inmates to Their Cells

About 7:15 P.M., all of the hostages were released and the inmates began returning to cells. They were placed in whatever cells in Group II or III that seemed to be the most usable at the time. As many as four or five inmates were placed in a cell. Some inmates were returned to the modular units.

A head count was attempted four or five times, but none of the totals was correct. An identity check was not ordered, nor was an immediate shakedown. Radios, keys, tools, knives, and razors were missing and the hallways were covered with debris and weapons.

Still, the institution was declared under control at 10:30 P.M. The 11:00 P.M. local television news reported the superintendent's statement that the facility was secure. Inmates watched this report on televisions in their cells. Food was distributed between 3:00 A.M. and 4:00 A.M.

Aftermath: "Inmates Are Secure"

Crucial to what followed was the superintendent's perception of the situation in the blocks. First, the superintendent believed that the inmates were locked in cells, could not get out, and posed no immediate threat.[72] He had assigned responsibility for securing the inmates to a captain with 18 years of experience at Camp Hill.[73] Over a two-hour period, the captain radioed reassuring reports to the superintendent, telling him that the inmates were locking up cooperatively. Those inmates found to be in cells that did not lock securely were moved to another one. At 9:15 P.M., the captain reported that all six cellblocks were secure. The major confirmed this over the radio.

Second, the Superintendent later stated that he had confidence in his chain of command with regard to providing him reliable information:[74]

> I truly believed that the information I was getting was accurate . . . So, confident in my staff's ability to assess the situation and give me information I needed, I began to focus on the problem of returning the institution to normal.[75]

Furthermore, his confidence had been reinforced by the experience of the riot just hours earlier: "The information that had come to me through the chain of command had been accurate, it allowed us to resolve the first riot."[76] The superintendent saw no reason to doubt that staff would continue to provide him accurate information.

Third, until the start of the second riot, the superintendent continued to receive information that was consistent with the captain's original assessment:

> There were no reports that inmates were out of their cells; there were no reports of defective locking mechanisms; . . . there were no reports of warnings of a second riot being possible.[77]

Elaborating on this point, the superintendent stated that the following day, 20 of his staff members accompanied him to the commissioner's office to take a call over a speaker phone from the governor. About this meeting, the superintendent remarked, "nobody said anything about potential problems."[78]

Finally, the superintendent perceived a need for a cooling-down period before a shakedown was attempted. He recalled two incidents in Camp Hill's history. One was the 1987 RHU incident described above, which had resulted in the termination or disciplining of six officers. The other occurred in 1983, when inmates attacked and nearly killed a sergeant. In response, according to the superintendent, inmates were dragged from their cells by officers, forced to run through a gauntlet, and "savagely beaten."[79] (The superintendent had not been at Camp Hill at the time, but relied on a department report of the incident, which he described as "frankly nauseating."[80])

The superintendent drew a parallel to the current situation:

> These two incidents were the result of an attack on one officer. What happens when you got 36 who have been hurt and who have been taken hostage and who have reportedly been sodomized, who have been beaten out in the open? You have an extremely volatile emotional climate . . . We had a lot of very tired, very scared, very upset staff. We had a lot of very tired, scared, upset inmates who fully expected physical retaliation.[81]

For these reasons, the superintendent concluded that a shakedown should wait at least another day, perhaps two. After the fact, no decision was more heavily criticized, but at the time, the superintendent felt relatively sure that the decision was the right one.

In following the superintendent's reasoning, it should be kept in mind that he had just emerged from an enormously stressful situation. He, like his staff, was exhausted and relieved that the incident was over. In that context, four points can be made.

First, the superintendent accepted reports from the blocks that were relatively abstract. Instead of demanding to know the condition of the blocks in their particular details, he was willing to accept as sufficient the statement that the blocks were "secure." The problem was that the term "secure," unless further qualified, is open to misinterpretation. The captain, in later testimony, explained that during the inspection of the blocks he was asked over the radio if the blocks were "secure."

> It strikes me funny that I was asked a question of that nature. And anybody that knows in corrections, that depending upon the circumstances, "secured" can mean many different things. And in that [particular] circumstance, it meant the inmates were locked in their cells.[82]

The superintendent, on the other hand, interpreted the captain's use of "secure" this way (as he recalled it later):

> Now when you say "secure" in corrections, there's only one thing you can possibly mean, and that is the inmates are in their cells and they cannot get out, they cannot escape. There is [sic] no if's, and's, or but's about it, it's not a term that's open to interpretation. When a commissioned officer [that is, the above-quoted captain] says, these inmates are secure or the cell block is secure, he only means one thing, the inmates are locked up, they cannot get out.[83]

Thus, while the captain never meant to report that the inmates could not possibly get out of their cells, the superintendent was sure that the captain had told him exactly that. (Of course, given the weakened condition of the locking mechanisms, it seems that the institution had not been "secure" for some time before the riot, if the word means that it is completely impossible for inmates to leave their cells.)

A second point is that the superintendent expressed seemingly contradictory assessments of his staff's capabilities in the situation. On the one hand, he claimed to have full confidence in their ability to assess the situation accurately; if there were any problems, they would surely inform him. On the other hand, he observed his officers to be very tired and very emotional; they could not be trusted to conduct a shakedown. The two assessments do not square easily. If staff were too exhausted and upset to use good judgment in conducting a shakedown, it would seem to follow that their perceptions of the situation might be clouded by the same emotional state.

This raises a third point. The superintendent perceived staff to be potentially both reliable and unreliable. Thus, one would anticipate that the superintendent would undertake an especially active effort to ensure that incoming information from staff was accurate and that he understood its meaning and limitations. This does not seem to have occurred. The superintendent could have gone to the blocks to check for himself, but he did not.

Fourth, the superintendent points out that staff could have brought problems to his attention when they met with the commissioner to receive the call from the governor.[84] Still, one can imagine that this would have been difficult for staff to do. The purpose of the meeting was to receive the governor's commendation. The commissioner was present. To flag operational problems in such a meeting might be perceived as being contrary to the spirit of the meeting, perhaps even impertinent. Also, the structure of the meeting may have further inhibited an open discussion of problems. The commissioner and governor maintained a dialogue, with the Camp Hill staff members listening over a speaker.

Finally, the procedure the captain used to assess whether the blocks were secure seems to have been inadequate. The captain entered a cellblock and, himself staying up front, directed a contingent of correctional officers and lieutenants go up and down each tier. Each cell door was pulled to check that it could not be opened. Yet, several key factors were overlooked:

- The cellblocks were dark because the overhead tier lights had been knocked out during the riot. In some blocks, the only lights were in the inmates' cells, and when they turned them off, it was pitch black.[85] Correctional officers had to operate with flashlights. If inmates were able to jam closed an otherwise broken cell door, it could pass the captain's inspection. The darkness would have made this more difficult to detect.
- During the riot, six sets of keys had been taken from correctional officers and not recovered.[86] Because of the nature of the locking mechanism, an inmate could not use keys to release himself, but if one inmate managed to get loose with the keys he could rapidly release many others.
- In many of the blocks, the security panels that protect the locking mechanisms' rods were missing. The potential was high that inmates would be able to reach out of their cells, grab the rods, and open cell doors.[87]
- When the captain was making his rounds, there were pockets of inmates scattered in various parts of the institution, including the furniture factory, education building, chapel, and rear gate. The captain stated that he was unaware of this fact when he declared the institution "secure."[88] These inmates were, by the early morning hours, moved to cells. However, the conditions of their cells

could not have been taken into account in the initial declaration that the prison was secure.

The administration saw it differently. Confident that the facility was secure, the superintendent began to focus on "the problem of returning the institution to normal."[89]

Decision for State Police to Exit

The next issue to be faced was the number of state police officers that should remain at the prison. A little after midnight, the municipal police had been released, leaving 260 state police. Between 1:00 and 3:00 A.M., the superintendent, the two deputy superintendents, and the ranking Pennsylvania State Police officer discussed the security needs of the institution. (The Adams commission reported that the major of the guard had also been present, but he himself denied this.)

The three Camp Hill administrators all believed that the inmates were "secure," that is, "are in their cells and cannot get out." In that case, any disturbance that broke out would be confined to a single cell, and a small contingent of officers would be sufficient to control such a disturbance. Between 2:00 and 3:00 A.M., then, most of the state police officers were released from duty, leaving a platoon of 27 officers and a captain. (Actually, this platoon was relieved by fresh personnel at eight-hour intervals.)

The state police platoon was originally deployed to the staff dining hall, but later that night the staff said they wanted to return that room to its regular use. A new site was discussed. The state police captain rejected a location in the education building in the area of Groups II and III, because he believed officers could be trapped there. So, the platoon was in fact relocated to a staff training house (Manor House), a quarter mile from the prison, beginning at 9:30 A.M. the following day (October 26). It was expected that the platoon would be withdrawn entirely that midnight.

From Riot Response to Riot "Recovery": Morning of Thursday, October 26

On Thursday morning, prison officials shifted from an emergency-response mode to a recovery mode. A damage assessment was conducted. It showed that there had been injuries to 36 Camp Hill staff, one state trooper, one firefighter, and seven inmates. Eight staff had been held hostage and 31 staff had been trapped inside buildings, some of which had been on fire.[90] Damage to the facility was extensive, as noted above. Six sets of keys were still missing.[91]

Maintenance crews arrived early in the morning, but only put in a half a day of work. They removed the vehicle from the perimeter fence, repaired the fence, removed another burned vehicle, and then were put on hold for the rest of the day. They were told not to make repairs to the blocks or to clean up the debris in them, because the state police first had to photograph and videotape the blocks for investigative purposes.[92] The maintenance crews were dismissed at 3:30 P.M.

The superintendent assigned the deputy for operations the task of identifying a dozen staff members who had played key roles in resolving the disturbance, so that they could meet with the commissioner later in the afternoon. "I spent a considerable amount of time with that," the deputy later stated.[93]

Superintendent's Rushed Meeting with the Inmates

At 1:00 P.M., the superintendent and his two deputies met with the same inmates who the previous day had negotiated with the deputy for treatment. At the start of the meeting, the superintendent told the inmates that the meeting would be limited to one hour.[94] By meeting's end, it was clear to the superintendent that the inmates' primary concern was the change in the sick-line policy.[95] The superintendent agreed to review the matter and get back to them in a few days.

At 2:00 P.M., the superintendent and his staff ended the meeting so that they could take the call from the governor scheduled for 2:30. Apparently, the inmates felt that nothing had been accomplished at the meeting. They were frustrated and angry.[96] One of the inmate negotiators later testified that he had felt that the meeting had been "a waste of time" and that he had nothing positive to tell inmates when he returned to the blocks.[97] While the inmate negotiators were being returned to their blocks, officers overheard comments such as "something is going to happen tonight," "it's not over yet," and "the war isn't over yet." The officers' reports, both written and verbal, were passed on to a captain, who in turn passed them on to the major of the guard.[98]

Disarray on the Second Shift

When the 2:00 to 10:00 P.M. shift assumed their duties, the officers assigned to Groups II and III felt immediately uncomfortable with the situation, especially now that the state police were no longer on the grounds.

One problem was that they were shorthanded. The normal complement for Groups II and III was 26 officers, but only 16 had reported for duty. Staff injuries incurred the night before had kept some of the officers from reporting. Also, the entire staffing schedule had been thrown off balance, because numerous off-duty officers had responded to the riot the evening before and had stayed all night.[99]

Also worrisome were the conditions in the blocks. The floors were strewn with debris. One officer would later comment, "there were weapons laying everywhere. Wherever inmates dropped them, that's where they laid. Nothing was picked up."[100] There were still no lights in the cellblocks.

Most of the officers suspected or knew that the locking mechanisms could be compromised. Officers later claimed that they reported these conditions to the upper echelon administration, but the administration claimed that they did not receive the communication.[101]

The lieutenant in charge of Group II and Group III notified all the block officers not to go down the tiers, but rather to stay at the front of the blocks. If they saw movement, they were to notify him, lock their blocks, and report to E Gate.[102]

Meanwhile, on the other side of the prison, inmates in the RHU had been highly disruptive through much of the afternoon, setting small fires in front of their cells. The deputy for operations and a captain went there to assess the situation. The deputy asked the lieutenant how things were going. The lieutenant responded "terrible."[103] When the deputy returned to his office, he called the state police lieutenant at Manor House. The deputy told her that tension was high in the facility, that she should stay on standby, but that he wanted to inspect Groups II and III before asking her to bring her platoon back into the prison.[104]

At 6:00 P.M., the superintendent conducted an interview carried by local news stations. During this interview, he made several remarks to the effect that the institution was secure and that the inmates' demands would not be met. Many inmates perceived the news conference an affront to them.[105] When the newscast ended, an audible roar went up inside the facility.

Second Riot Begins, October 26, 7:00 P.M.

The deputy for operations along with a captain drove to Groups II and III to assess the mood of the blocks.[106] They went first to J Block. The deputy saw an inmate running down a tier toward the back of the cellblock. The deputy told the captain to stay there with the officers and that he would return to the control center to call the state police.

Soon after that, inmates simultaneously poured out of their cells in large numbers. The lieutenant issued a radio call to officers in the blocks to evacuate the blocks, lock the first (front) doors as they were leaving, and then exit the yard through E Gate.[107] Two officers apparently misheard the instructions and locked themselves inside their blocks. Inmates soon overpowered them.[108] The officers in F, G, and J blocks had no door keys (they were taken from them the night before),[109] but a sergeant and another officer were able to lock those blocks. All but the two officers who had locked themselves in left their blocks just before the inmates took control, and left the yard through E Gate.

The attempt to lock inmates in the blocks was ineffective, presumably since they still had the door keys. Inmates entered the yard in large numbers. They ran toward E Gate, which had not been repaired since the first riot, and through it into the remainder of the prison.

Adams argues that, because the inmates released themselves so swiftly and in concert, the riot was probably planned and organized.[110] According to an eyewitness, the inmates were moving in a military-like formation after they passed through E Gate, half of them peeling off for the modular area and the other half heading directly toward the control center.[111]

Control Center, Dormitory Units, and C Block Attacked

Correctional staff secured the door to the control building just before inmates reached the door.[112] The building was the prison's operational command post. Inside were the deputy for operations, the major, three captains, an unarmed state police corporal, plus other treatment staff and correctional officers. (The superintendent had gone home to rest.) In addition, about a dozen nonhostile inmates were present. The entire group locked themselves in the secure control room area.[113]

On the outside, inmates tried to batter open the front door and shoved lit mops through the barred first-floor windows in an attempt to smoke the staff out.[114] Inmates then tore out a first-floor air conditioner and entered the building. They set fires, and thick smoke began to fill the first floor.

The smoke forced the group in the control room to move to the second floor, initially passing through a small key-pass window and then up a stairwell filled with dense smoke. At this point, there were about 40 people on the second floor: 27 Camp Hill staff members, a state police corporal, and 12 inmates.[115] The staff began to chain doors closed and barricade them.[116] Inmates gained access to the rooftops of the Group I buildings and, from there, started to break into the second floor of the control center.

As these events were unfolding, other rioting inmates attacked the dormitory units. Some of inmates assigned to the dormitory units put up resistance and defended their buildings as best they could. Several inmates aided dormitory unit officers by dressing them in inmate clothing to help them escape. Rioting inmates set fires to Dormitory Units 1 through 6, which completely destroyed them.[117] Inmates from units 7 and 8, who were participants in an intensive drug treatment program, successfully fended off the rioters at considerable risk to themselves.[118]

Other inmates ran loose throughout the compound, setting fires that destroyed the furniture factory and heavily damaged the gymnasium, education building, and a half-dozen other smaller structures.[119] The inmates in C Block released themselves by breaking through cell walls. About 7:30 P.M., inmates rushed the main gates; corrections staff fired warning shots forcing them to retreat.[120]

State Police Rescue

Meanwhile, the state police officer trapped on the second floor radioed Manor House for immediate help. Correctional staff made several calls to the sergeant at the front gatehouse, explaining that their situation was desperate. They reported that smoke was filling the room and it was becoming difficult to breathe. Inmates were beating on the walls trying to get in.[121]

The 25-officer state police contingent arrived at the main gate and sought permission to enter the institution to effect a rescue. The commissioner of corrections and the superintendent were at the gatehouse by this time. The state police officer in command later stated that there was a delay at the gate of from three to four minutes.[122] The superintendent said that the state police were delayed only as long as necessary to develop a plan and ensure that any armed contingent knew where to go and what to do.[123] The superintendent correctly observes there were

> 12 to 14 hundred inmates on the loose . . . You just don't grab bodies and [put] them through a gate . . . If you do that, . . . you run the risk of inmates getting weapons and you run the risk of the people that you're trying to save dying because you panicked and threw people in without a plan.[124]

The delay, in the superintendent's estimation, was time well spent and ensured the mission's success.[125]

This delay became the subject of great controversy, however, because the gate sergeant later claimed that the commissioner and superintendent had stubbornly refused to allow the state police contingent to enter the prison at all. (Both those officials flatly denied this.[126]) The sergeant claimed that he himself had opened the gate against orders after the superintendent had left the area. Other correctional staff, including commissioned officers, later testified that the superintendent's indecisiveness had endangered the lives of fellow officers and only the sergeant's action saved them.[127] Echoing this view, the Adams commission stated in its report that the delay "may have endangered 40 to 50 lives."

In any case, the state police contingent entered the main gate and they formed a thin skirmish line from the gate to the control center. Several correctional officers and arriving municipal police joined the line.[128] A municipal police officer, using an automatic weapon, fired warning shots into the ground to prevent inmates from advancing toward the control center.[129]

When the state police arrived at the control center, the staff trapped on the second floor lowered a rope of linked-together garrison belts.[130] A shotgun and handgun were attached and pulled up.[131] A few minutes later, a ladder was brought in and propped next to the control center. The trapped personnel escaped by knocking out an air conditioner; a captain had succumbed to smoke and had to be carried out.

Command Posts and Tenuous Negotiations

After leaving the gatehouse, the commissioner went to the department's administration building to establish a department command post. The superintendent went to his office to establish the command post for the institution and was joined by the deputy for operations, after his rescue from the control center.[132]

Over the next several hours, 875 state police officers arrived at the prison.[133] Personnel from other state prisons, municipal police, firefighters, and emergency medical teams also arrived and were deployed around the perimeter.[134] The Pennsylvania Emergency Management Agency was notified of the riot by the county's Office for Emergency Preparedness.

Inmates contacted prison officials using radios stolen the previous night. State police negotiators, with the assistance of the deputy for treatment, began to negotiate about 10:45 P.M. (According to his own account, the deputy was assigned to the negotiating team but felt it wise to stay in the background.[135]) The negotiators threw a telephone (with a long cord) over the perimeter fence to provide a direct line between them and the inmates.

Negotiations continued through most of the night. Inmates expressed concerns related to crowding, correctional officers' treatment of them, the quality of food, and medical treatment.[136] At various times, inmates stated that they wanted to meet with the governor, commissioner, or superintendent. The commissioner responded that he would meet with inmates only after the hostages had been released and the inmates returned to their cells.[137] The inmates demanded to hear this directly from the commissioner, who actually went to the command center to convey this message in person. However, the inmates then said (without explanation) that they did not want to talk to the commissioner.[138] Inmates also requested that Amnesty International representatives be brought into the institution.

As negotiations were being conducted, inmates set fires throughout the compound, using gasoline from the industries shops as an accelerant. The gate between the gymnasium and the commissary was barricaded with debris soaked in gasoline. At one point, inmates used a homemade litter to carry an injured hostage to the yard, allowing state police to retrieve him.[139]

Assault to Retake the Institution

About 4:00 A.M., the negotiations appeared to be stalled. The negotiators sensed that the inmates were not interested in achieving a resolution.[140] Hammering could be heard in K Block (the location of the inmate negotiators), suggesting that inmates were barricading themselves in for a long siege. Also, the hostages had not been seen for several hours, and the state officials did not know their condition or even if they were alive.[141]

The state police commander at the scene and corrections officials developed a tactical plan, whose goal was to demonstrate the state's resolve to conclude the incident soon and to pressure inmates to resume serious negotiations.[142] This would be accomplished through a show of force and a tightening of the perimeter. If the inmates threatened a hostage, however, state officials were prepared to back off.[143]

At 6:45 A.M., three columns of state police officers were formed. One column, facing E Block, created a diversion by shouting to draw the inmates' attention. The two other columns prepared to enter the institution via the rear of the prison. One column entered the kitchen from its rear entrance; inmates lit fires in the kitchen's front entrance, blocking the column's advance. An airport fire "crash truck" was used to break open a barricaded fence near the gymnasium, allowing the third column to enter the yard between Groups II and III.

Inmates began throwing rocks, debris, and firebombs at the officers.[144] The officers responded with warning shots fired at the ground, wounding four inmates. The rest of the inmates retreated into the Group II and III blocks. The state police removed the wounded inmates for medical treatment.

The state police then formed a skirmish line between E and H blocks. At this point, the chief inmate negotiator told the state negotiators over the phone (falsely, as it turned out) that one hostage had been killed and that other hostages would be killed unless the movement of troops stopped.[145] The state police commander ordered his officers to halt and a standoff prevailed for a few minutes.

State officials then decided to give the inmates an opportunity to surrender. It was announced over a state police cruiser's public-address system that inmates wishing to surrender should, as the designation of their block was called out, release their hostages, enter the yard area, and lie face down on the ground.[146]

At 7:44 A.M., the inmates in E and H blocks began to comply, hanging white sheets and towels out of cell windows and then entering the yard. Other blocks followed their example. As they lay on the ground, inmates were frisked, handcuffed, and then taken to the main stockade field. The last hostage was released at about 9:00 A.M. from K Block.

After state police and institution staff had made a sweep of the blocks to ensure that all hostages had been released, the institution was declared under control at 10:00 A.M., Friday, October 27, 1989.

Aftermath

Thirty-four staff and 32 inmates had been injured during the second riot. Five officers had been taken hostage, one of whom was seriously injured and required hospitalization.[147]

Securing the Facility

Over the weekend, inmates remained on the yard under the supervision of armed state police.[148] The six blocks in Groups II and III were swept clean of debris and all inmate property. Four of the six units were found to be usable. Arrangements were made to transfer 774 inmates to other state facilities and another 800 inmates to federal prisons on a temporary basis.[149] By Sunday evening, all inmates were off the yard.

In the blocks, inmates were placed four to a cell, kept handcuffed, and manacled in pairs.[150] Mattresses, blankets, and toiletries were not provided, and inmates were left clad with little or no clothing. The cell doors were triple locked: two chains with two locks, plus the normal locking device of the door.[151]

Camp Hill office staff and counselors began fielding telephone calls from the families of staff and inmates. Over a three-week period, the number of calls reached 10,000.

Keeping the Institution Secure

For several months most of the institution remained locked down. Inmates were fed in their cells and exercised in small groups in handcuffs and restraints. Armed state police officers were initially stationed in the cellhouses; after a few days they were moved to a building outside the perimeter. In addition, a special complement of 25 state police assisted perimeter patrols 24 hours a day. An additional 15 state police investigators worked at Camp Hill for weeks to collect evidence for the prosecution of some 157 inmates involved in the riots. Emergency response teams from several other state institutions were stationed at Camp Hill on a rotating basis, serving one-week tours to help provide supervision for inmate recreation and shower schedules.

Investigations and Morale at Camp Hill

Over the two riots, 24 staff were taken hostage and 100 staff were injured. After the riot, 70 correctional officers and 30 other staff members went on disability because of physical or psychological problems stemming from the riot.[152] Six months later, this number had been reduced by about half.

Damage to the facility from the two riots was over $15 million. That cost, plus overtime for correctional personnel and Pennsylvania State Police, was estimated to be in the range of $40–$50 million.[153]

The riots were a statewide embarrassment to the Department of Corrections. The governor appointed a blue-ribbon commission to investigate the riots. He explained that had inmates rioted only the first night, he would have wanted only a routine review. "But when you have two nights in a row, worse the second time around, that becomes a unique situation that requires a unique response."[154] The state's Senate Judiciary Committee and House Judiciary Committee each held hearings and issued reports.

The riots exacerbated the division between Camp Hill's administration and its correctional staff. Each side criticized the other in public hearings before the two legislative committees. The administration blamed the staff for inaccurately reporting that the blocks had been secured after the first riot;[155] the staff charged the administration with endangering lives by delaying the entry of the state police contingent.[156]

Actions taken after the second riot also generated controversy. Facing numerous lawsuits, the commissioner ordered inmates reimbursed for the property that was removed from the cellblocks. The payments were small; they were given only to inmates who were not charged with participation in the riot; and they saved the state money by avoiding legal fees that would have been larger than the amount dispensed. Still, some staff and politicians complained that the commissioner was rewarding inmates for their misbehavior at the taxpayers expense.[157]

In January, the governor recommended to the commissioner of corrections that the superintendent, the deputy for operations, and the major of the guard be terminated from service to the department, and that the deputy for treatment be transferred to another institution.[158] The commissioner carried out these recommendations (although the major retired before his dismissal) and then resigned his position during a dispute over whether he had withheld information from the Adams commission.[159]

Change and Restoration

Following the Camp Hill riot, the Pennsylvania corrections system was restructured. Changes in philosophy and organization were made at all levels from the central office to the individual housing unit. The result has apparently been a substantial improvement in the system's morale, professionalism, efficiency, and ability to obtain necessary resources.

With the resignation of the commissioner in February 1990, all officials with authority over the Pennsylvania Department of Corrections and Camp Hill prison before the riot had been removed or had resigned from office. One of those released later commented that his decades-long career in corrections had been, suddenly, brought to a halt.[160]

In April 1990, the governor named Joseph D. Lehman (then deputy secretary of corrections for the state of Washington) as commissioner of corrections. Under Lehman's direction, the agency embarked on an effort to create a new departmental culture, characterized both by shared goals and by acceptance of employee input and innovation. The department also became more proactive with regard to its external environment. Initiatives included the following:

Vertical Integration through Regionalization

For some time, Pennsylvania had been in transition from a system in which each superintendent operated his or her facility more or less autonomously, to one in which the central office established policy and direction. To further advance that change, the department was divided into three regions (formerly there had been two) and the three regional deputy commissioners were given greater line authority. This clarified the lines of authority between the central office and the institutions.

Decentralization through Policy Assessment Committees

Traditionally, the Department had operated on the principle that lower echelon staff were excluded from higher level decisions. Now policy assessment committees were established whose mandate was to involve staff at all levels of the organization in policy debate and formulation.

Information Collection and Utilization through SCAN

The department's research unit established a statistical reporting system (SCAN). Using SCAN, the central office can identify problem areas faster than is possible with normal reporting procedures. The information was shared with those in the field, allowing for a joint search for solutions.

Implementation of Unit Management

In effecting unit management in all but four facilities (as of this writing), facilities were divided into smaller units within which both security and treatment staff were expected to establish policy together as a team. To facilitate this, the central office was reorganized along lines that would assist unit management at the local level.[161]

Revamping Emergency Preparedness

Previously, each of the state's 14 prisons had developed their own emergency plans independently. The result was a great deal of inconsistency in overall philosophy, organization, strategy, and tactics. Some prisons were well prepared; others were not. Further, by both historical practice and formal agreement, the state police would take the lead when force was needed to quell a disturbance. This arrangement tended to encourage the department to underprepare.

The commissioner obtained funds from the National Institute of Corrections (a division of the U.S. Department of Justice) to hire a consultant to assess the department's statewide emergency planning and preparation. Subsequently, a new emergency response infrastructure was created. A committee of six superintendents developed a new departmentwide emergency management policy manual. A new emergency response training program was developed for executive staff and superintendents. CERTs were given additional, more intense training, and new equipment to establish uniformity across facilities.

Each institution was required to designate one person to oversee and, in fact, champion the emergency preparedness program. The unwritten assumption, the commissioner explained, was that the person had to be immoderate in his or her dedication to the program, a "fanatic," in the positive sense of the word.

Finally, all 7,000 department employees were given some form of emergency response training. This apparently had a very positive effect on morale, and gave the staff a sense of "being in control again."[162]

External Relations

Previously, the department of corrections had operated as though it had little or no role in influencing its external environment. Commissioners rarely appeared at the capitol, unless requested to do so. One consequence of this was the shortfall of resources that plagued the department during the 1980s.

The new commissioner took a much more active role in the policy process. A first key issue was sentencing reform, especially greater use of sentences short of imprisonment. New lines of communication were opened to citizen groups and foundations concerned with criminal justice policy.

At Camp Hill, a new superintendent was appointed who apparently regained the support of the correctional staff.[163] Two months after the riot, the state legislature provided funds to rebuild and upgrade the prison. New cellblocks were built and existing ones renovated and hardened. Barriers were constructed to divide the yard into zones and limit inmate movement. An additional 100 officers were hired.

Further plans were made to change the mission of the Camp Hill. The prison would become the state's sole reception center for new inmates, which would define the prison's primary mission. In addition, it would house a smaller number of general-population inmates and inmates undergoing drug and alcohol treatment.[164]

5

Mack Alford Correctional Center, Oklahoma

May 13–15, 1988

The May 1988 riot at Oklahoma's Mack Alford Correctional Center did not take prison officials by surprise. Before the disturbance, and in the course of its development, prison officials took what seemed to be reasonable and correct actions to prevent it, and then to limit its expansion.

But expand it did. Over a two-hour period, inmates were able to seize eight hostages and take over two-thirds of the prison.[1] The causes of this riot lay not so much in the conditions of confinement or the structural features of the situation as in the spiral of conflict itself. Despite the absence of substantive issues, a negotiated settlement was achieved, raising the more general question of what negotiations are about.

The Prison and Its Prisoners

Mack Alford Correctional Center is a medium-security prison located in the southeastern quadrant of the state. The prison opened in the 1930s as a satellite to the Oklahoma State Penitentiary, the state's maximum-security unit for men, 35 miles to the north. Over the next three decades the facility's mission changed several times: It became, in turn, a hospital for patients with venereal disease, a German prisoner-of-war camp, and a training school for juvenile delinquents. In 1968 it was again made an annex of the penitentiary, and in 1973 it became a separate prison. In March 1986, its name was changed from Stringtown Correctional Center to its current one in honor of Mack Alford, who had served as its warden for 24 years.

In the few months before the disturbance, the prison's population grew from 530 to 670 inmates (its rated capacity was 540). Sixty percent of the inmates were white, 29 percent African American, and the remainder mostly Native American or Hispanic.

Interior fences divided the prison into three sections (see Figure 5-1). The northernmost section contained 10 nonresidential buildings, including a gym, a chapel, a canteen, three vocational training buildings, and the old administration building. The shift commander's office, located in the old administration building, was referred to as "the captain's office."

The middle section, or North Compound, contained two dormitory housing units, called West Building and East Building, as well as the inmate and staff dining halls. The dormitories each held about 165 inmates. Within the West Building was a six-cell restrictive housing unit for protective-custody inmates and others requiring temporary detention.

In the South Compound were two more housing units, New Building and South Building, each holding about 170 inmates in cells with solid steel doors. The cells had been designed to house one inmate each, but at the time of the riot most housed two. South Building also contained a five-cell detention unit in which were inmates serving time for disciplinary infractions.

Although more secure than the open-air dormitory units on the North Compound, the South Compound buildings were considered by corrections officials to be inferior in construction. The cell walls were constructed from plaster. An inmate could poke a hole in the wall and conceal contraband in the wall's interior. The walls had been patched many times over the years, making detection of hidden items nearly impossible.

The North Yard and the South Yard gates, which provided passage between the compounds, were kept open during the day and locked at 10:00 P.M. when the yards were closed. Four towers were situated on each side of the prison. The main administration building, which included the warden's office, was on the east side of the prison outside the perimeter fence.

By all accounts, warden Mack Alford had, during his long tenure, exercised highly autocratic rule in the old-warden tradition. He demanded great personal loyalty and usually got it. Prison staff were shocked by his unexpected death (from a heart attack) while breaking up a fight on the yard in 1986. His successors had a hard time moving out of his shadow and avoiding unfavorable comparisons with the legendary Alford. One officer, for example, stated:

> Mack Alford did take time out to walk around and see how everybody was doing, praise you on your job . . . I haven't seen our new warden enough to even tell you anything about him. He never communicated with us very much.

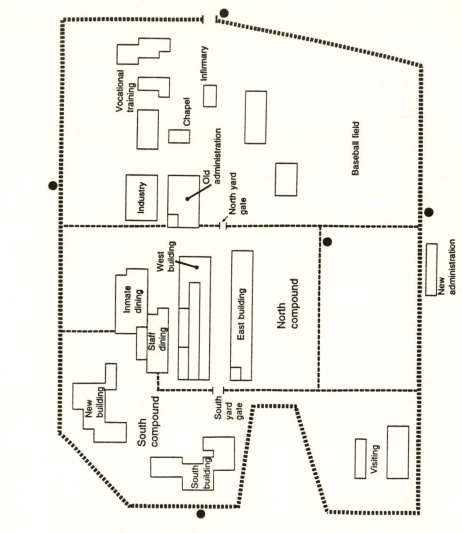

Figure 5-1 Mack Alford Correctional Center.

In September 1987, the prison was converted to a unit management system. Some officers said that this had improved morale among both staff and inmates. A sizable fraction, perhaps a majority, however, disliked the new system and complained that unit management had undercut their authority. In their view, case managers were far too lenient toward inmates and failed to back up their authority. But the kind of open hostility between staff and administration that existed before the riot at Camp Hill was not in evidence here.

In postriot interviews, inmates voiced two types of grievances. First, some inmates complained about the prison's amenities, especially the food (poorly prepared) and the laundry services (laundry returned unclean or wet, or lost). Prison officials conceded that there were problems in these two areas and were working to remedy them. (A new food service supervisor was hired, and the 40-year-old laundry equipment was being replaced.) Still, many inmates described the prison in evenhanded terms, one inmate going so far as to call it "the best medium institution in the state."

The level of dissatisfaction with the food and laundry services was not particularly intense by prison standards, and not enough to produce a riot. More important were the feelings of racial hostility. Some white inmates felt that African-American inmates, especially Black Muslims, received favored treatment. A white inmate active in the riot said, "Whatever them f——king Muslims wanted, they got. The warden and major let 'em have whatever they wanted. And they was running us in the ground." African-American inmates, in turn, complained of racial hostility directed against them by white inmates.

Corrections officers working at Mack Alford were subject to two different chains of command, depending on where and what shift they worked. Unit managers, who reported to the deputy warden, supervised all correctional officers, counselors, and case managers assigned to their unit, except night-shift officers (midnight to 8:00 A.M.). Officers working the night shift, and all officers not assigned to units, reported to the shift commander, a captain. The captains reported to the major who worked under the deputy warden. The major and his subordinates, therefore, were responsible for all aspects of security, transportation, and communication outside the housing units.

Initiation: Inmate Mobilization and Countermobilization

On the morning of Friday, May 13, 1988, two African-American inmates housed in the New Building allegedly broke into the rooms of two white inmates and stole items purchased from the commissary. The burglary was witnessed by a white inmate, a cellhouse orderly, who did not report it. The victims discovered that their property was missing when they returned to their rooms around noon, and the news spread.

Two other white inmates (not the theft victims) took it upon themselves to launch an investigation. They pressured the orderly to name the thieves, threatening to kill him otherwise. The orderly still refused. Regardless, the two white inmates believed that two African-American inmates, one a Muslim, who had been suspected of earlier thefts had committed this one as well. Later in the afternoon, the two white inmates asked the informal leader of a group of Muslim inmates what he knew. The Muslim leader said he would look into it.

About 6:00 P.M. the first signs of trouble became visible to prison officials. A New Building officer observed a group of 20 African-American inmates gathering in front of his unit, most of them Muslims. On a nearby picnic table was a pile of commissary items, including cigarettes and a case of soda. At the same time, groups of white inmates were milling nearby.

The officer reported these developments to the captain on duty, the shift commander for the swing shift, from 4:00 P.M. to midnight. The captain walked to New Building around 6:10, accompanied by a sergeant, to see for himself. He asked the Muslim leader what his group was doing. The inmate replied that they were just passing time.

While this conversation was taking place, however, the inmate orderly who had witnessed the theft had gone to the captain's office to ask that he be placed in protective custody because of the death threats against him. The captain was called back to his office to handle this. The orderly confirmed that the two inmates suspected by the white inmate "investigators" had indeed committed the thefts.

On telephoned instructions from the captain, the New Building officer called the Muslim leader into his unit to ask him again what was going on. This time the inmate leader confirmed that his group had brought the commissary items to "pay a debt" owed by some younger inmates. And, in fact, once the commissary items were handed over to the victim of the theft, the Muslim group dispersed.

But tensions remained. A white inmate later told investigators:

> Yeah, they got their stuff back. But [we were] still gonna run them off the yard for the simple fact that they stole . . . We don't tolerate thieves in the penitentiary.

As soon as the group of African-American inmates left, about 25 white inmates gathered in the same area. Their attention seemed to be focused on the section of New Building housing the two alleged thieves. Every so often, a white inmate from the group walked into the building and looked around to see who was there. The New Building officer reported these developments to the captain's office, identifying three inmates as the agitators. In fact, two of these three would initiate and lead the riot.

Around 7:00 P.M. the New Building officer encouraged one of the suspected thieves to ask for protective custody, but, though he was obviously very frightened, he refused. Forty-five minutes later, the deputy warden, who had spent the day in Oklahoma City at a training seminar, dropped by the prison and talked with the captain by phone. They agreed that the two African-American inmates should be removed from the unrestricted inmate population, but they had no place to put them. The prison's 11 detention cells were filled; for various reasons, none of the 11 inmates could be released, and no other secure area was available. The deputy warden decided to put off a solution until Monday, and left the prison, leaving the captain in charge.

A few minutes after this conversation, the New Building officer called the captain's office to report that the situation was getting worse. Several inmates had warned him that there would be "major trouble" unless the two African-American inmates were removed from the yard. The sergeant who took the call responded that the deputy warden had postponed the transfer until after the weekend.

At 8:00 P.M., 15 African-American inmates, including both the suspected thieves, were loudly taunted by white inmates as they left New Building to eat a late-evening Ramadan meal. After the meal was over at 9:00 P.M., the Muslim inmates told the two alleged thieves that they were taking them to the captain's office and that they should request protective custody status. Both refused because, they said, they had not done anything wrong. The two suspects then did not return to the New Building, but went instead to East Building in the North Compound. The Muslim leader thereupon informed the captain, through a correctional officer, that the Muslims would no longer protect the two suspects and urged that they be removed from the yard before they were killed.

Around 10:00 P.M., the two suspected thieves returned to New Building, each carrying a golf putter from the North Compound's miniature golf course; they were disarmed by the New Building officer. Meanwhile, a crowd of 300 inmates had gradually collected on the yard, now mostly white with some African-American inmates off to the side. They shouted taunts at the two suspects, who responded in kind and then rearmed themselves by breaking off broom handles to make clubs.

Alarmed by the growing tension, the New Building officer radioed the captain's office for help. Accompanied by five officers, the captain went to New Building, disarmed the suspected inmates, moved them to a different room, and posted two officers at the door. He then called the deputy warden at home to explain the situation and got authorization to call in the emergency squad, which consisted of 10 officers under the command of the major. By this time, the crowd had become even larger and more unruly; estimates of its size varied from two-thirds to 90 percent of the prison's 670-inmate population. The captain personally ordered the assembled inmates to return to their units, but no one would move. He then called his office to have the count bell sounded (ordering inmates to their cells), about 15 minutes before its regular time. When only a few responded, the captain then began to write down inmates' names, making it clear that those who remained would face disciplinary action. Faced with this threat, the inmates vacated the area.

By 10:30, the incident appeared to be over; the count was completed and the inmates seemed to have settled down for the evening. The captain discussed the situation with the major and the deputy warden, who had both returned to the prison. The three concluded that the problem inmates—the two alleged thieves and the three reported white agitators—should be removed from the prison that evening. A little after 11:00 P.M., the deputy warden received permission from the central office to transfer the five inmates to the Oklahoma State Penitentiary, 35 miles to the north. Officers brought the two African-American inmates to the administration building, and they were driven to the penitentiary without incident.

The transfer of the three white inmates was given more careful attention. It was decided to wait until just after the arrival of the midnight shift but before the departure of the evening shift. At 11:45 the major briefed the captains of both the arriving and departing shifts on the procedures that would be followed. They were to use a "low-profile" plan. Each inmate would be brought to a van by only two or three officers. If an inmate did resist, the officers were to back off and report to the major. The inmates seen as least threatening would be removed first; this, the major believed, would take some of the "fight" out of those whose turn would come next.

Accordingly, two officers went to East Building and told the first of the white transferees to pack his belongings. The inmate walked to his bed but then bolted down a flight of stairs and across the yard into the West Building, where another of the transferees resided. One of the East Building officers pursued him, and a West Building officer joined in the chase.

The West Building officer found the two inmates in a back wing on the second floor. With 50 inmates looking on from their beds, the officer approached the two uncooperative transferees. One of the two pushed the officer to the floor and put a knife at his throat. One inmate said to the other, "we need to get some coffee and cigarettes, 'cause this is gonna take awhile."

Response and Expansion: Other Hostages, More Territory

The time was 11:50 P.M., and two inmates held a single hostage, two shifts of correctional personnel were on duty, and three senior prison officials were present to take charge of the situation. And yet the disturbance had only begun to escalate. The forces of control initially attempted to negotiate with the inmates on a personal basis before they had mobilized enough force to prevent the disturbance from spreading. This gave the hostage takers the opportunity to recruit others and spread disorder throughout the prison.

When they heard that a hostage had been taken, the swing-shift captain and a lieutenant immediately went to the scene. With the knife pressed against the hostage's throat, the inmates said the captain could stay but ordered the lieutenant: "We're going to kill this motherf——ker if you don't leave!" He backed off to the housing unit's lobby. A few moments later, the major entered the section. One of the hostage takers yelled, "Come on down here, motherf——ker, you're the one we really want." The major immediately left for the captain's office, leaving word with officers in the lobby that the captain should call him as soon as he could.

One of the inmates told the captain (who was himself an African American) that he was not going to the penitentiary over those "mother-f——king, thieving Muslims" and that "all you niggers are alike anyway." The inmate then ordered the captain to leave the section because he had "no answers," and demanded to speak with a different captain, for whom one of the two had worked as clerk. The swing-shift captain said he would try to find him, although, he noted, he was not on duty, and left the section at 12:15 A.M.

In retrospect, nothing had been accomplished by these attempts at personal persuasion. On the contrary, the inmates had taken the initiative, dictating who they would and would not speak with, making demands with which high-level correctional officers complied. In going to and fro in response to the inmates' commands, these officers consumed valuable minutes that they could have used to isolate the disturbance in a single building or a single room.

Meanwhile, in the captain's office, the major briefed the deputy warden. The deputy warden ordered the emergency squad called in, along with the prison's three designated hostage negotiators; deployed the midnight-shift officers to strategic locations; and notified the warden and the central office of the hostage situation.

Having returned to the lobby, the swing-shift captain called the deputy warden who told him that the two inmates were not to be allowed to leave the West Building. At that moment, however, the hostage takers ordered the hostage to his feet, saying, "You stop for anything, I'll kill you," and marched him out the front door of West Building, unhindered by correctional officers. They headed toward East Building. One inmate held the hostage by his arm, and the other held him by the back of his collar, pressing a knife to his neck. As they were crossing the yard, a third inmate ran out of East Building, produced a long knife, and said that he was joining them. As the group entered East Building, one of the hostage takers ordered the three correctional officers present to get out of the building, which they did.

The three inmates took their hostage to the second floor of East Building, made him change into inmate clothes, took his keys and radio, and put him in a chair. Using electric cord, an inmate tied a hangman's knot and looped it around the hostage's neck.

They found five other inmates willing to follow their lead and told them to barricade the doors and cover the windows with blankets. Chairs and locker boxes were piled in front of entrances. This seizure of East Building marks the point at which the three hostage takers became the leaders of a full-fledged riot.

General pandemonium broke out in East Building. Some inmates destroyed property and broke windows. One group broke into the case manager's office and trashed and lit fires in it. Other inmates called for West Building inmates to join them, and some did.

The swing-shift captain had remained on the phone with the deputy warden, reporting the events as he saw them occur. After the hostage takers had moved to the East Building, the deputy warden issued several orders designed to limit the scope of the disturbance. He told the swing-shift captain to secure the doors in the West Building and keep rioters out. He also instructed an officer to take a key from the emergency key box to open a rarely used auxiliary door on the west side of the West Building that led to a small enclosed yard. If inmates were able to break into the West Building, the officers could use this escape route and be evacuated from the side yard.

The deputy warden also ordered that both the South Yard and North Yard gates were to be kept locked and that radio silence was to be maintained. The phone connection to East Building was disconnected.

The deputy warden determined that there were 17 officers in the compound—three in South Building, four in New Building, and seven in West Building, and the three who had evacuated East Building and were now standing in the North Compound yard. He ordered the East Building officers and two others to obtain rifles and redeploy to perimeter posts and to the unstaffed south tower.

At about 12:45, one of the trained negotiators, who had arrived at the prison and been briefed by the deputy warden, briefly talked with one of the rioters over a walkie-talkie. The inmate said that they would kill the hostage if officers tried to enter the building or if the phone lines were not reconnected. He added that any further discussion would have to wait until arrival of the particular off-duty captain whom they had demanded earlier. Prison officials soon discovered, however, that the captain was on vacation and could not be located immediately.

About 1:00 A.M., the two inmate leaders began to discuss what to do next. One reportedly said to the other, "We started this, now what's our demands gonna be . . . We gotta have something [to demand]." The other inmate responded, "Damn it, the only thing I want is I'm not going to the walls [Oklahoma State Penitentiary]." The two inmates did agree, however, that they needed more hostages. Furthermore, the fires that had been set in East Building were beginning to burn out of control.

Fifteen minutes later the two inmate leaders and a dozen other inmates stepped out of East Building, holding the hostage in front of them as a shield against sniper fire, and headed toward the South Yard gate. The gate, of course, was locked, and they could not open it. One of the inmates asked the hostage if any of his keys would open the gate. He replied that the key to the gate was always kept on the south side. The inmates yelled to the South Compound officers that, if they did not open the gate, they would cut off the hostage's head. The officers did not respond.

At this point, one of the inmate leaders decided that they had been in an open area too long and were vulnerable to sniper fire from the south tower. (In fact, some prison staff later argued that sniper fire at this point would have ended the incident.) One of the inmate leaders ordered the group to head toward West Building to see if more hostages could be taken there. Informed of this, the deputy warden called the warden and obtained permission to send the emergency squad, which the major was then assembling, onto the yard. He then called the captain inside West Building to warn him that the inmates were approaching the main entrance but that armed assistance was coming and a key to a side entrance was also being brought.

Inside the unit there was debate over what to do. About a dozen inmates had stayed in the West Building lobby to side with the officers, saying that they would not allow the hostage takers to destroy their property and living quarters. One of them urged the swing-shift captain to open the front door and "we'll take care of them." Several of the inmates began to make weapons for the anticipated fight. The captain decided otherwise and ordered a large metal filing cabinet to be shoved in front of the door. All of the officers, assisted by several inmates, braced themselves against the barricade.

Meanwhile, an officer brought the emergency key to the west side door, which was intended as the officers' escape route. But it would not work. The deputy warden called the north tower to see if another key was available. None could be found.

The rioting inmates tried to force open the front door. At one point, the door opened about a foot; one of the rioters stuck his arm through and swung a knife widely, slashing one of the West Building inmates in the shoulder. But the barricade held firm.

For the moment, the rioting inmates were stymied. The officers and inmates inside West Building had repelled their attack, they could not get through the locked gate to South Yard, and fire was beginning to consume East Building, so they could not return there. They had only one hostage and were in a vulnerable position on the yard.

Then one of the inmate leaders remembered that he had the hostage's keys. He asked the hostage if any of the keys would open another West Building door. The inmate pressed the knife against his neck, telling the officer he would be killed if he lied. The officer replied that one of the keys would open a fire escape at the south end of the building.

Leaving the hostage under guard outside, nine inmates took the key and entered West Building via the fire escape. The door brought them into the restrictive housing unit, and they released some of the inmates being held. Two gates separated the restrictive housing unit from the rest of West Building. One had been opened by officers during the early stages of the disturbance and had not been relocked. The second was secured only by a hasp and padlock and was easily kicked open.

The officers, still occupied with securing the front entrance, were taken by surprise. Three inmates overpowered the swing-shift captain. Outnumbered and outarmed, the captain of the midnight shift ordered the other officers not to resist. The inmates now had seven hostages, including two captains. Back in the captain's office, the deputy warden realized that more hostages had been taken when an unidentified inmate answered the West Building phone.

The deputy warden called the officers in the South Compound. He told them to double check that the gate was locked and thereafter to stay inside their buildings and out of sight. If the rioters came to the gate, the officers were not to communicate with them in any way.

The inmates left the West Building, heading, again, for the south gate, but now with seven hostages rather than one. An evening-shift sergeant in the South Building somehow missed, or disregarded, the deputy's instructions and walked to the gate. The inmates told him that they would kill their hostages unless he opened the gate. The sergeant initially refused. The inmates then forced the captain of the midnight shift to "order" the sergeant to open the gate. The sergeant again refused, but then asked the captain of his own shift, "[captain's name], do you want me to unlock this gate?" The swing-shift captain replied, "[sergeant's name], open the gate." The sergeant complied and was immediately taken hostage.

At about the same time, other inmates were entering the South Compound through a broken window in the south side of the mess hall. Whether this occurred just before or just after the gate was unlocked cannot be determined now. Pouring into South Compound in two streams, the inmates quickly took over South Building and took the officers still there as hostages.

Nothing done by prison officials before, during, or after the riot stirred more postriot controversy than the unlocking of the South Yard gate. In postriot interviews, some corrections officers stated that the sergeant's decision to unlock the gate was a courageous act, in which the sergeant sacrificed his own safety to save the lives of others. Others saw it as a violation of security procedures that contributed to the expansion of the riot and the taking of additional hostages.

It is unclear now why the sergeant went to the gate in the first place, particularly since the deputy warden had anticipated just the sort of situation that arose and had ordered that no personnel approach the gate. A second issue concerns the sergeant's obedience to the swing-shift captain's "order" to open the gate. Department policy on this is clear: a prison official taken hostage exercises no authority.[2] (Although if the two captains had been in a position to issue valid orders, the midnight-shift captain would have had just as much authority over the sergeant as the other one.) Apparently, however, the swing-shift captain enjoyed the deep respect of his officers, including this particular sergeant, and this loyalty outweighed the training and policies that, as clearly as they could, instructed the sergeant to ignore the "order."

It may be that the decision was not so crucial, in fact, since (although the sergeant apparently did not know this) other inmates were entering the South Compound through a window in the mess hall about the same time as the confrontation. Thus, the inmates arguably could have taken over the South Compound regardless of the sergeant's actions. On the other hand, fewer inmates may have gone to the South Compound if they had had to crawl through a window. The opening of the gate may have permitted the critical mass of inmates needed to seize the South Compound and hold it for two days.

The deputy warden found out that South Building had been taken over when an inmate answered that telephone. He then ordered officers to evacuate New Building and to go to the fence underneath the south tower where they could be protected by the officers with rifles. Another officer from South Building managed to join them, and the group was evacuated over the fence about an hour later using fire ladders. The electricity was cut off to South Building.

At about 1:40 A.M., Saturday, May 14, inmates controlled two-thirds of the prison. They established their base in South Building. The hostages were moved to the building's detention unit.

Prison under Siege: Day One

The next 24 hours were a standoff, one intensely frustrating to corrections officials. The inmate leaders' actions were difficult to predict, erratic, and always charged with the possibility of violence against the hostages. Inmates issued demands, corrections officials met those demands, but then inmates balked at the last moment. Meanwhile, the hostages were alternately well treated and terrorized.

Inmates in South Compound

For several hours rioters left the South Yard gate open, allowing North Compound inmates to join them freely. Some South Yard inmates also left northward to avoid the riot. About 300 inmates were on South Compound in the first hours after its seizure. Many of them just roamed the yard, while others engaged in acts of vandalism. Inside the two housing units, South Building and New Building, inmates smashed windows, broke doors off their hinges, turned desks over, and burned the files from the cabinets of case managers. Some inmates burglarized other inmates' cells. One inmate would later report that he had been raped by three inmates. Several inmates used weight bars to knock holes in South Building's interior walls and knock out exterior windows so they could watch for assault teams. Several fires were started in South Building but were quickly extinguished by inmates. But later in the morning, a fire in New Building was allowed to burn unchecked.

After the initial rampage, many of the inmates began to move to the North Compound, probably to avoid identification as riot participants. This included some of the inmates who had been most active in destroying state property. Around 3:30 A.M. one of the two inmate leaders yelled "last call," meaning that the South Yard gate would be locked. Sixty-nine inmates stayed in the South Compound; the nonparticipating inmates were cleared from North Yard and moved to a ball field.

One of the three riot leaders was put in charge of the hostages. He ensured that the hostages were treated relatively well, at least when they were inside the housing units. They were supplied with food, drink, and cigarettes to the extent that these items were available. A fan was turned on.

Three hostages were released during the first few hours of the riot. One of the two inmate leaders had promised the first hostage that he would be released if they could get more hostages, and he was in fact let go at 1:40 A.M. About 20 minutes later, the midnight-shift captain was released because of a badly sprained back.

A third hostage was released about 4:30 A.M., also for medical reasons. The prison's medical administrator approached one of the inmate leaders at the fence and told him that one of the hostages might die under the stress because he had a heart condition. The inmate leader at first refused to let him go, but was persuaded by an inmate who said they could be charged with murder if the officer died.

The inmates told the hostages that they would be killed if an assault were made, and the officers said later that they believed it. Inmates made sure that access to the hostages would be difficult for state authorities in the event of an assault. They kept the hostages primarily in the detention unit cells in South Building, the most secure and least readily accessible area. Inmates barricaded an office and a hallway that led to the unit, and all of the hostages except the swing-shift captain were dressed in inmate clothes. From time to time, one or two hostages were moved to other locations unknown to prison officials in the South or New Building.

From time to time terror against the hostages was used to coerce prison officials into granting specific demands. On Saturday morning, for example, inmates spotted officers with shotguns stationed on North Yard. The swing-shift captain was brought onto South Yard and forced to kneel; three inmates held knives to his neck, and a fourth yelled that they would cut the captain's head off unless the guns were removed. The officers were withdrawn, and the captain was returned to his cell.

Command and Control

Since the outbreak of trouble on Friday afternoon, command at the prison had changed hands three times. The swing-shift captain had been in charge of handling the initial racial confrontation, although he had consulted the deputy warden by telephone. Later, as the incident crossed the line from confrontation to open rebellion, the deputy warden and major had both been called to the prison. The deputy warden assumed overall responsibility for guiding the response, while the major, as commander of the prison's emergency team, directed tactical efforts.

At midnight the warden arrived at the prison and set up a command post in his office. For the next two and a half days, he would direct the riot response, staying at the prison continuously and catnapping no more than an hour at a time. The major continued to supervise the tactical effort, while the deputy warden assumed responsibility for the nonparticipating inmates and for food, housing, and other support for the emergency response personnel.

Meanwhile, the deputy director of corrections opened an emergency command center at the central office in Oklahoma City at 12:35 A.M.; the director arrived about an hour later. Command in the central office operated through several preestablished committees:

- The Operations Task Force, chaired by the director, was the key decision-making group.
- The logistics committee ensured that the emergency response efforts were adequately staffed and had the necessary vehicles, housing, and equipment.
- The intelligence committee assembled and evaluated information that could assist with the resolution. For example, the committee developed profiles of the hostage takers based on information from both the department's own records and out-of-state records.

Each committee met in a separate room, and a sign was posted on each of the doors with the names of those persons permitted in the room.

As envisioned by the director, the role of the central office in an emergency is to assist, not direct, the efforts of the warden. The Operations Task Force served as a think tank and sounding board for the warden. Mack Alford's warden took full advantage of this and was in almost constant contact with the central office to discuss his strategy.

In addition, the central office sent two deputy directors and the inspector general to the prison. They arrived at the prison about 3:50 A.M. on Saturday morning. One of the deputy directors worked directly with the warden, serving as a strategic advisor and taking charge when the warden needed relief. The second deputy director spent much of his time on North Yard as a sort of forward command observer. A phone line was strung from a spot on the north yard to the warden's office, and the deputy director provided the warden with up-to-the-minute information on events on the compound. Also, negotiators would report to the deputy director, who in turn would then relay developments back to the warden. The warden's directives to personnel on the yard also passed through the deputy director. The inspector general initially assisted in this deputy director but later became directly involved in the negotiations with the inmates. Meanwhile, seven other state prisons sent emergency response teams to Mack Alford, including the Oklahoma State Penitentiary. The state highway patrol also sent an emergency response team.

Negotiations

After the takeover of South Compound, the riot leaders insisted they would only talk to the captain whom they had asked for earlier (and who had not yet been found) and refused to speak with any prison official present. To initiate negotiations, or at least find out what the inmates wanted, prison officials recruited two seasoned and respected inmates from the nonparticipants, one of whom was a friend of one of the riot leaders. This was obviously a very unusual practice, but one prison official would later explain it was helpful because the inmate go-betweens "could go up to the fence and talk to them without them going crazy thinking we were about to come through the fence." The two cooperating inmates said they would try to convince the rioting inmates to give up.

The two inmates were taken to the South Yard gate, where they talked to the riot leaders through the fence. At first one of the rioters insisted on holding out for the captain of their choice, but finally, one of the inmates convinced a riot leader to speak with two department officials.

This meeting took place about 4:30 A.M. Representing the department were the inspector general from the central office and a trained hostage negotiator from the penitentiary. The inmates demanded to meet with a member of the American Civil Liberties Union, a state senator, and the wardens of two other state prisons. They also stated that they wanted to be transferred to a federal prison and have the transfer made in the presence of a U.S. marshal.

In postriot interviews, the inmate leaders said that they wanted to transfer to a federal prison because they feared they would be beaten if moved to the penitentiary, and they also believed African-American inmates did not "run everything up there in the Fed joint." After an hour of conversation, one of the inmate leaders became hostile toward the officials and insisted they would only talk with the particular captain they had asked for.

At about 6:00 A.M., this off-duty captain arrived at the prison, having been located an hour before. He had had drinks the night before and was a bit groggy at first, but soon regained his composure. He was briefed by the warden and two department officials, who instructed him to negotiate through the fence and not to enter the South Compound itself.

Ignoring these instructions, the captain asked the inmates at the South Yard gate to open it and he went into the yard. Some of the inmates began to argue that he should be taken hostage. The inmate leader who had been the captain's clerk responded, "No you guys, you can't have him. I worked for this man four years, and I gave him my word he could come in here." The inmate leader threatened to kill anyone who tried to take the captain as a hostage.

The inmates told the captain that if the prison were rushed, they would kill the hostages. They also told him that about 15–20 inmates wanted to be moved to a federal prison. After a half hour of discussion the captain left the yard to confer with the warden and then returned to the yard. A few minutes later, about 7:40 A.M., the inmates released a hostage as a show of good faith.

Contacted by the state corrections department, the Federal Correctional Institution in El Reno, Oklahoma, said they would be willing to take these inmates on a temporary basis and dispatched a bus staffed with correctional officers to pick them up. With the federal prisons now involved, agents from the U.S. Marshal's Service and the FBI were sent to the prison, both arriving around noon.

At about 2:00 P.M. the captain returned to the South Compound gate accompanied by the two federal agents. When the inmate leader determined that they were actually federal agents, he released another hostage. Speaking through the gate, the captain told the riot leaders that their demand for the transfer would be granted, that a federal bus was on its way to pick them up, and that they should make a list of those who wanted to go. He also assured the inmates that the federal agents would remain to monitor the inmates' safety.

Then, unexpectedly, one of the two inmate leaders quietly unlocked the south gate. He grabbed the FBI agent and tried to yank him into the compound. The agent was barely able to pull away, and the inmate quickly relocked the gate.

This was a signal that resolving the riot by rational bargaining would not be so easy. Later that afternoon, two inmates brought a hostage officer to a picnic table in front of South Building. They held his hand on the table, told him they were going to cut off a finger, and made him scream as a knife was slammed into the table inches from his hand. An inmate poured hot sauce on the hostage's hand as fake blood. This scene was not linked to any demand. The sniper spotter in the south tower came close to ordering shots, but saw the event for what it was and withheld fire.

About 6:30 P.M. the federal bus arrived, and the warden arranged to have it driven to a point on the North Compound where inmates could observe it from the South Building. One of the two inmate leaders brought the hostage captain from the detention unit to the fence. The captain negotiator told the inmate leaders that their demands had been met and explained to them the procedures that would be followed for boarding the buses. But, again unexpectedly, an inmate leader responded that they could take the bus and "stick it." The inmates returned to the South Building, taking their hostages with them.

About an hour later the inmate leader returned to the fence with another demand: They wanted the media to be present when they boarded the buses. Only this, they stated, would ensure that they would not be harmed; if this demand was not met, the deal was off.

The warden refused. His decision was based on the principle that the media's presence in a hostage situation encourages prisoners to take hostages in the future. In fact, he had previously issued a written directive that hostage takers were not to be given access to the media. Moreover, he believed the inmates had been given adequate safeguards. As a compromise, the warden offered to have the transfer videotaped in the presence of the two federal agents. The inmates were not persuaded.

With negotiations stalemated, inmates now issued a new demand: They wanted soda and ice cream by 6:45 P.M. or they would cut off a hostage's finger.

The central office ordered a message sent to the inmates: "If you harm the hostages in any way, we're coming in." The inmates' next actions were even more ominous. Four inmates brought a hostage to the yard. One inmate held a knife to his throat, while another inmate combed his hair, tucked his shirt in, and gave him a "last cigarette." As the 6:45 deadline approached, an inmate asked the hostage if he had a last request. (Keeping his wits about him, he said Coke and ice cream sounded good to him.)

Meanwhile, prison officials readied their assault teams and alerted snipers stationed in the west dorm. But the deadline passed without violence, and the hostage was returned to his cell 10 minutes later.

Later that evening the inmates again demanded soda and ice cream and, in addition, coffee, cigarettes, and milk. If these were not produced by dark, they would "send a finger out." Again the assault teams were readied; again nothing happened.

Around 10:00 P.M. the inmates again demanded to talk to the media. Officials rejected the demand. The negotiating captain told the inmate leaders that if they did not board the federal prison bus it would return to El Reno. Around 11:00 inmates began to throw rocks at emergency lights in the North Compound and at the few officials there. All evacuated the compound except the deputy director, who used a chair to protect himself from the barrage.

At 1:00 A.M., the warden directed the captain to tell the inmates they had one last opportunity to board the bus and that it would not be brought back. There was no response, and at 1:30 A.M. the bus departed. The first round of negotiations had not produced a settlement. Further developments would have to wait for Sunday morning.

Prison under Siege: Day Two

Between Saturday night and Sunday morning, 27 inmates surrendered by either climbing the fence or going through the broken window in the South Dining Hall. This left 60 inmates in the South Compound. As the second full day of the disturbance began, prison officials had become increasingly pessimistic that a peaceful resolution could be achieved. Prison officials felt that they had met the inmates' key demands on Saturday and it had gotten them nowhere. They had warned the inmates to board the federal bus or lose their chance for good, and they had meant it.

Further, officials sensed that inmates were coming to enjoy the event, especially the notoriety they were getting in both the national and local media. They seemed to have little incentive to end the disturbance. Indeed, in the first conversation of the day at 7:20 A.M., one of the inmate leaders told the negotiating captain that there would be no discussions that day. They had plenty of food and water, they said, and were willing to hold out several days to get their demands.

On the other side, fatigue was setting in among the correctional forces of all ranks. Fresh tactical teams had been brought in, but now they, too, were getting tired. The strain on the Mack Alford staff was great. A south tower officer, for example, had worked an 18-hour shift, gone home for two hours of sleep, and then returned to duty. Prison and central office officials were becoming concerned that errors of judgment might be made. One central office official commented:

> You could see our patience was starting to get a little thin. At the time we sent the buses back, we had been at this for 22 hours. They were tired and we were tired.

Finally, prison officials had not seen two of the three hostages since midafternoon Saturday. Their safety was of great concern.

Tactical Efforts and Assault Plans

For these reasons, plans for a possible assault were discussed in the warden's office early Sunday morning. In addition, prison officials carried out a tactical plan to apprehend some of the rioters by stealth.

At 6:00 A.M., correctional officers cut a hole in the fence behind New Building and moved a 15-person emergency squad into the building. The idea was to apprehend any inmate who might wander in. When an inmate walked in, officers would grab him from behind, put a hand over his mouth, handcuff and gag him, and then take him out the hole in the fence. Over the next three hours, eight inmates were apprehended.

Around 9:00 A.M., an inmate entered the building but managed to escape and tell an inmate leader what had happened. Another inmate was sent to investigate. When he encountered the emergency squad, he pulled a knife from his waistband and advanced on the officers despite orders to halt. An officer fired a shotgun round at the inmate but missed, and the inmate ran out of the building yelling that officers were in it.

Meanwhile, the two inmate leaders were talking to the negotiating captain at the fence, having brought with them the hostage captain. When they heard the shotgun blast, the inmates put knives to both sides of the hostage's neck. The negotiating captain, himself unaware of what the blast meant, was able to convince the two inmates that it was an aerosol can exploding in a fire. Still, one of the inmates said that if New Building was not vacated in five minutes, they would bring a hostage into the yard with a rope around his neck and execute him. The two inmates returned the hostage captain to his cell and the emergency squad was withdrawn from New Building. (Later in the day, inmates set fire to New Building and, unlike the previous day, refused to cooperate in putting it out. The fire burned out of control most of the afternoon.)

As the day progressed, several white supremacists appeared to be becoming dangerously assertive. "White Power" was painted on a picnic table, and a sign with the same message was hung on South Building. (Another sign, "DOC has not met our demands and has lied to you," was also displayed.)

Officials were especially concerned about the hostage captain, who, they feared, might be injured or killed because he was an African American. (In fact, an inmate had threatened to kill him late Saturday night but had been warned off by the two inmate leaders.) Securing his release became the warden's first priority.

Around 2:00 P.M., the warden held another meeting in his office to plan a tactical assault. They went over blueprints of buildings and discussed possible entry points. Each emergency team was assigned to a tactical task. The Mack Alford squad would be responsible for retaking the South Building because of the officers' familiarity with the building, especially its detention unit, in which the hostages were being held. The highway patrol would retake New Building. Officers from the Oklahoma State Penitentiary would be split, half backing up the Mack Alford squad and half backing up the highway patrol. Emergency squad members from two other prisons would secure the yard and handle inmates as they came out of the building.

After the meeting, the major gathered all of the commanders of the emergency squads, gave them maps of the prison marked with the probable locations of the hostages, and instructed them about the division of duties. Shots were to be fired only if an officer was injured.

Negotiations

The negotiating captain continued to meet with the inmates throughout the day, but little progress was made until early evening. At 7:30 P.M. inmates issued a new set of demands. They called for the restoration of the electricity to South Building, the services of a particular American Civil Liberties Union attorney, a federal bus, 50 sodas and 50 ice creams, five cartons of cigarettes, and media coverage. If the sodas, ice cream, and cigarettes were provided immediately, and their other demands were agreed to, they would release the hostage captain.

As these negotiations were taking place, three state legislators who represented nearby districts arrived at the prison and offered their services as negotiators. Prison officials were hesitant to accept their offer of assistance, if for no other reason than it would be inconsistent with standard negotiation strategies in corrections. But they accepted in the hope that the legislators might provide a new angle, one that could break through the impasse.

As prison officials envisioned it, the legislators would act more as observers than negotiators, reassuring the inmates that they would not be mistreated. To the extent that they would become involved in actual negotiations, the legislators would focus on issues of how a surrender might be arranged.

The deputy warden briefed the legislators, making sure that they would not agree to something that might pose a security problem either in the release process or in the future. The deputy director who was stationed on the yard discussed the importance of periodically reporting to him the status of the talks, so he could report events to the warden as they unfolded.

At 8:00 P.M., the captain along with two other prison officials returned to the South Yard to make a counterproposal. The inmates would be given ice cream and soda in exchange for the release of the hostage captain. After his release, three state legislators would talk with them. The electricity also would be turned on. Prison officials offered a compromise on the issue of media coverage: They would allow television technical crews in the yard but not reporters. The crews could film the release but would be kept far enough away from the inmates that they could not conduct interviews.

At 10:00 P.M., the lights were turned on, and the inmates received their sodas, ice cream, and cigarettes. The captain was released unharmed. He was taken first to the infirmary and then to the warden's office for debriefing.

Ten minutes after the captain's release, inmates walked to the fence to negotiate. One hostage was brought to the gate and the second was shown from a window in South Building. This reassured prison officials that both were uninjured. The three state representatives approached the gate, accompanied by a major from the highway patrol. The negotiating captain also was there.

An inmate leader told the legislators that, if prison officials did not use force that night, they would surrender in the morning. They also advised the captain that they would move the hostages around that night, post sentries on the roof of South Building, and patrol the perimeter. Prison officials told the inmates that they would accept no more property damage that night. Negotiations ended at midnight.

Surrender Ritual

On Monday morning there were 50 inmates left on the yard. At 8:30 A.M., two media crews were allowed into the North Compound, each monitored by two officers. The warden instructed all emergency squads to move off the compound and away from windows or otherwise out of sight.

At 8:40 A.M., the three state legislators, the negotiating captain, and the major from the highway patrol were in position to observe the surrender. A bus arrived at 9:00 A.M. Forty-five minutes later six inmates began talking with the legislators at the fence. The legislators were told that all 50 inmates wanted to come out.

While the legislators were still talking to the inmates at the gate, eight heavily armed troopers moved in behind them. The inmates apparently believed that an assault was starting. A group ran back to South Building. One of the hostages was grabbed by the hair and pulled out of the building with a knife to his throat. Several inmates began to argue with several other inmates over whether the hostage should be killed right then and who would get to do it. Inmates finally realized they were responding to a false alarm.

At 10:00 A.M., four inmates brought a hostage to the gate opened by one of the inmate leaders. He was released and walked out by himself. Twenty minutes later, the last hostage was released. Soon after, the inmate leaders and other inmates left the yard. Nine inmates who were considered to be the most active in the riot were put on a bus by themselves and taken to another state prison. Emergency squad personnel brought the 41 remaining inmates out of the compound one at a time, stripped and searched them, fed them sandwiches and cold drinks, and handcuffed them. They were then placed on vans for transportation to the penitentiary.

The yard was secured at 11:50 A.M.

Aftermath

Two hundred inmates were temporarily housed in a cellhouse at the Oklahoma State Penitentiary. Nine inmates, including the three leaders, spent one night at another prison and were then transferred to the penitentiary the next day.

Over the longer run, employee morale and commitment to the department seem to have been made more solid by the riot. All of the hostages returned to work after the riot and continued their employment. The department's executive leadership took the position that, while mistakes had been made, staff had risen together to resolve the crisis. A ceremony was conducted in which the hostages were introduced before the assembled state legislators and given a standing ovation.

Fire and vandalism destroyed much of the prison. In developing plans to reconstruct the prison, the central office involved Mack Alford prison staff in developing plans for its reconstruction. A delegation of Mack Alford employees, including managers, correction officers, case managers, and maintenance workers, visited several Ohio prisons to survey different architectural designs. The director commented, "What they got [at Mack Alford] is what they designed. They feel like they own it."

II

CONTRACTED RIOTS

6

Coxsackie Correctional Facility, New York

August 1–2, 1988

Collective violence is a continuation of politics by other means, says sociologist William Gamson.[1] It is as "instrumental in its nature as a lobbyist trying to get special favor for his group or a major political party conducting a presidential campaign." The Tillys maintain that urban riots, like the ones in the U.S. cities in the 1960s, deserve a "strongly political interpretation."[2]

The argument—or image—is not implausible, even for prison riots. We know that inmates have used riots to advance political agendas, as the Atlanta riot illustrates. It is a mistake, however, to spin such occurrences into a general theory of what prison riots are like and are about.

This disturbance in a New York prison is very far from politics. It would be a stretch of some length to argue that the key demand, a telephone call by the inmate leader to his stepfather, flowed out of collective interest. By any reasonable standard, the means used were grossly disproportionate to the ends sought. The outcome was not any sort of prison reform, other than tighter security, but rather long prison sentences for the instigators.

Coxsackie Correctional Facility and Its Special Housing Unit

Opened in 1935, Coxsackie Correctional Facility is a maximum-security prison located 30 miles south of Albany.[3] Its inmates, generally speaking, are young, aggressive, and known to have a high proclivity toward violence. On August 1, 1988, the prison was operating at its full capacity of 961 inmates. Within the fenced perimeter there are 30 buildings, most of which are connected by an enclosed corridor.

The riot was confined to the prison's special housing unit (SHU), a separate single-level building for inmates who have violated prison rules (see Figure 6-1). The SHU is remote from the rest of the facility but is connected to it by a 100-foot-long "SHU corridor" that runs off a main corridor (see Figure 6-2). At each end of the SHU corridor is a single solid steel door with a small glass viewing panel. Each door is manually opened with a different security key.

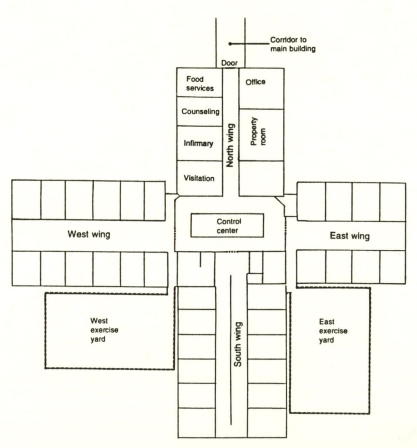

Figure 6-1   Special housing unit, Coxsackie Correctional Facility.

Figure 6-2 This photo looks down the SHU control hallway toward the fire hose; the control room is at the left and the visiting and recreation rooms are off to the right. The hallway on the right leads to unit offices, the sick call area, personal property storage, and, at its end, to the corridor where the negotiations transpired. *Source*: Department of Correctional Services, State of New York.

This SHU itself has four wings running off a centrally located control room. The south and west wings each have 12 single cells, and the east wing had eight single cells. The north wing contains administrative offices. Separate corridors lead from each wing to the control center. At the end of these corridors nearest the control center are sliding security grilles. An officer inside the control center operates them from a control panel, thereby regulating movement in and out of the wings. Nine feet separate the security grille and the control center.

Inmates and Security at the SHU

The 32 SHU inmates had an average age of 21, the oldest being 26. Most had exhibited violent behavior, both before and after imprisonment. Eighteen were serving sentences for robbery, three for burglary, three for murder, two for assault, and the remainder for an assortment of other violent crimes. Three were serving life sentences, and the average maximum sentence of the rest was about 8 years. The vast majority had been placed in the SHU because of assaults on staff or other inmates, while a few had attempted escape or had been found in possession of a weapon. Eleven of the inmates were Hispanics, 18 were African Americans, and three were whites.

Security procedures in the SHU were tight, at least on paper. Inmates stayed in their individual cells almost around the clock, eating their meals there. They were permitted out of their cells only for showers, visits, and one hour of exercise per day.

SHU inmates exercised in two small fenced exercise areas that were accessed through security doors, one off the east wing and the other off the west wing. Movement to and from the exercise yard was closely regulated. According to the written protocol, one inmate was called out for recreation at a time. He backed out of his cell with hands on head, was frisked, and was then escorted to the yard. Once in the yard, he walked to the far end and held the fence. This procedure involved three officers: one at the cell, one to escort the inmate through the two interior doors to the yard, and one at the chain-link gate that opened onto the yard.

Once all the inmates scheduled for recreation were holding the fence, the gate was closed and the recreation period started. The process was reversed at the end of the period. During the exercise period, an officer observed the yard from a position between the outside door of the SHU building and the gate to the fenced exercise yard.

In short, great attention had been given to the design both of the building and of the SHU's security procedures with a view to forestalling a disturbance by its violent inmates. Yet several factors lowered, in some measure, the actual security level of the unit.

The first general problem was a serious shortfall in the training and experience of the line and supervisory personnel actually present in the unit. On the day of the incident, none of the four officers regularly assigned to the SHU was on duty. Two were on vacation and two had regular days off. While each of the four relief officers had previously worked in the SHU at least once in the past, they were not as familiar with written policy and operational procedures as the regular SHU officers.

Several months prior to the disturbance, the sergeant in charge of the SHU had been suspended for reasons unrelated to SHU operations. A replacement had not yet been selected, and another sergeant, with responsibilities elsewhere in the facility, had taken over the supervisory duties on a temporary basis. This sergeant visited the unit daily but only briefly and, it would appear, usually during the latter part of the shift.

Post orders were not always available or updated to reflect what was expected on the various SHU posts.[4] The facility was in the process of writing and updating post orders at the time of the incident, but the task had just begun. As a consequence, relief officers learned their duties by asking and observing regular staff at those posts. When the relief officers were shown the procedure for manning the SHU, they may have been taught how to perform certain procedures in a seemingly convenient manner rather than by strict policy and procedure.

It so happened that even the top leadership of the prison reflected an absence of continuity on the day of the riot, although there is no evidence to show that this directly promoted the riot. The superintendent had been assigned to the institution in early July, the month prior to the incident, and the deputy superintendent for programs was in his second week at the facility. On the day of the incident, several senior-level staff members were absent from the facility, including the deputy superintendent for security and the first deputy superintendent. Their responsibilities were assumed by lower ranking officers.

The general lack of experienced line and supervisory personnel had probably contributed to the falling off of compliance with SHU's operating procedures. Over time, SHU procedures designed to ensure the security of staff and inmates had been altered by staff for the sake of convenience. For example, security gates and doors within the unit were left open when written procedure indicated they should have been kept closed and locked. In addition, officers and supervisors were apparently unaware that some security gates could (as a safety device) be kept from closing by exerting pressure against them.

In addition to the general lack of experience and continuity on the personnel front, there were some specific flaws in the management of the physical plant. For one thing, the SHU was cleaned by its own inmates. As it turned out, the inmate who emerged as the nominal leader in the takeover of the SHU had been a porter in the SHU for some time prior to the incident. While out of his cell, he had been able to learn how the doors were opened, observe staff movement and practices, and assess where and how the security controls were situated. Further, this inmate was known to be particularly dangerous and had been placed in the SHU for assaulting another inmate.

Finally, about three-fourths of the walls of the SHU control room were made of glazing (wire-reinforced plate glass). The common understanding was that this glazing was "impact resistant," that is, could withstand blows by inmates. Yet in two other New York prisons with SHUs of similar construction, inmates had broken the glazing. Funds had been requested by the department to replace the glazing in all similarly constructed SHUs, including Coxsackie. At the time of the incident, funds to correct the deficiencies had not been approved (see Figure 6-3).

Relations between Staff and Inmates in the SHU

Relations between inmates and staff in the SHU were tense. According to officers, inmates hurled urine, feces, and other debris at them as they passed their cells. In general, officers perceived the inmates to be loud, unruly, and strenuously difficult to manage.

For their part, the inmates felt harassed and verbally abused by at least some of the staff who were regularly assigned to SHU. In postriot interviews, inmates made two specific allegations. First, they charged that officers had physically abused them. One inmate claimed that he had been beaten up and knocked unconscious by officers.[5]

Figure 6-3 The SHU control room at Coxsackie was extensively damaged during the incident; the wire-reinforced glass was quickly breached by the inmates as the disturbance got underway. *Source*: Department of Correctional Services, State of New York.

The evidence, however, seems to discredit these allegations. In the nine-month period leading up to the riot, correctional officers completed only three incident reports involving the use of physical force, all of which appeared justified.[6] Nurses, counselors, and supervisory staff who visited the SHU had discovered no injuries. Furthermore, in the nine-month period leading up to the riot, none of the 28 grievances filed by SHU inmates charging harassment had been sustained, though about half had been appealed to an independent oversight commission (New York State Commission of Correction). One inmate filed almost half of the grievances, with many of them frivolous on their face.

The second major allegation was that staff doctored their food, spitting or stepping on it.[7] In postriot interviews, staff strongly denied the allegation. They did, however, acknowledge that they were aware of this rumor. One officer reported that he ended his practice of making amicable comments when delivering the food, such as "enjoy your food," because inmates interpreted any statement as having sinister implications.[8] Still, the inmates were convinced that their food had been tampered with.[9]

After the riot, inmates had an interest in alleging preriot brutality in order to justify the rebellion. It is not clear that they believed the allegations before the riot. Still, hostility in the SHU was certainly intense. Inmates apparently had reached a point where retaliation was contemplated against some of the regularly assigned SHU officers. Yet none of those officers was on duty when the riot began, a fact undoubtedly known to inmates.

Initiation

At approximately 10:30 A.M. on Thursday, August 1, 1988, seven inmates from the east wing and seven inmates from the west wing were completing an exercise period in their respective yards. The other 18 SHU inmates remained in their locked cells. During the exercise period, the officers supervising the two yards had observed nothing unusual in the inmates' conduct or demeanor. Now, per procedure, the inmates faced and held the exercise yard fence at the point farthest from the gate through which they would pass to return to their cells.

The officer observing the east yard unlocked and opened the SHU door that led to a small vestibule area within the SHU. The next door in, which separated the vestibule from the east wing, was electronically controlled from the control center. The officer in the control room unlocked it. One officer remained on the East tier to await the return of the inmate. A second went to the area just outside the exercise gate.

The officer who had been observing the yard swung open the chain-link gate, and the other officer called for the first inmate to come forward to go inside the SHU building. The inmate walked toward the gate with his hands in his pockets, still according to procedure. But when he was about three feet from the officer who had opened the gate, he took his hands out of his pockets and punched the officer in the face. The officer activated his personal alarm as he fell, and the second officer signaled for help from the officer on the east tier.

Two other inmates in the exercise yard rushed to join the assailant, and the three inmates began to shove the second officer back into the building. The officer on the wing, coming to assist, collided with the officer being pushed back, and the two officers fell to the floor. An inmate took one of the officers' batons and began to club them.

The officer in the control room could see the inmates assaulting the officers and set off an alarm in the institution's main control room. The sliding barred gate that separated the east wing from the control center area ought to have been closed, according to procedure. But it was not. The officer in the control center activated the closing mechanism, but the three inmates got there in time to hold it open.

The Facility's Initial Response and Riot Expansion

Responding to the alarm, a sergeant and five officers arrived at the solid steel entrance door to the SHU, about two minutes after the first alarm went off. However, they did not have the key to open it. Looking through the small security window in the door, the sergeant could see the three loose inmates. He radioed for more assistance and for the keys to the SHU door. Two of the three inmates came to the SHU entrance door and shouted through it that they had control of the unit and would kill any staff who tried to enter. They then moved toward the housing areas.

Meanwhile, the officer at the gate, the victim of the initial assault, regained his feet and closed and locked the gate to the exercise yard, thus securing the four remaining inmates on the yard. This officer then went inside the SHU and headed for the control room, but was attacked by a baton-wielding inmate on the east wing.

The officer in the control center, observing the struggle, activated the security gate that separates the control center area from the east wing. The officer managed to put himself on the east-wing side of the gate and the inmate on the other side, adjacent to the control center. Thus, the officer was safe temporarily in the east wing, while the inmate stood outside the control room.

The inmate first demanded that the control room officer open the security gate to the east wing. When the officer refused, the inmate began to strike the control room security glazing with a baton. On the second blow, the glazing broke. The control room officer decided to exit the control room through an emergency hatch in the ceiling. Having already collected most of the keys kept in the control room, he began to climb the ladder to the escape hatch. Part of the way up, he remembered that the master control key was still in its slot in the security console.

He returned to the control panel and turned the key to the "off" position in order to remove it. The key, however, was attached to the console by a chain. (The chain had been installed four years earlier to prevent officers from inadvertently walking off with it at the end of their shift.) Before the key could be pulled away, the inmate kicked out enough glass to allow him to climb into the control room and overpower the officer. An inmate then opened all the SHU cell doors using the control panel. With most of the 32 SHU inmates now loose, and keys in their possession, rioting inmates were able to seize the four remaining correctional officers in the unit and on the west yard with little resistance.

The inmates secured the hostages' hands with handcuffs and shoelaces. One officer had his wrist and ankle handcuffed together, and all of them were stripped of their personal property. The officers were moved to two locations, a property (storage) room off the north wing corridor and an area immediately in front of the SHU exit door. During the first hour of the riot, they were moved back and forth between those two locations.

The Decision Not to Assault

The sergeant outside the SHU door had been able to see most of these events through the window in the door. Additional officers began to arrive at the door, raising to 10 the number of uniformed officers present, some of whom had batons.

At 10:37 A.M. a captain arrived at the SHU door simultaneously with a door key that had been obtained from the prison's arsenal. The sergeant favored an immediate assault to retake the SHU and rescue the hostages, believing on the basis of his experience that these younger inmates would retreat in the face of physical force. But the captain did not like the odds. He did not know how many inmates were free within the cellblock but the numbers were growing quickly; they had the other officers' batons, and probably makeshift weapons as well by now. And if the assault failed, they might be taken hostage themselves and the riot might expand to other parts of the prison. The captain ordered the group to jam the lock and went to confer with the superintendent.

Response by the Facility and the Department

Inmates throughout the rest of the facility were returned to their housing units and were secured for the course of the disturbance with only minor problems. Fifteen armed correctional officers were stationed around the facility's perimeter. Three armed officers were placed on the SHU's roof.

Meanwhile, the superintendent called the central office in Albany to explain the situation. By 11:30 A.M., four department officials were on their way route to Coxsackie: the commissioner, deputy commissioner for operations, the assistant commissioner with responsibility for overseeing the facility, and the director of the crisis intervention unit (CIU, the hostage negotiations unit). According to a log of the incident, it was anticipated that the commissioner and deputy commissioner would "take over from superintendent's office" when he arrived.[10]

Coxsackie's Correctional Emergency Response Team (unit of officers trained in riot control and tactical operations) was activated, as were two others from Albany and from the nearby Eastern Correctional Facility.

The riot was eventually resolved through 14 hours of negotiations, which occurred in three phases.

Phase 1: Negotiations Begin at the SHU Door, 10:50 A.M. to Noon

By 10:50 a deputy superintendent was at the SHU entry door, being briefed by the captain. He began to talk to some of the inmates on the other side of the door, one of them an apparent leader. As they were speaking, the deputy superintendent could see one of the officers, who had been brought out to the SHU corridor door from property room, being threatened with a knife at his throat. The officer was then surrounded and beaten by about 10 inmates and finally returned to the property room.

The negotiations, if they can be called that, were at this point chaotic. At the SHU door, inmates shoved each other for a chance to talk to, or more often yell at, prison officials on the other side about having been abused. Threats were shouted at the hostages.[11] The prison officials responding at the door were the deputy superintendent, who carried out some of the conversation in Spanish, and a sergeant.

At about 11:10 A.M., an inmate called officials over a prison telephone, claiming that he was in charge. He issued two demands. One was that the

SHU's electricity, which had been turned off, be restored. The second demand, which would eventually become central to the riot's resolution, was to allow him to make an outside telephone call. Later in the negotiations, prison officials would learn that the inmate wanted to speak to his stepfather.

After the demands were made, inmates paraded an officer at the SHU entrance, threatening to kill him unless the electricity were turned on. At 11:45 A.M., five minutes after the inmate issued their demand for electricity, the superintendent ordered it turned on.[12]

During this initial conversation, four of the five hostages had been positively identified by the deputy superintendent. At least two of the hostages were known to have sustained head injuries, although the severity of their condition was uncertain. One was thought to be possibly unconscious. The fifth hostage was not first seen until noon.

A forward command post was established in the facility's barbershop because of its proximity to the SHU. A line was opened from this post to the command post in the superintendent's office. From here, an open line was established with the Albany-located Emergency Operations Center (EOC), the department's command post in the event of an emergency.

In this situation, however, the role of the EOC would be circumscribed to one of coordinating logistical support. The department's leadership, including the commissioner, would take charge of the incident on site.

Phase 2: Department Leadership Assumes Control, Noon to 3:30 P.M.

The CIU director arrived at Coxsackie at about 11:10 A.M. The commissioner and deputy commissioner for operations arrived about an hour later. From about noon on, the commissioner took direct control of the resolution from a command post established in the superintendent's office. The commissioner also kept the governor and other key state criminal justice officials informed of the situation. While the commissioner was directing the response to the incident, the superintendent assumed responsibility for maintaining order in the rest of the facility. The CIU command center was established in the deputy superintendent's office, and the barber shop was kept as forward command post.

Course of Negotiations

Once at the command post, the commissioner directed staff to discontinue conversation with the inmates over the telephone and, from then on, to conduct all negotiations through the SHU door. Officials asked inmates to accept a "hostage" phone with a direct line but the inmates refused to take it.

The deputy superintendent, who had been negotiating since the beginning of the incident, continued in that role for the first two hours. About

12:30 P.M., a Spanish-speaking CIU team member relieved the deputy superintendent. From that point until the third phase, CIU members conducted the negotiations.

The inmate who initially claimed to be in charge was able to exercise a measure of authority in the situation. From conversation between him and prison officials, the riot's resolution became focused on two issues. First, the inmate leader wanted an outside telephone line so that he could call his stepfather. Second, he asked for written assurance that there would be no reprisals from department staff. This had to be guaranteed by a representative of the central office.

No other coherent demands emerged. Still, some inmates made it clear that the nominal leader was not speaking for them. Various inmates would come to the SHU door to voice their opinions, in apparent disregard of the nominal leader. Throughout the course of the riot, inmates could be heard arguing and fighting among themselves. To a large extent, the negotiations consisted of attempts by prison officials to calm the inmates by repeating reassurances that they would not be harmed if they gave up.

Treatment of Hostages

Over the next 10 hours, the hostages were separated and moved to locations within the SHU. They were placed in cells and handcuffed to cell doors and grille gates.

From time to time inmates assaulted the hostages, usually when they were in front of the SHU door and visible to officers on the other side. Some inmates threatened the officers with death and sexual assault, but neither threat was acted upon. Other inmates made efforts to lessen their ordeal, dressing their wounds and offering cigarettes.

In the early afternoon, the inmates forced the hostages to make calls over the facility's internal phone system. One of those calls was received by the facility's telephone operator at 1:20 P.M. The hostage told her that he was the only uninjured hostage and that he needed to talk to the superintendent or receive a call back from someone in authority. Soon after this, the commissioner ordered that the only communication with those inside the SHU would take place through the negotiation process.

Still, inmates yelled through the SHU windows to the staff that had formed a perimeter around the unit. At one point, an officer heard an inmate claim that one officer had been stabbed, one officer had a broken arm, and two officers had head injuries. This was only partly true, but prison officials did not know that at the time.

Assembling Intelligence

CIU members began to collect and collate information about the SHU inmates. Soon after the riot started, counselors pulled the file-folder records on all of the SHU inmates. CIU members interviewed the head of the facility's psychological unit, as well as correctional officers and sergeants familiar with the SHU inmates. An officer began reviewing grievances filed by SHU inmates over the previous three months. From these sources, a list of the unit's 10 most violence-prone inmates was compiled, which included the inmate leader. Also, efforts were made to collect information on the relationship between the inmate leader and his stepfather. The CIU director relayed the assembled information to the staff in the command post.

Phase 3: Negotiations Lead to Settlement, 3:35 P.M. to Midnight

The CIU negotiators attempted to get inmates psychologically committed to conditions that, if met, would constitute adequate safeguards against staff beatings. In particular, they focused the inmates' attention on an assistant commissioner whom they described as a person of authority, willing and able to ensure their safety.

At 3:35 P.M. the assistant commissioner arrived at the prison from Albany. He was briefed on events and went to the SHU entrance door, making his first attempt to talk with the inmates around 4:00 P.M. He introduced himself to the inmates, stating, "You wanted to speak with someone from Albany. We want to get this over with and get the hurt people out."[13] The inmate replied, "We don't want to be hurt. Our concerns are the men who are hurt."

A few minutes later, the inmate leader brought two hostages, and a little later a third hostage, to SHU door. The assistant commissioner could see that they had sustained head injuries and numerous bruises and were bleeding. Still, each hostage nodded to him to signal that he was all right. About a half an hour later, around 4:30, a fourth hostage was seen, apparently not seriously injured.

By 4:45 P.M., prison officials had been able to locate the inmate leader's stepfather and had him on the phone. The stepfather agreed to speak with his stepson, and that he would urge him to release the hostages and surrender. At 5:00 the assistant commissioner told the inmate leader that he had his stepfather on the phone. The inmate leader responded that this was not enough to effect a surrender, explaining that they now wanted written assurances against being assaulted. At 6:00 P.M., the assistant commissioner told the inmates that he had the written reassurances that they had requested. He received no response.

At this point, prison officials had met the inmates' demands. Yet, for another six hours, inmates refused to surrender. The period was marked by several incidents, in which one thing or another disturbed or provoked inmates, and officials responded as best they could.

Around 6:30 P.M., a sergeant and seven officers went to the SHU roof, from where they hoped to monitor what was being said within the SHU. Inmates heard them and believed that an assault had started. The negotiators attempted to reassure the inmates that there was no one there, but the inmates refused to speak further with the negotiators for a time.

About 8:20 P.M., inmates released an officer. According to both inmate and officer accounts, this occurred because inmates feared that the officer might die from the injuries he had sustained. (In fact, he was the least seriously injured of the five hostages.) Apparently, one of the hostages had been able to convince the inmates that the hostage's release would be a show of good will.[14]

Once released, the officer provided information that suggested that a tactical assault would be very difficult. The inmates had barricaded the control room, had chained shut one SHU door entrance, and had acquired numerous weapons, including a dozen batons, helmets, gas masks, and riot shields.[15]

The officer was taken to a hospital but his injuries were not serious enough to require him being admitted.

At 8:50 P.M., officials allowed the inmate leader to speak with his stepfather, a call which was monitored by officials. The conversation did not go smoothly and was hostile from both ends. The inmate told his stepfather to call the media and have them brought to the prison. When the stepfather advised him to surrender, the inmate responded, "Don't preach to me." Prison officials told the inmate to end the conversation after three minutes.

Between 9:00 P.M. and a surrender at midnight, prison officials had to work through a host of difficulties and delays. At one point, the inmates said that they would release the hostages when they heard verification of the agreement on the news. Negotiators succeeded in steering the inmates away from the issue and it was dropped. Again and again at the inmates' prompting, the assistant commissioner reassured the inmates that they would not be harmed. Around 10:00 P.M., for example, the assistant commissioner told the inmate leader:

> No one is going to lay a hand on you. I made arrangements to get you guys some food. No one is going to hurt you, read the letter . . . I'll be right here. I will supervise the entire thing. Nobody is going to hurt you. You got my word. I can't give you any more.[16]

At 11:00 P.M., the inmates told prison officials that they wanted to wait until 6:00 A.M. and added that they wanted a video camera and the prison's chaplain. Prison officials produced both. When the video camera was put in place, the inmates now insisted that the video camera had to be a media camera. The chaplain spoke to the inmates, and they told him they did not want to release the hostages that night because "we're scared."

At about 11:50 P.M., the inmates apparently changed their minds and told officials that they wanted to surrender that night. At midnight they began to remove barricades from the SHU door. Then they decided to wreck the SHU control center as best they could. Their theory was that this would ensure their transfer out of the unit to another institution. At

12:30 inmates began to file out of SHU with the hostages mixed among them. Two inmates and one officer were carried out on stretchers. Ten minutes later, all the inmates had surrendered.

Aftermath

Two inmates were treated in outside hospitals but not admitted.[17] The remaining inmates were taken to the gymnasium, where they were kept 20 feet from each other, instructed not to talk, and guarded by one or two correctional officers per inmate. Each inmate was examined by a member of the medical staff and interviewed by the state police, the New York State Commission of Correction, and the Department of Correctional Services' investigative unit.[18] In the course of the morning they were transferred to other institutions.

Seventeen inmates were prosecuted and convicted for their actions during the riot. They received additional sentences ranging in length from two to fifteen years.

The four officers who were released were taken to a hospital. They had been badly battered but none of their injuries was life threatening.

7

Kirkland Correctional Institution, South Carolina

April 1, 1986

One of the lessons of previous chapters is that the same problems that lead to prison riots, such as a breakdown in communication between administration and staff, also make it more difficult to limit or terminate the riot. The Kirkland riot shows the opposite side of the coin; the prison was generally well managed before the disturbance, and so was the resolution.

The Prison and Its Inmates

Kirkland Correctional Institution, opened in 1975, is a medium-security facility located on the outskirts of the capital city of Columbia, South Carolina.[1] Adjacent to it are the headquarters of the department of corrections. The prison was opened in 1975. It has a campus-type layout, with detached buildings spread across grass-covered grounds (see Figure 7-1). On the west side of the grounds are seven housing units; on the east side are an administration building, an inmate industries building, a cafeteria, an infirmary, and a psychiatric unit for mentally disturbed inmates. In a central location is a large multipurpose building with an inmate store, library, barber shop, and academic and vocational classrooms.

On the eve of the riot, Kirkland housed 950 inmates in space meant for 448 inmates. To accommodate the overload, many cells designed for

121

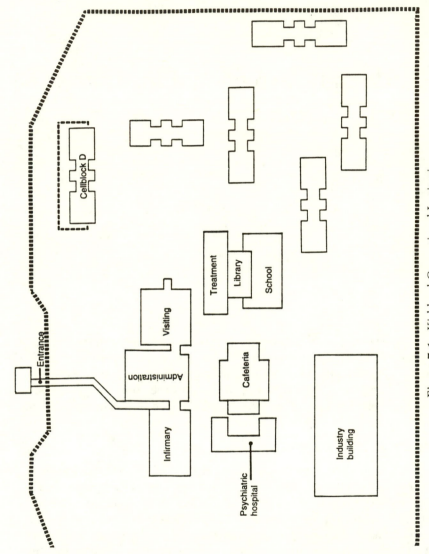

Figure 7-1 Kirkland Correctional Institution.

122

two inmates held three. Still, the atmosphere of the facility seemed positive; in fact, Kirkland had never experienced a major disturbance. Kirkland's unit-management system, under which teams of correctional staff and management staff were given responsibility for maintaining particular housing units, had apparently helped foster a positive relationship between staff and inmates. The warden was liked by and respected among staff. The department's director of security had conducted a security audit of the prison a few weeks before the disturbance and reported that the morale was high among both employees and inmates. To him, the prison appeared to be well managed, and there were no indications that a riot was imminent.

This positive atmosphere, however, did not extend to Housing Unit D, the prison's 73-bed administrative segregation unit. Although Kirkland was built as a medium-security prison, it housed a number of high-risk and dangerous offenders. This was because the state's maximum security center, which had traditionally housed the state's most violent inmates, had been closed under the terms of a consent decree settling a lawsuit about overcrowding. Those inmates were transferred to other prisons throughout the system, including Kirkland.

Unit D was not overcrowded, and each inmate was assigned to a single cell. Still, hostilities were intense, especially in a separate bay of eight cells called the substantiated security risk (SSR) section of Unit D. The eight SSR cells were reserved for the prison's most violent and disruptive inmates, primarily those with histories of assaults on staff and other inmates.

Inmates in SSR were constantly at war with the correctional officers and with the prison. They would often collect their own urine and excrement and hurl it through the bars at officers or spit on them as they passed. Some inmates set fire to their mattresses or other debris in their cells.

The abuse took a toll on correctional officers. "Everyone coming in contact with the clientele we had in Unit D [was] burned out," one Kirkland supervisor stated. "There wasn't a fresh crew of people that I could put in there." According to a department report, correctional officers assigned to the unit experienced high rates of stress-related illness and turnover.[2]

In August 1985, prison officials began to renovate Unit D to make it more secure. Maintenance crews installed heavier doors and window grilles. However, the original 1975 electric locks, which had suffered a great deal of wear over the years, were retained in the new doors. This led to an incident in which an inmate was able to break out of his cell and stab an officer.

In response to this incident, the warden ordered sliding dead bolts to be installed on each cell door in SSR as a backup for the electric locks. He also ordered sliding metal plates to cover the ventilation slots to prevent inmates from throwing urine and feces on officers.

Prison officials decided against securing the dead bolts with padlocks. They were concerned that cells secured with padlocks would be a fire hazard, a worry given especially great weight because a fire a number of years back had killed two Kirkland inmates. In addition, officials were confident that an inmate could not open the dead bolt from inside his cell, and no inmate was allowed into the bay area.

The South Carolina Department of Corrections is unusual both in the stability of its upper echelon management and in the degree of attention that its top officials have given to the issue of riot preparedness. In 1982 the department acted to strengthen its emergency preparedness unit by dividing it into three operational divisions. Situation Control Teams (SITCONs) were designated to be trained in the use of negotiation to resolve emergency situations and were also given the responsibility of debriefing hostages after their release. Reserve Emergency Platoons (REPs) were to be trained in the use of crowd control techniques and emergency perimeter security. Correctional Emergency Response Teams (CERTs) were trained in specialized tactical force, such as the use of sniper fire. A CERT would have the initial responsibility to contain and control a crisis area.

Each of the state's prisons has locally based REP and SITCON teams. The SITCON teams each have five members; the number of REP members depends upon the size of the institution, ranging from 16 to 52. Three facilities (including Kirkland) had a CERT. Though each REP, SITCON, and CERT team is based at a particular facility, it also contributes to a departmentwide emergency operations structure. At his or her own discretion, a warden can deploy the facility's own emergency response team. If the warden requires additional help, he or she can request assistance from units based at other facilities.

Riot Initiation

At about 7:00 P.M. on April 1, 1986, an SSR inmate asked a correctional officer for some aspirin. While the officer went to get it, a second inmate escaped from his cell. Apparently, he had jammed the electric lock on his cell and then somehow opened the dead bolt, perhaps by reaching through a ventilation slot. When the correctional officer returned with the aspirin, the inmate approached him from behind, armed with a prison-made knife, and threatened to kill him unless he turned over his keys.

The officer shouted for help, but the three officers in Unit D's control center could not hear him. The officer, who was armed only with a tear gas canister and trapped by himself, dropped his keys and ran to alert his co-workers. Once past the wing's security grille, the officer phoned the D Unit's control center to summon help. The officers there, in turn, triggered the institution's emergency alarm system.

Since this was the evening shift when inmates were not allowed out of their cells, the officer had had no need to carry more than one key, the one to the wing's entrance. However, the post orders did not specify which keys should be carried on which shift. On that particular evening he had been carrying the cell keys for SSR and the adjoining wing of Unit D, and the inmates proceeded to release these inmates, 32 in all.

Expansion

About 20 minutes after the first officer was seized, some of the prisoners used a metal chair leg to break the padlock on a fire exit door and entered a fenced-in recreation yard. There they used a weight-lifting bar to break the lock on a door leading back in to a corridor in another part of Unit D. They were then able to release more prisoners by breaking the lock on another fire exit door.

At about 7:35 P.M. a group of inmates scaled the fence of the Unit D recreation yard and escaped onto the main compound. Just outside the fence was a heavy metal tool box secured by a large lock, which contained tools for the ongoing renovation of the unit, including acetylene cutting equipment, bolt cutters, crowbars, power saws, metal grinders, and sledge hammers (Figure 7-2). The inmates smashed the lock and took possession of the tools.

Figure 7-2 Construction equipment and tools that were left inside the security perimeter in a locked toolbox were accessed by inmates during the Kirkland incident. The tools shown were recovered in shakedowns during the process of securing the facility after the riot. Immediatly after the incident, tool-control procedures were revised to require that all construction tools be removed from inside the perimeter when not in use. *Source*: Al Waters, Director, Internal Affairs, South Carolina Department of Corrections.

The control center alerted the officers stationed in the six remaining housing units, instructing them to lock themselves behind the entrance grilles and wing gates in their units. Under most circumstances, these locations would have been safe even from an angry group of inmates. The rioting inmates in this situation, however, were able to use the heavy tools to break into all six housing units, release about 700 inmates in the general population, and take hostage or trap 20 correctional officers and two counselors. Inmates vandalized and set fire to the administrative offices that are in each housing unit and also set fire to the multipurpose building.

Still, for the most part, the general inmate population did not take part actively in the riot.[3] This may have been because most were not especially angry with the administration.

Administration's Response

At about the time that inmates were climbing over the Unit D recreation yard fence, Kirkland's chief correctional officer arrived at the prison. He was the senior officer in charge but, with 20 officers trapped, had only a few officers available. He assigned several to perimeter posts and one to the roof of the administration building. The instructions for the officer on the roof were to prevent inmates from seizing buildings yet untouched: the administration building, infirmary, cafeteria, prison industry building, and psychiatric center. The officer took with him a shotgun and a walkie-talkie.

With the idea of adding more officers to the roof, the chief called the psychiatric center to direct the two available officers to report to the administration building. Unknown to either the chief or the officers, however, about a dozen inmates had crossed past the administration building and were in the vicinity of the psychiatric unit. Seconds after the two officers had left for the administration building, the inmates overpowered them, handcuffed them, beat them, and moved them back into the housing area. The chief also told his command center to call the department's director of security and to ask that he mobilize all available REP members. The director of security, who received this call at home, issued this order call and then left for Kirkland.

At 8:00 P.M., large numbers of inmates began moving east, in the direction of the administration, industries, cafeteria, infirmary, and psychiatric center buildings. As the inmates neared these buildings, the correctional officer stationed on the roof of the administration building fired a warning shot above their heads. This was actually a violation of official procedure, which said that only the warden had the authority to give an order to fire. But the inmates retreated back to the housing area, and the riot was successfully confined after that point to the west side.

By 8:20 P.M., department officials had established a command post in the warden's office in the administration building. Present were the commissioner, deputy commissioner for operations, regional administrator, deputy regional administrator, director of security, and the warden, as well as the captains of the department's three emergency response teams.

Most of those in the command post had worked with each other for years, some for as many as 20 years. "We're all good friends, longtime associates," one administrator stated, "[and thus] we didn't have to impress each other, no posturing."

Early Hostage Release

At 8:45 P.M., the regional administrator, who was now at the command post, answered a call from an inmate who said that he had two hostages and he wanted to meet with someone in authority. When the regional administrator asked who he wanted to talk to, the inmate responded, "You, alone, in front of [the administration building] in 20 minutes."

At the appointed time the caller and another inmate brought out two hostages handcuffed together. The inmates told the regional administrator that their only demand was a promise that inmates would not be injured. He responded that the department would do what was necessary to restore order but that no one would be hurt as long as inmates did not try to injure any hostage or inmate. He also asked the inmates about the number and condition of the hostages; the inmate provided no clear information but stated that he would have the remaining hostages released if the department would not intervene and let him handle it. The regional administrator said that if this were to occur it would have to happen quickly and that he should call him back. The regional administrator then left with the two hostage officers, who were freed from their handcuffs and sent to the infirmary.

Critical Point

At 9:10 P.M., the regional administrator received a phone call in the command post from one of the 11 officers who were trapped in a security office in Unit D. He reported that the inmates were trying to break in on them and that they had weapons and a cutting torch. The officer also reported that several fires had been started in the building and that the smoke was making it difficult to breathe and see.

The regional administrator asked the officer if they could leave the building via a rear door if enough help arrived to cover them. He answered that they could but that inmates were close to breaking in on them. The regional administrator told the officer to watch the rear of the building and to prepare his group to leave quickly.

The regional administrator briefed the others in the command post, and everyone quickly agreed that the officers trapped in Unit D had to be rescued immediately. The REP captain would later remark that he wanted to go onto the yard with no fewer than 100 officers, but that the 35 now assembled would be the bare minimum for safety.

Ultimatum and Deployment

At 9:15 P.M., the warden collected his thoughts and made the following statement over the institutional public address system:

> [We] will take necessary steps to quell the disturbance unless those involved cease their violent acts. The riot squad has been deployed with shotguns. They have been instructed to use all necessary force to quell this disturbance, to include deadly force. Lie down on the ground where you are. I am not playing games. I am dead serious.[4] (abbreviated; statement repeated by Warden)

As the warden's message was being broadcast, a 35-officer REP group led by the department's REP captain and the chief at Kirkland left the administrative offices building heading toward Unit D. The captain was unarmed, but the other REP members carried shotguns loaded with birdshot. The team went through the rear gate of the Unit D recreation yard and freed the trapped officers through Unit D's emergency exit door, located between the building's wing gates.

Five REP members accompanied these officers back to the administration building; the remaining 30 re-formed with other REP members just arriving and began moving inmates toward the main recreation yard at a rapid pace. There were a few moments of uncertainty when the officer who was supposed to be carrying the yard gate key could not find it. At that point, some words were exchanged between inmates and the officers, and the REP captain ordered the team members to rack their guns and ordered the inmates to lie on the ground. The inmates complied, and a team member was dispatched to get bolt cutters, but within minutes the officer discovered that he had had the key all along.

The warden made a second statement over the public address system at 9:40 P.M. After repeating part of his earlier statement, he said,

> If you are not involved and do not want to become involved, report to the recreation field immediately. I repeat, if you are not involved and do not want to become involved, report to the recreation field immediately.[5]

Many inmates responded and moved to the main fenced recreation area. Apparently, they were just as happy to be done with the riot, perhaps because of the above-noted lack of hostility toward the administration. Others were routed to the fenced recreation yard by the REP squad as they performed sweeps of the yards and buildings. Eventually, about 600 inmates were placed there. Another 100 inmates had remained in their housing units to avoid the disturbance. A smaller group of inmates, mostly those fearful of other inmates, was moved to an area near the industry building. Although this latter group was not restrained by fencing, its members were primarily concerned with their own safety and wanted no part in the riot.

By 10:15 P.M., officials considered the prison to be sufficiently in control that fire trucks could be moved into the compound. They extinguished fires in the housing units and the multipurpose service building. By 11:30 P.M., the facility was considered fully secured.

The nine additional hostages were released throughout the evening. A group of 30–40 inmates helped hide some of the trapped officers or helped them escape. One correctional officer, for example, was given inmate clothes and, with the assistance of several inmates, was able to run across the yard to escape. The remaining hostages were freed by the emergency response team as they swept the buildings and yards. The SITCON team debriefed all of the hostages and trapped staff members, as well as some of the inmates who provided protection to officers.

Aftermath

Around midnight, prison officials inspected the housing units and found that, while the office areas had been destroyed, the units could still safely house inmates. Inmates were ordered to move in groups of 10 from the recreation yard to their housing assignments, one housing unit at a time. Housing unit managers were present to identify them. This process took about six hours. Eight inmates identified as the most active in the disturbance were put in security vans for transportation to a nearby facility. The prison was fully locked down by 6:00 A.M. on April 2. A shakedown was conducted later in the morning, and a second and third time about a week later.

To remedy the problems that allowed the riot to spread, the electric locks on all Unit D doors were replaced with manually operated deadbolt locks; the warden issued new policies that required officers to carry only those keys they needed; and the use-of-force policy was changed to allow the senior person on duty to make the decision. Two fences were installed around Unit D, making this area inaccessible, or at least less accessible, to rioters. The department issued an order that no construction tools would be allowed to remain inside an institution, regardless of the inconvenience this might cause construction crews.

Ten months after the riot, 32 inmates pled guilty to or were convicted of riot-related charges. Their sentences ranged from six months to fifteen years, to be served after completion of their current sentences. In total, more than 100 years of additional prison time were given. Other inmates were disciplined through the department's internal discipline committee.

The riot's direct cost to the state was about $1 million. This included $730,000 for repairs to the facility (see, e.g., Figure 7-3), plus additional expenses related to overtime, workmen's compensation, counseling, and fire fighting.

One year after the riot, only one of the 22 employees trapped or taken hostage had left the department. The turnover rate of this group was lower than the turnover rate for employees elsewhere in the department. Department officials we interviewed attributed this in part to mandatory "stress debriefing" or counseling sessions for the hostages and others exposed to potentially traumatizing experiences.

Figure 7-3 Although the cinderblock construction of this building (Unit A II) meant that only furniture, files, and other non-structural elements burned, the damage was still severe. *Source*: Al Waters, Director, Internal Affairs, South Carolina Department of Corrections.

Perhaps equally important were the efforts of corrections officials in the postriot adjustment process. Kirkland's warden, for example, took an active part in one of the postriot counseling sessions.[6] He thanked those taken hostage and the other participants for their efforts, and answered questions about the incident and related security matters in the department. Just as there are good reasons why a general visits his wounded troops in the field hospital, corrections officials cannot delegate "recovery" to mental health workers alone.

8

Arizona State Prison Complex, Cimarron Unit

June 21, 1990

This one-hour disturbance by inmates at Cimarron Unit of the Arizona State Prison Complex at Tucson initially pitted inmates against inmates. It began as a fight over a cigarette lighter and escalated into a giant brawl. When prison officials intervened, inmates turned on them, and force had to be used to end the disturbance.

Cimarron Unit

The Arizona State Prison at Tucson is a complex that houses 2,400 inmates in four semiautonomous units. A warden administers the complex as a whole, with each unit under the direction of a deputy warden. A number of support services are shared. For example, the Tactical Support Unit, a unit specially trained to handle riots, is staffed by members from the entire complex.

The riot was confined to the Cimarron Unit, the last of the four units to come on line (in 1986). Department officials considered the cell blocks at Cimarron to be more secure than those in the state's other medium-security facilities. Thus, Cimarron received the more difficult to manage medium-custody inmates, including gang members.[1] The unit's 780 "heavy medium" inmates were serving terms from one year to triple life. This number of inmates was only somewhat above the unit's design capacity of 744.

The Cimarron Unit is divided into north and south divisions, each containing two cell houses, separated by a fence with a gate. Buildings 1 and 2 are in North Yard, and Buildings 3 and 4 are in South Yard (see Figures 8-1, 8-2). The entire unit is surrounded by two 12-foot fences topped with razor ribbon wire, and a 14-foot fence surrounds the entire complex (except a minimum-security unit).

Racial/Ethnic Antagonism

Cimarron inmates tended to segregate themselves along racial and ethnic lines. African-American, white, and Hispanic inmates would congregate separately in the dining areas, recreation yards, and other public areas. Tension among the groups was palpable and would, from time to time, break out in overt hostility. In September 1987, 16 African-American and white inmates got into a brawl over a gambling debt.[2] Two years later, about 80 inmates were involved in a disturbance that began when an African-American inmate and a white inmate fought over exercise equipment.[3] In March 1990, 108 African-American inmates in the Cimarron Unit signed a petition to the U.S. Justice Department alleging "unfair treatment" and "arbitrary and capricious harassment and verbal abuse" of African-American prisoners.[4]

Cimarron had also suffered some racial tension among its staff. In the fall of 1989, what apparently had begun as racial joking among correctional officers had escalated into an incident of insults and name-calling. Two African-American officers had also filed claims for $5 million against the department for alleged racial harassment. In April 1990, after a department investigation of racial harassment, two white officers were fired, one was demoted, and about 10 others received disciplinary letters.[5] One of the officers disciplined for racial slurs was found to have connections to the Ku Klux Klan.[6]

The Events of the Riot

On June 13, 1990, two Hispanic prisoners beat an African-American inmate with a weight-lifting bar. This incident apparently intensified hard feelings between the two groups, and five African-American inmates were assigned to other prison units because they allegedly advocated taking reprisals for the attack.[7]

About five days after this incident, an African-American and a Hispanic inmate got into a scuffle over a cigarette lighter, with the African-American inmate getting the best of the Hispanic. The next day, June 21, at around 5:00 P.M., 120 inmates from the north side were being served their evening meal, under the supervision of two correctional officers. At

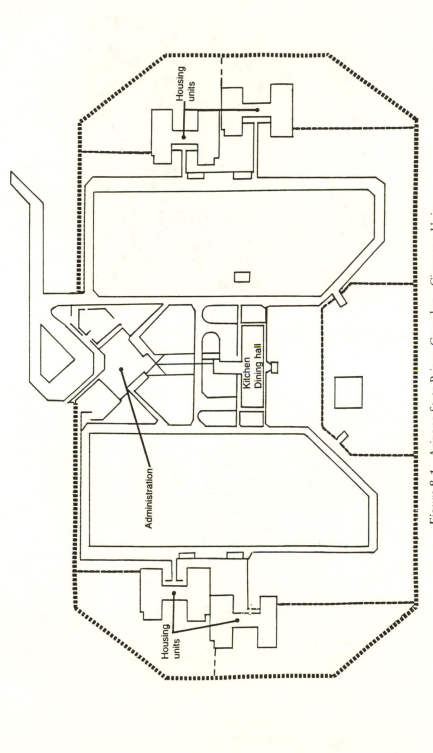

Figure 8-1 Arizona State Prison Complex—Cimarron Unit.

133

Figure 8-2   The front entrance to the Cimarron Unit's Adminstration Building. *Source*: Arizona Department of Corrections.

the beverage counter, the Hispanic inmate resumed the earlier argument with the African-American inmate and then grabbed a wooden mop handle wringer and swung it at him, but hit another African-American inmate, apparently by mistake.

Quickly, African Americans and Hispanics took sides and began throwing food, trays, and utensils at each other. This escalated into a free-for-all fistfight. White inmates joined in on the side of the Hispanic inmates. The two officers present tried to break up the fighting but were unsuccessful, so they called over the radio for backup, left the dining hall, and secured the dining hall door to contain the situation.

The shift commander, a lieutenant, responded to their call for backup within a minute's time. He and another officer began to enter the dining hall. Inmates overpowered them at the doors and poured out onto the north recreation yard. The inmates, 100–120 in number, divided themselves into two opposing groups, the African Americans against the whites and Hispanics.[8] Other inmates on the yard joined in.

Cimarron Unit had at this time not yet been fully landscaped, and rocks of all sizes would commonly work their way up through the dry soil to the surface. There was also a lot of construction debris still present on the yard. Inmates on both sides armed themselves with rocks, two-by-four pieces of lumber, and mop handles from the dining room. Racial threats were yelled back and forth, and stone throwing began.

Officers ordered inmates to return to their housing units, but to no avail. The lieutenant and the officers on the scene tried to separate the groups, but just when they thought they were about to accomplish a separation, the inmates resumed fighting. This happened two or three times. Meanwhile, the lieutenant had ordered all the other inmates in the prison to return to their cells, and this order was obeyed without incident, except by the inmates on the yard.[9]

Weapons Are Ordered for Use and South Yard Inmates Become Involved

The lieutenant issued orders calling for a tear-gas gun, a shotgun, and the activation of the Tactical Support Unit. Two officers went to retrieve the munitions from the control room located in the administration building.

About the same time, 50–100 inmates from South Yard rushed the gate that separated North and South yards, apparently in an attempt to get into the North Yard action. A female officer attempted to secure this gate but the inmates overpowered her before she could do so. They pinned her briefly against a wall, injuring her knee, but did not take her hostage. With the addition of these south-side inmates, some 400 of Cimarron's 800 inmates were involved in the disturbance on the North Yard.

The two officers obtained from the armory a gas grenade gun, a vest that stores shotgun and gas shells, and a 12-gauge shotgun loaded with birdshot as well as a box of shells. As the two officers emerged from the building, a group of white and Hispanic inmates began to approach them. One of the officers dispersed them by firing a warning shot into the air, and two officers brought their weapons to the lieutenant and sergeant on the North Yard.

Other officers from adjoining units in the complex began arriving to assist with the crisis, bringing the number of officers to about 30. Elsewhere on the yard, a white inmate tried to break down a gate leading to a tool storage area in the corner of the yard. Two officers apprehended the inmate, but let him go because they were outnumbered and unarmed. In the struggle an officer injured his ankle.[10]

Inmates Turn on Staff

At this point the inmates began to perceive the officers with guns as their primary antagonists, instead of each other. The Hispanic and white inmates began to retreat toward their housing units. The 40 African-American inmates, however, turned their aggression toward the staff. They began to hurl stones at the officers, and 10–15 of them began to advance on the staff.[11] A warning shot was fired by the officer with a shotgun, but the inmates continued to advance, yelling obscenities and hurling rocks. An officer then fired a tear-gas round, and then a second. The wind dissipated the gas.[12]

The crowd of African-American inmates began to yell specific threats against the staff, to the effect that they would rush them, take their guns, and kill them. Some of the inmates began to move around to the sides of the officers' group. The lieutenant feared that he and the other officers might be surrounded and quickly pulled his group back.[13] Three shots were fired into the crowd of black inmates, now at a distance of about 40 yards. The shots were aimed at the concrete in front of the prisoners so that the pellets would ricochet up toward the inmates' lower extremities.[14] But the dust cloud from the first shot made it difficult to place the second and third shots, and one inmate was hit directly in the chest by one of the shells.[15] Fourteen other inmates were injured by the ricocheting pellets.

Rock throwing continued, but the danger to the officers abated. One of the officers aimed his gun at the inmates to discourage any attack.

The officers held their ground in this situation for about 40 minutes. Meanwhile, backup department security staff arrived, and then an armed Tactical Support Unit, taking control of the situation. The two Cimarron officers with weapons were relieved of them. About 40 minutes after the first shot, the situation was under full control.[16] The injured inmates were hospitalized; six officers were found to have suffered minor injuries.

Aftermath

Corrections officers searched and locked down inmates; the detention unit was cleared of inmates, and the most active rioters were confined there.[17] Families of inmates who had been injured or who were involved in the disturbance were notified by the prison, and a telephone line was opened to take their calls. All incoming and outgoing movement was canceled, and the entire prison remained on lockdown for three days. Property damage was insignificant, under $500 in all, and normal activities were resumed by July 6.

The department conducted an investigation of the incident, interviewing staff and inmates and requiring written reports from all staff who were present. In addition, because African-American inmates had been shot by white officers, and in view of previous racial problems at Cimarron, the director of corrections arranged for a separate investigation to be conducted by the state's Department of Public Safety. The shootings were found to have been justified.

An electronic closing mechanism was installed on the gate between the North and South yards, the yard was planted with grass to prevent the exposure of rocks, and officers were directed to move inmates to and from the dining hall in smaller groups.

9

Idaho State Correctional Institution

September 28, 1988

This disturbance received no great attention and produced no legislative hearings or blue-ribbon commission. Yet for every "noteworthy" riot, defined loosely as something akin to an Atlanta or a Camp Hill, there are dozens more like this brief but deadly disturbance. It is hard to identify "underlying causes" for this riot, but we can identify factors that enabled a small incident to expand and disrupt the entire prison.[1]

The Prison

Located a few miles south of Boise, the Idaho State Correctional Institution (ISCI) was planned in the early 1960s and completed in 1973. It was designed as the 375-inmate medium-security component of what would become a three-prison complex. According to one senior corrections official, when the ISCI was being planned, the emphasis was on creating a "rehabilitative" environment without, in hindsight, sufficient attention being given to security concerns. Thus, the interior walls were built with cinder blocks without steel bars to reinforce them.

The minimum-security component, the South Idaho Correctional Institution, was in operation at the time of the riot, but the Idaho Maximum Security Institution was under construction when the riot occurred. ISCI was actually Idaho's highest security prison, and its population in-

137

cluded close-custody inmates, inmates with administrative segregation and detention status, and those awaiting execution. The institution also served as the reception facility for all male prisoners sentenced to the department of corrections.

The prison has an open-campus layout with free-standing buildings on a large compound. The perimeter consists of two fences; there are five towers on the perimeter and a sixth tower located in the middle of the four main housing units.

Predisposing and Facilitating Conditions

During the period leading up to the disturbance, ISCI was not a prison in turmoil. There had been no significant policy changes. The warden had been appointed only three months before, but our interviews suggest that he had quickly earned the respect of both staff and inmates. The two deputy wardens had considerably more experience at the institution.

The prison was overcrowded at the time of the riot, with 500 inmates occupying space designed for 375, and double celling was in effect in two of the housing units. The riot, however, occurred in Housing Unit 9, which housed only one inmate per cell.

Prior to the disturbance under study, ISCI had experienced several serious disruptions. A major riot occurred in 1980 when the entire institution was lost for a brief period before being retaken, and several smaller but significant disturbances took place later in the 1980s. In 1986, inmates seized control and destroyed much of Housing Unit 8, which served as the administrative segregation and death row unit. During that disturbance, inmates were able to gain access to the interior of the cellblock and to all the other locked cells by breaking through the unit's interior cell walls, which (as previously noted) were made of unreinforced cinder block.

As a result of that disturbance, steel plating was installed throughout Unit 8 to prevent inmates from breaking out of their cells. Funds were not available, however, to renovate the three remaining housing units, which were built of the same unreinforced cinder blocks. Besides, it was expected that higher custody inmates would be transferred to the maximum-security prison when it opened, which would reduce the danger of violent disturbances at ISCI.

Housing Unit 9 is designed in the form of a T, with three single-story wings (or tiers) running off a centrally located control room (see Figure 9-1). The three tiers, labeled A, B, and C, each has 26 cells.

At the far end of each tier is an emergency security door that exits to the outside. At the other end, nearest the control room, was the tier's dayroom. Inmates were permitted to use only the dayroom adjacent to their tier. A security door, called the E door, connects each dayroom with the vestibule that surrounds the control room and leads to the main door out of the unit and into the main compound. The E doors were normally

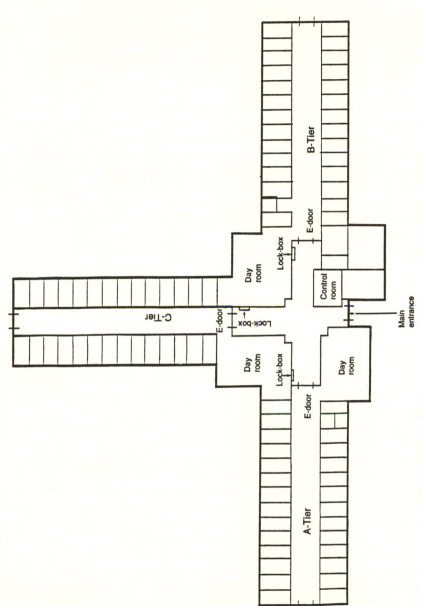

Figure 9-1 Housing Unit 9, Idaho State Correctional Institution.

kept locked. From the control room, staff could look through the small glazed window in the E doors into the corridor, but the small windows did not permit staff to see into the cells themselves. "Lock-boxes," which secured the controls that locked the cell doors in a tier, were mounted on the wall on the control-center side of the E door.

During times when the inmates were permitted out of their cells, three correctional officers were assigned to the unit. One officer was posted in the control room, while the other two officers supervised the inmates who were watching television, engaging in other dayroom activities, or showering.

The 78 inmates in Unit 9 were classified as close custody. This meant that they were supervised more closely than the medium-custody inmates at the facility, but their movements were not as restricted as those inmates who were confined to Unit 8, the segregation unit. According to the staff, many of the inmates had been in the institution for a number of years, were serving long sentences, and had been troublesome and hard to manage.

The Incident

The incident broke out in Unit 9 on Sunday afternoon, September 28, 1988, at 2:40 P.M. No unusual events had occurred in the previous week or during the morning. At about 2:00, an officer smelled alcohol in C tier and went to investigate.

Most of the inmates were watching television either in their cells or in the dayroom, but one inmate was found to be drinking a prison-brewed alcoholic drink. The officer reported this to the prisonwide control room. The shift commander, a lieutenant, ordered that the inmate be removed to detention in Unit 8.

The officers began to remove the inmate from the tier, without taking the precaution of ordering the rest of the inmates back to their cells or, for that matter, waiting for the inmates to return to their cells for the afternoon count. Several other inmates on C tier, who had also been drinking, began to object and shout. Sensing that they were about to have a serious problem in the unit, the officers instructed the inmates on all three tiers and dayrooms to return to their cells to be locked up. The inmates on A tier and B tier complied, but 10 of those on C tier refused.

The 10 inmates began to destroy the dayroom. Then they began to break out the glass windows between the dayroom and the control room. The two officers on the tiers locked the A- and B-wing inmates in their cells and secured those lock-boxes, and then retreated to the control room. From there, one officer wrote down the names of the disruptive inmates, noting as best he could what each was doing.

Inmates then lifted the heavy table in the C tier dayroom, which had not been secured to the floor and, using it as battering ram, began to knock down the E door. The officers realized that they were about to lose the unit and hastily went up the ladder and out the hatchway onto the roof of the unit. Approximately 15 seconds later, the inmates broke into the control room itself.

The officer in a tower that observes the hatchway had been notified that the officers were evacuating their unit. The tower officer covered their exit and was prepared to stop any inmate who tried to come up that hatchway. The officers climbed to the roof and remained there for some time until a ladder was brought to the building.

While the inmates had taken the control room, they did not have the keys to get into A and B tiers. They used a fire standpipe, which was being installed and had not yet been secured to the wall, to try to break into the A- and B-tier lock-boxes. While the pipe did not give them enough leverage to open the lock-boxes, it was used to break through the cinder-block walls into the dayrooms and then the corridors of A and B tiers. Once inside the A and B tiers, with the cells doors still locked, they began to knock holes in the walls to the cells, which they could do because of their flimsiness (Figure 9-2). While several cells were partially broken into, only one cell was eventually opened.

The Response

Once the severity of the trouble in Unit 9 had been realized, a general alarm was sounded throughout the institution. The lieutenant on duty moved the inmates who were in the dining hall and gym or at other activities back to their housing units. Inmates assigned to Unit 11, which is immediately adjacent to Unit 9, were secured in the gymnasium. During the remainder of the disturbance, the inmates in the other units created no problems for the staff.

By about 3:50 P.M., the warden, deputy warden for security, and numerous other staff had arrived at the prison. The institution's Corrections Emergency Response Team (CERT) members were telephoned and told to report to the institution. Also, the Idaho State Police, Boise City Police, and the county sheriff's office were called to respond.

At about 4:00 P.M. the director of the department arrived at the institution. The director, who had been with the department for more than five years, assumed direct command of the response effort. While a command center had been established in a deputy warden's office, per the response plan, it took a secondary role. The director, clearly in charge, moved throughout the administration building and issued orders from wherever he was situated.

A 16-person team consisting of armed institution staff, city police, and county deputy sheriffs was deployed to confine the disturbance to Unit 9. The institution's fire unit arrived and was standing by outside the perimeter in case they were needed. Staff were assigned to reinforce the institution's perimeter in the vicinity of Unit 9.

Inmates broke out some of the windows on A tier, and several inmates began to call out to the surrounding staff from the unit windows.

Figure 9-2   The Control center in ISCI's Unit 9, into which this window looks, was destroyed by inmates during the 1988 riot. While the bars on the windows were not broken, inmates were able to gain access to the Control Center by breaking holes in the cinderblock walls. *Source*: Department of Correction, State of Idaho.

The deputy warden engaged one of the inmates in a brief conversation in which the only demand was "free movement through the yard." The inmate attempted to lure the deputy warden closer, hoping that other inmates out of sight of the deputy warden could throw something at him. Other inmates were overheard talking about blocking the entrances to the unit.

     At about the same time, the staff surrounding the unit heard noises coming from the window of a cell on B tier. A group of inmates were attempting to break into the cell of another inmate who was pleading with them to leave him alone (Figure 9-3). Staff approached close enough to

Figure 9-3   ISCI inmates were able to break holes between cells during the disturbance in 1988. This hole in the wall of Cell 48 allowed inmates to enter and murder another inmate. *Source*: Department of Correction, State of Idaho.

the window, about three feet above the ground, to see through it and to hear cries for help from the inmate as the two other inmates gained access to the cell and began stabbing him.

An officer radioed the director and asked to fire his shotgun to stop the assault, but permission was denied. Several factors mitigated against opening fire: metal slats obscured the line of sight, making it difficult to distinguish the assailants from the inmate being attacked; at that distance, the shotgun pellets would spread, making a precisely targeted shot impossible; if a shot did injure someone, prison officials could not get first aid to him; and perhaps most important, it was not fully clear that the assailants were actually assailants. They were assailants, however, and they actually killed a victim.

Thirty minutes later, at approximately 6:15 P.M., the CERT team moved to the yard and two officers were posted on the roof of Unit 11, one with a rifle and one with a 12-gauge shotgun with birdshot loads. A county paramedic unit entered the compound through the rear gate and was deployed behind Unit 7, awaiting further instructions.

Fire and Rescue Efforts

Water was beginning to flood the unit's floor, posing a threat of electrocution. The warden ordered that the water to the unit be turned off. A few minutes after the water was turned off, large amounts of smoke were observed coming from fires started by the inmates inside the unit. At this point, the main task confronting officials shifted from controlling a disturbance to one of both controlling the disturbance and rescuing inmates from a potentially lethal fire. Some of the inmates were still locked in their cells.

The institution's fire unit moved to the front of Unit 9 and began shooting streams of water through the broken windows in A tier in an attempt to put out the fires. The state police's Special Weapons and Tactics (SWAT) team, along with the director, warden, and other staff, moved from the administration building to the yard. The director ordered that the Boise Fire Department be requested to respond to the institution. After initially indicating that they would not respond, the fire department sent three trucks, nearly 25 minutes after the initial request.

An assault team consisting of ISCI personnel, state police, county deputy sheriffs, and Boise City Police was assembled adjacent to Unit 9. The plan was first to evacuate those inmates who were nonparticipants. Led by the ISCI CERT team members, the officers opened the security door (which was not barricaded) at the end of B tier and started to enter the unit but found the smoke too thick to allow safe entry. The door was left open for a few moments but no inmates exited. It was decided to lock the B tier security door and try to enter through the security door at the end of C tier, where there was little smoke.

Using a bullhorn, the lieutenant in charge of the ISCI CERT team called to the inmates on C tier to come out with their hands over their heads. The security door was opened and the inmates began filing out through the door, where they were taken into custody. The officers then entered the tier and verified that all inmates had been removed from the tier.

From there, the officers moved to the area adjacent the control center. They could see that fires were still burning in an office, a supply room, and the A-tier dayroom. These fires were extinguished with the help of a fire hose.

The officers then moved toward B tier. The inmates had battered the lock-box to the extent that it would now not open with a key, but a crowbar gave the officers enough leverage to pry it open. The locking mechanism to the cell doors was still operable, and the officers released the inmates and evacuated them through the open security door. During this process, it was confirmed that inmates had indeed killed one inmate in his cell.

The officers then turned to A tier. The lock-box here had been extensively damaged by the inmates, rendering it inoperable. The electricity was turned off and the officers opened each cell manually, removing the inmates through the B tier security door.

The inmates who had been removed from the unit were ordered to remove all their clothing and to sit quietly in a small exercise yard behind the unit. Later, they were escorted to a secure exercise area, and then to Unit 7 for confinement. The inmates who were believed to have instigated the disturbance, as well as those who were thought to be responsible for the inmate's death, were confined within Unit 8.

Members of the state police who had been providing perimeter security support were released from their assignments, and the state police SWAT team, which had been on the yard, returned to the administration building.

With the institution secured, the additional law enforcement units were released. The director met with members of the news media. One representative from the media was taken on a tour of Unit 9.

In the aftermath, 30 disciplinary reports were written. Eleven inmates were prosecuted, and five were found guilty. One of the inmates who murdered the inmate found dead during the disturbance was given a life sentence.

III

CONCLUSIONS

10

Before the Riot

It is unrealistic to expect that any process can produce a riot control plan that anticipates all possible occurrences. Unexpected turns of event force officials to improvise. The riot may be of much greater scope than thought possible, or it may occur without warning. In matters of organization and strategy, corrections professionals are still learning and sometimes disagree. They must make instantaneous decisions with incomplete information; almost inevitably, hindsight will reveal some of these decisions to be mistakes.

But this does not mean that riot resolution must be left to chance or that riot control plans are useless exercises. Vigilance by correctional staff may thwart a planned rebellion. A rapid mobilization of force may prevent an incident involving a few inmates in a small area from mushrooming into a full-scale disturbance. In appropriate circumstances, either negotiation or the use of force may result in a speedier resolution with fewer casualties.

By summarizing the lessons of our eight cases, we hope to suggest actions that prison officials may take to avoid riots, limit their scope and duration, or recover effectively from them.

Riot Avoidance

Some riots come as a complete surprise (e.g., Talladega, Kirkland, Coxsackie, Idaho State Correctional Institution [ISCI] at Boise); others flow rather directly out of a snowballing set of events in which the forces of disorder gain momentum (e.g., Mack Alford, Cimarron); still others take place in situations known to be unusually dangerous and with a significant degree of warning (e.g., Atlanta, Camp Hill). These three configurations present different opportunities for riot avoidance.

Riots with No Warning

The riots at Talladega, Kirkland, Coxsackie, and ISCI occurred without significant warning. All but the ISCI riot occurred in high-security units. The ISCI riot began in a unit that had been constructed as medium-security housing, but the inmates housed there were classified as close custody, that is, more dangerous and difficult to manage than medium-custody inmates.

Where violent and rebellious inmates are concentrated, prison officials rely in large part on the physical elements of security to prevent violence. Typically, inmates are restricted to their cells for most of the day; they move to and from their cells under physical restraints (e.g., handcuffs); they are not allowed to congregate in groups of more than a half-dozen and sometimes not at all.

Hostilities in such units, even when well managed, are often intense. This was the case at Coxsackie and Kirkland. Tensions were also high at Talladega, where they were related not only to the violent dispositions of the inmates and the restraining environment, but also to the detainees' anticipation of being deported.

Riots in high-security units are primarily a function of opportunity. They occur when one or several inmates are able to initiate a disturbance by taking advantage of a weakness in or a momentary lapse of the system of security, *and* are subsequently able to spread the disturbance by defeating other security systems. Avoiding such riots, then, is a matter of strengthening and making more foolproof the structures and systems that provide security.

EXPERIENCED STAFF AND SUPERVISION

The continual presence of experienced staff in a high-security unit, both line officers and supervisors, is a sound security practice that failed in three of these four riots. At Coxsackie, the officers regularly assigned to the high-security special housing unit (SHU) were absent on the day of disturbance. The replacement officers were unfamiliar with the unit's procedures. Furthermore, responsibility for supervising the unit, normally vested in a sergeant assigned full time to the unit, had been temporarily assigned to a sergeant who had duties elsewhere in the facility. One of the postriot procedural changes was that a sergeant was to be present in the unit at all times; relief officers were also given more thorough orientation to SHU procedures.

The Bureau of Prison's (BOP's) report on the Talladega incident recommended that, in the future, more senior and experienced supervisory staff be assigned to high-security units than had previously been the practice. This would "enhance the application of proper correctional practices in every aspect of the unit's operation."[1]

At Kirkland, Unit D's correctional officers had experienced high rates of stress-related illness and turnover, apparently related to the hostility exhibited toward the staff by inmates within the unit.

POST ORDERS

A unit's post orders specify the duties to be followed on each post by the assigned officers. Prison officials must anticipate that inmates, especially those in high-security units, will probe officer behavior for weaknesses. At Coxsackie, the post orders were incomplete and not updated. Relief officers learned of their duties by observing or asking regular officers and staff at those posts, but errors crept in during this word-of-mouth process. Security gates were left open when they should have been closed, and the keys to the control panel were secured to the panel. One of the riot's leaders had worked as a porter in the unit and had been in a position to observe these lapses. These factors were important in the expansion of the initial hostage incident.

At Kirkland's Unit D, the post orders did not specify which keys the evening duty officer should and should not carry when entering the unit. The keys to the cells' doors were not needed, but the officer first taken hostage was in fact carrying them, which permitted the incident to expand. After the disturbance, the warden issued a new policy limiting the keys officers carried to those actually used on that shift. In addition, the department instructed all wardens of maximum- and medium-security prisons to review their key control procedures.

At Talladega, the case manager, responding to a report that inmates were loose on the exercise yard, neglected to lock a door behind him. Had the door been locked, the rioters would have been confined to an enclosed yard with, at most, three hostages.

At ISCI, correctional officers removed an inmate from a unit while other inmates in that unit were not confined to their cells. Had the officers required all inmates to be in their cells before the inmate was removed, the rebellion could not have developed. On the other hand, after the disturbance began, a correctional officer, acting on his post orders, was able lock down two of the three tiers, limiting the scope of the disturbance.

PHYSICAL PLANT ISSUES

Problems associated with the facilities' structures were associated with all four of these riots. At Kirkland, an inmate jimmied the electric lock on his door and (apparently) reached through a ventilation slot to slide open an unsecured dead bolt. (After the disturbance, the electric locks were replaced with manually operated dead bolts.) A toolbox, left inside the perimeter, was breached and its contents used to expand the riot.

At Talladega, a transformer outside the rear door obscured vision from the rear door of the unit, giving two inmates a hiding place. The door leading from the unit to the exercise yard could not be slammed shut quickly from inside the unit.

At Coxsackie, the control console's wire-reinforced plate glass did not withstand an inmate assault. Prison officials were aware of the potential danger associated with the window. Funds had been requested for its replacement but had not been approved.

The physical problems at ISCI stemmed in part from the use of medium-security buildings to house close-security inmates. It was known in advance that the interior walls, made of unreinforced cinder blocks, could be breached during a disturbance. However, prison officials did not retrofit the unit. Doing so would have been expensive; in addition, a new high-security facility was scheduled to open soon. Also, inmates used a large unsecured table placed in the dayroom to smash through walls, allowing them to gain access to the unit's control center.

A single weakness in a security system in a unit housing high-custody inmates may open the door to a violent incident. The more numerous or frequent such lapses are, the greater is the likelihood that several of them may combine to set the stage for a prison riot of large scope. The exact moment such a combination will occur may be difficult or impossible to predict.

Escalating Conflict

The disturbances at the Mack Alford Correction Center and the Cimarron Unit of the Arizona State Prison at Tucson both flowed from a snowballing set of events. The early stages of these incidents followed a common pattern:

- On the days of the disturbances, personal disputes among inmates inflamed preexisting intergroup tensions. At Cimarron, a quarrel over a cigarette lighter led to a beating; at Mack Alford, two inmates allegedly stole property from the cell of another inmate.
- The conflicts gained momentum. At Cimarron, the inmate receiving the beating sought revenge with a mop handle. At Mack Alford, several inmates "investigated" the crime. A group gathered to retrieve forcibly the stolen items.
- Mutually hostile groups mobilized their forces. At Cimarron, a fight broke out along racial lines in the mess hall. At Mack Alford, large numbers of inmates confronted each other on the yard.
- After officials intervened, inmates redirected their hostility against the staff. At Cimarron, the brawl in the dining hall moved to the exercise yard and there was transformed to a hostile confrontation with officers. At Mack Alford, the disturbance began when an officer, without backup, pursued an inmate who resisted being transported to another facility. That inmate and another inmate took the officer hostage, marking the beginning of the disturbance.

Riot avoidance, in these situations, lies not so much in physical security (although this may be important) as in managing the escalation process. At Cimarron there was little opportunity initially because the officers in the cafeteria were quickly overwhelmed. Once on the yard, the skirmishing groups resisted efforts of correctional officers to intervene, making use of rocks that were present on the yard. (One of the postriot reforms was to grass over the yard to reduce the number of rocks.)

At Mack Alford, prison officials had, over a six-hour period, skillfully managed a potentially explosive situation. This was made more difficult by a shortage of detention cells. Just when resolution seemed near, several judgment errors were made: (a) A correctional officer chased a defiant inmate without backup and, (b) after the officer was taken hostage, the first response was to try to negotiate his release, rather than to isolate and contain the incident. This permitted a small-scale disturbance to expand to a full-scale riot.

Riots with Warning

The Atlanta and Camp Hill riots did not take place as random incidents, or after the escalation of minor quarrels, but on occasions when everyone knew the institutions to be in crisis. Yet it is common for prison officials to hear predictions of riots in their facility: It will happen today, tomorrow, unless the food improves, the prison is less crowded, or correctional officers are given greater authority. Often, such warnings float on a sea of exaggeration or hearsay. They also may be deliberate attempts to create a crisis atmosphere, either for its own sake or to force change in one direction or another.

How may prison officials recognize a facility that is truly on the brink of a disturbance? The American Correctional Association identifies 27 "indicators of prison tension that often precede riots and disturbances."[2] They include

- increases in lockups, disciplinary cases, and requests for transfers;
- warnings by inmates to officers that they should take vacation or sick leave;
- a decline in attendance at popular events, such as movies;
- inmates making "excessive and/or specific demands" or other "unusual and/or subdued action";
- an increase in demands by employees for greater safety; and
- an increase in employee turnover.

To our knowledge, no one has validated this (or any other) list of riot indicators. This is not to suggest that such lists are without value, only that more work needs to be done. One problem with the ACA-list is that an increase in "prison tension" is not the only source of prison disturbances and, arguably, not the most predictive one. Other circumstances, such as level of adherence to daily security procedures, may be more foreshadowing. Items that measure those (possibly more predictive) circumstances must be developed and validated. Moreover, the ACA-publication gives little guidance as to how to use such a list. The 27 indicators should not be thought of as a separate category of intelligence but simply another source of information that must be confirmed, evaluated, and integrated with other sources of information.[3]

The events leading up to the November 1987 riot at the U.S. Penitentiary at Atlanta illustrate the difficulties of distinguishing valid warnings from false ones. As described in chapter 2, during the two-day period immediately preceding the Atlanta riot, officials had reason to believe that a disturbance might occur. The repatriation agreement with Cuba provided a motive to riot, and the riot at Oakdale demonstrated the readiness of at least some detainees to act on that motive. In fact, at 6 A.M. on the morning of the riot, prison officials met and discussed whether to proceed with normal operations or to lock down the facility, and they decided to open it for breakfast as usual.

Prison officials were aware of at least some overt warnings from detainees and from correctional officers that a riot was likely, but these warnings were considered unreliable. The BOP's report on the riot stated:

> [T]he Atlanta Administration had become desensitized to detainees' threats to take over the institution. During numerous occasions throughout the past seven years that detainees were housed at Atlanta, staff had received informant information or intelligence that the Cuban detainees were going to take over the [industry building] the next day, only to have normal operations.[4]

Apart from reports by informants, there was other evidence that a riot was impending. Detainees in one unit had remained dressed overnight, outgoing mail was reported to be several times heavier than normal, and much of the outgoing mail contained photographs.[5] In retrospect it appears that inmates were mailing out their photographs to avoid their being lost or destroyed in the riot, but at the time the increase was explained as being the result of a new program that allowed detainees to have pictures taken of themselves. Staff, however, had seen detainees remove their family photographs from their lockers.

Other signs of an impending riot appeared later that morning: A group of inmates resisted going to work in the morning, and detainees at breakfast were unusually quiet. It would be unfair, however, to conclude that the Atlanta officials were unmindful of the possibility of a riot. The BOP's report makes it clear that the warden met several times with his executive staff and department heads to determine if "reliable information [had] surfaced indicating the detainees would react violently."[6] Still, the evidence they had was never quite enough. According to the report,

> Institutional activities such as recreation and meals throughout the weekend appeared normal and routine. Only one inmate requested to be locked up in Segregation over the weekend and no observable increase in commis-

sary purchases had taken place over the past week. *None of the traditional indicators of trouble in a prison environment were [sic] present.*[7] (emphasis added)

However, there is no agreed-upon list of "traditional indicators of trouble." And no such list could possibly act as an infallible oracle. The presence of "traditional indicators" might well mean danger, but the absence of such indicators does not necessarily ensure safety, not in the face of other "nontraditional" evidence or in a situation where tensions are known to be high. Furthermore, evidence collected within the prison has to be taken together with the understanding of what kinds of situations or grievances are likely to produce riots.

When inmates' hopes are raised and then dashed, when inmates' sense not merely of deprivation but also of injustice is high, when policy makers outside the prison are seen as potentially sympathetic to the inmates' cause, then riot is in the air. And the Atlanta officials knew that the detainees had reached this point. In such circumstances, reports and evidence that normally would not be "proof" that a riot is imminent should be given much greater weight; it becomes especially important that prison officials take the situation into their own hands.

Response to Threat of a Riot

If a riot appears imminent, prison officials may take two types of actions to prevent its occurrence. Administrative actions might include a lockdown of a unit or the entire facility; transfer of suspected instigators to a segregation unit or to another facility; cancellation of activities that give inmates the opportunity to congregate, such as recreation or work; increasing the number of correctional officers on duty, or bringing them to a higher state of alert; and a search for contraband. Diplomatic actions include efforts to convince inmates that a riot would be costly to them personally, counterproductive for reform, and/or unnecessary because their grievances will be addressed in the future. Elements of both approaches can be combined, of course.

In the Atlanta case, officials felt themselves forced to choose between administrative actions and diplomacy and chose diplomacy. They reasoned that a lockdown might not be effective: A portion of the detainees were housed in dormitory units, which could not be locked down, and the cell doors in the administrative segregation section were old and possibly defective.[8] Besides, they thought a lockdown might further inflame the detainees and precipitate "the very riot a lock-down [was] intended to prevent."[9]

This concern often arises, but we know of no study that estimates how often precautionary lockdowns actually precipitate riots. Furthermore, when prison officials conclude they can not lock down the prison as a precaution, the situation is grave. If they can not lock it down to prevent a riot, how much more difficult will it be to contain the riot were it to break out? Perhaps the relevant authorities ought to make clear to prison officials that they can call freely upon the system for additional resources to implement precautionary lockdowns. The cost to the system of mobilizing to put down a full-blown riot will be many times greater.

On the other hand, the relevant authorities should be cautious not to promise more resources than they can actually marshal. Further, as the history of Atlanta points out, once a facility is locked down, troubles may smolder over the long run.

Riot Preparation

Riot preparation includes the acquisition of resources (organization, equipment, information) for use in a riot situation; the development of a strategy for the use of these resources; and the mental readiness to respond to an incident. Its importance is hard to overstate.

Our case studies suggest to us that the key issues that corrections officials face in riot preparation include matters related to the organization's core commitments; command structure; the premises and commitments that establish the "rules" for dealing with a riot situation; the development of plans; and the training of personnel.

Organizational Core

There is a tradition in the study of public agencies that emphasizes the importance of an institutional "core," meaning a group of key individuals who have internalized the values and mission of the organization.[10] It is the activity of this group, rather than abstract principles or written guidelines, that ensures an agency's work will embody its mission. The departments under study varied in the extent to which an institutional core took charge of riot preparation. The case of the South Carolina Department of Corrections is especially instructive.

At the time of the 1986 Kirkland disturbance, South Carolina may have been unique in U.S. corrections in the commitment of its commissioner to riot preparation. Throughout his 20-year tenure (1968–1988), William Leeke stood at the forefront of the field of emergency preparedness in U.S. corrections. In 1968, Commissioner Leeke chaired the committee of the American Correctional Association that was responsible for revising the first edition of its manual on prison riots.[11] Research for the report was done by the South Carolina Department of Corrections under a grant awarded to the department by the Law Enforcement Assistance Administration (LEAA).[12] Soon after the release of the American Correctional Association publication, Commissioner Leeke initiated a research project on the history and causes of prison riots, again funded by LEAA and conducted within the department. In 1973, the department published a monograph on its findings.[13] We mention these details because they offer concrete evidence of a level of commitment to emergency planning well beyond the ordinary.

At the time of the 1986 Kirkland disturbance, there existed within the Department's central office a core group concerned with emergency preparedness. It included the deputy commissioner for operations, who took on the responsibility for writing policy papers that established guidelines for managing emergency situations, establishing the command structure, and operating a training program. Under his leadership, the department conducted an innovative program for training institutional managers in the management of emergency response efforts. This program included seminars for wardens and deputy wardens and on-site drills. During the Kirkland disturbance, both the commissioner and deputy commissioner participated in the decision-making group that directed the response.

One way to view the reforms prompted by the Atlanta/Oakdale disturbances is that they were essentially an effort to create a core group with a primary commitment to emergency preparedness. At the national level, the hub was the newly established Office of Emergency Preparedness (OEP). It oversaw the implementation of the recommendations made by Atlanta/ Oakdale afteraction review teams. It also developed other programs to increase emergency preparedness, such as site visits to observe mock emergency drills and development of a helicopter-based deterrence system.

At the facility level, this commitment was secured through new training programs. The OEP found that the facility-based Special Operations Response Teams had developed a high level of esprit de corps, recognition, and status within facilities. The challenge was to achieve the same for the Hostage Negotiation Teams.

It seems reasonable to assert that the Kirkland, Talladega, and Coxsackie disturbances were resolved more effectively because of the existence of a core of individuals in each agency committed to emergency planning.

Premises and Commitments

By this we refer to the limitations that are imposed in advance on the actions of officials and officers in response to a disturbance. Such limitations may be established to prevent officials from making "inferior" choices, either because it is thought that the existence and knowledge of such limitations will affect the course of the disturbance, or on principle.

The imposition of such directives has risks, since it limits the flexibility of prison officials in tailoring their strategy to the situation at hand. Poorly thought-out limits may be hopelessly complex (a game tree with many branches, each representing a choice that depends upon previous ones), irrelevant (establishing principles so broad that they provide little guidance in actual situations), or impractical (mandating a course of action whose premises do not hold in the situation).

Still, the American Correctional Association manual on riots points out that some fundamental premises should be agreed upon in advance.[14] The manual suggests the following:

- Rioting inmates will be given no "illegal freedom."
- Rioters will not be granted immunity from prosecution or amnesty.
- A hostage or other prison official under duress exercises no authority.
- Keys and weapons are not to be surrendered.
- Drugs and liquor will not be provided.
- Transportation will not be provided to inmates that might allow them to leave the prison.

Consensus on these points is not firm. For example, the detainees at Atlanta were given amnesty for participation in the riot, and prosecutions were not pursued for the illegal takeover of the facility. Some would insist that the list include the principle that force is to be used immediately if a hostage is subject to physical harm or material threat of harm. On the other hand, force was not used at Coxsackie even though the hostages were being beaten, because the tactical advantages held by inmates were so great.

Problems associated with establishing workable premises and standing orders in advance arose in the early stages of the riots at Kirkland and at Mack Alford. At Kirkland, a correctional officer fired a warning shot over the heads of a group of inmates advancing on a section of the prison that, until then, had remained under the control of officials. The shot forced the inmates to retreat. A standing order, however, permitted the use of force only if expressly authorized by the warden, who had not yet arrived at the prison. As mentioned, after the riot, the standing order was changed to allow the senior official on duty to authorize the use of force.

In the early stages of the Mack Alford riot, inmates threatened to kill a hostage unless they were allowed to pass through an internal security gate that divided two housing compounds. The correctional officer on duty at the gate opened it and was himself taken hostage. An official in the central office would later point out that had there been a standing order (known to both officers and inmates) that no gate was ever to be opened under threat of force, the inmates might not have made this demand. He highlighted this point by noting that inmates did not demand that exterior gates be opened because they knew that such a demand would be summarily rejected.

Riot Plans

Riot plans are too often a weakly integrated compendium of policy statements, advice, memos, and agreements among agencies. Often, perhaps as a result, they are not fully understood or read frequently enough by those who are responsible for implementing them. Riot plans should be well organized, clearly written, and concise. Cumbersome plans will receive lip service before a disturbance and ignored when one arises.

The riot contingency plan should be a comprehensive guide that describes the special responsibilities to be met, the resources to be used, and the contribution of each individual or group involved. It must address the issues of command: which official shall be in charge of the resolution efforts, and how he or she will control the forces of the different agencies that will be involved. Part of the riot plan should be a procedure for how the riot plan book itself will be used during the incident.

It is also possible to develop a plan, or a variation on or elaboration of the general riot plan, in anticipation of at least some specific existing or anticipated crisis. A situation-specific plan can be more detailed in its anticipation of possible situations, planning of responses, and assignment of responsibilities; the abstract "be prepared for many contingencies" is replaced by "be prepared for X, Y, and Z, and this is what we will do in each case." Such a plan, once developed, can be circulated for comment, both up the chain of command and to those who have special expertise.

In none of the disturbances under study had a situation-specific plan been developed. It could reasonably be argued that one was needed at Atlanta. Three factors—the signing of the repatriation agreement, the onset of the Oakdale riot, and unrest among the Atlanta detainees—were indicative of a heightened likelihood of a riot. The reason no situation-specific plan was written was explained in a letter by a Department of Justice official to a congressional committee examining the disturbance:

> All Federal Prisons have emergency contingency plans. The Bureau of Prisons did not contemplate that should an agreement be struck with Cuba, existing emergency plans would need modification.[15]

While existing plans may not have needed modification, it may have been useful to have developed additional written plans specifically tailored to the situation at hand.

Training and Preparation

Any plan, however well designed, will achieve little unless those for whom it is designed know their duties and are fully prepared to act on them. Riot planning can be conducted in the central office for the agency as a whole, or in the warden's office for a particular facility. But mental, physical, and emotional readiness can be achieved only through field practice and instruction. Further, by its very nature, readiness is difficult to assess adequately and can be reliably measured only once an actual disturbance begins.[16] Still, training scenarios allow for surrogate measures.

Observing the training practices in each of the agencies under study was beyond the scope of the present study. However, several points did emerge.

JOINT TRAINING

The resolution of a prison riot often may require coordination among units that, under normal circumstances, have little or no contact. The state police and a department's tactical team, for example, may be asked to launch a joint tactical operation, although they have never trained together. Even within an agency, or a facility, different components of the riot response operation, such as the negotiation team and tactical team, may be insufficiently aware of the needs of the other components.[17]

Greater coordination can be achieved through joint training programs. The BOP, for example, is developing training exercises that integrate the activities of command, hostage negotiation teams, and tactical teams.

TRAINING OF COMMAND PERSONNEL

Supervisory personnel need to enhance their skill in the management of crisis situations. In general, managers must learn how to lower the temperature of the situation—reduce anxieties so that intemperate acts are not committed—while still advancing the interest of achieving speedy resolution. Specific skills include situation assessment, management of resources from multiple agencies, coordination of multiple teams, and strategic thinking in hostage situations, all under great pressures of time and consequence.

The South Carolina Department of Corrections has developed a rigorous training program for its wardens, deputy wardens, and other senior prison officials. An annual three-day training seminar combines classroom instruction with real-time field exercises. In addition, complex and demanding on-site scenarios are conducted in facilities. The scenarios are sprung unannounced upon those in command. Significantly, the deputy commissioner for operations often personally conducts these training scenarios. Later, participants write up their experience and offer any recommendations for improving the department's emergency procedures.

PREPARATION AS RIOT AVOIDANCE

The more prepared a facility is for a disturbance, the less likely it is that one will occur. One reason for this is that inmates may be deterred from trying to start a riot if they know that hostile acts will be met by a quickly deployed counterforce. The idea is expressed by the well-worn aphorism, "if you want peace, prepare for war."[18]

It would be useful to have a quantitative measure of this deterrent effect, to know how much the expenditure of resources lowers the probability of a disturbance and by what amount, but we are a long way from having this. A related issue is the threshold point beyond which additional expenditures yield no incremental deterrent effect. There may be, as well, a floor below which incremental increases are insufficient to provide a deterrent effect until the floor is reached.

A second reason that riot preparation is also riot avoidance is that a rapidly deployed show of force, an act made possible by preparation, can limit the scope of a disturbance. If the incident is contained quickly, it may later be viewed as a minor disturbance rather than a riot. In any case, a promptly contained incident will require only a fraction of the resources needed to resolve a full-scale riot.

Finally, officers in a well-prepared facility may be more attentive to the signs of disorder. Evidence for this was adduced by Larry Hirschhorn in a study of a high-security facility in turmoil.[19] He found that correctional officers who are chronically worried about their safety tend, paradoxically, to be less attentive to the actual dangers inherent in their situation. Hirschhorn goes on to argue that the establishment of a well-trained response team might help reduce anxiety among officers, thereby increasing their alertness and perceptiveness. Further (although not argued by Hirschhorn), prison officials, having committed resources to riot preparation, including training sessions for themselves and for staff, may be more conscious of their responsibilities for emergency preparedness. Thus, their vigilance may increase.

11

During the Riot

Command

A prison riot poses implicitly or explicitly the question of who will exercise authority over the forces of control. This encompasses the capacity to deploy the forces at hand, monitor their actions in the field on a continuous basis, deliver orders promptly and effectively, coordinate operations among the governmental agencies that are involved, and gather and interpret information on what inmates are doing and intend to do.[1] It is reasonable to assume that the task of command becomes more complex the longer a riot lasts, and the more agencies involved.

Brief disturbances that prison officials can handle with resources immediately at their disposal do not raise complicated questions of command. In the resolution of a prison riot, however, personnel may be brought in from the outside—police, FBI agents, negotiators, National Guard, medical personnel, and so on—who are not (without special arrangement) subject to the authority of the prison's officials. Moreover, a prison riot is the sort of public emergency in which higher officials may feel the need to step in and exercise command themselves. The notion (possibly an unfortunate one) may also be present that the very occurrence of a riot is a sign that the prison's own officials have "failed" at their job of maintaining order and that someone else must step in to take charge.

At any rate, it is rare that the problem of command is resolved by turning over the command of personnel and resources from other agencies to the unfettered discretion of the prison's chief administrator. The

162

question of how command will be exercised is often negotiated on the scene, and the issues of unity of command (how authority will be exercised over forces from different governmental units), level of command (which official in the correctional hierarchy will be in charge), and location of command (where the command post will be established) must generally be faced.

Unity of Command

Unity of command refers to the placement of all the personnel involved in the resolution of the riot under the direction of a single official.[2] Unity of command facilitates coordination of the efforts of all personnel toward common objectives. In its absence, coordination may still be achieved through voluntary mutual cooperation, but this may break down if disagreements occur.

Unity of command may be especially difficult to achieve when the agency in charge must draw on the resources of additional agencies, usually under a "mutual aid" arrangement. In effect, two or more organizations—with different traditions, equipment, experiences, personal relationships, and most important, lines of authority—are being asked to act as one. Problems can easily develop. For example, during the Camp Hill disturbances, tension developed between the corrections department and state police. Issues that should have been settled in advance, such as the ammunition that the state police would carry, had to be negotiated on the spot, consuming precious time.

In response to this problem, the Oklahoma Department of Corrections attempts to incorporate the heads of the various state agencies that may be involved in the resolution into the central office command center. For example, during the Mack Alford disturbance, the director of the state police was asked to be present in the command center. According to one department official, state police officers at a disturbance site were more responsive to the directives of the central office because they knew that their agency head was part of the decision-making process.

Unity of command can be impaired by divisions internal to the command personnel. While one individual is formally in charge, in fact command is almost always a team effort whose success depends in large part on the level of trust among its members. If this team has already been created in the course of preparation for a possible riot, fewer internal obstacles may arise. If not, the team and the trust must be created on the spot. The institutions in our study accomplished this task in varying degrees.

At Kirkland, the command group evidenced a strong level of internal trust within the group. Members supported each other and, at the same time, allowed open expression of views and impartial exploration of options. As a result, the command team could focus on the task at hand and act decisively.

At Camp Hill, by contrast, strains emerged among the corrections command personnel. In part, this may have been because the department was divided before the riot. Also relevant may have been the history of frequent turnover among upper echelon corrections officials in Pennsylvania.

At Atlanta, unity of command had to be forged in the course of the disturbance. A riot of that magnitude had not been anticipated, and working relationships and a chain of command had to be developed among the attorney general, the director of the Bureau of Prisons (BOP), directors of several other federal agencies, the regional director, and the warden. By the time of the Talladega incident, four years later, these working relationships had been consolidated and a riot command structure was implemented with few problems.

Level of Command

Directly related to unity of command is the question of which official or officials in the correctional hierarchy will be in command of the resolution effort. This may be the warden, a regional official, the commissioner, or even the governor of the state (or in the federal system, the attorney general). The facilities in our study displayed some variation.

At both Coxsackie and ISCI, the commissioner took direct control of the resolution. Significant decisions concerning the resolution were deferred (to the extent feasible) until the commissioner arrived on the scene. The commissioner became, in effect, both the overall authority in charge and the field commander. At Coxsackie, the commissioner stayed in the background, concealing his presence from inmates. At ISCI, in contrast, the commissioner entered the yard and directed the operation from there. During both incidents, the role assigned to the warden was to manage the rest of the prison while also providing information and other resources.

At Mack Alford the warden was given the primary responsibility of designing and executing the resolution. The commissioner saw his role as establishing a framework that would assist the warden. He served as a sounding board for the warden, providing advice and direction, met with state political leaders to assure them that all that could be done was being done, insulated the warden from political pressure as required by the situation, and mobilized resources and put them at the warden's disposal. The commissioner allowed the warden to make key decisions, as long as he continued to have confidence in the warden's performance.

Kirkland, Atlanta, Talladega, and Camp Hill represent somewhat different configurations. At Kirkland, the commissioner, members of his executive staff, and the warden assembled in a room. While it was clear that the commissioner was the ultimate authority, the group functioned more like an executive committee working jointly to develop a solution.

At Atlanta, both the regional director and the warden were at the prison soon after the riot began. It was decided then to give authority in the local situation to the regional director. Because of the duration of the riot, it was necessary to develop teams to rotate in and out of leadership positions. In Washington, the attorney general and the director of the BOP maintained direct oversight of the resolution.

After the Atlanta and Oakdale riots, the principle was established that the next higher level of authority above the warden, usually a regional director, would assume on-site control of a major disturbance. This strategy was implemented at Talladega. Also during this disturbance, the director of the BOP and the acting attorney general maintained the roles that had been established for those offices at Atlanta.

At Camp Hill, the commissioner took the position that the responsibility for the resolution rested with the warden. In practice, however, he involved himself in a number of important decisions, including the one to allow state police into the facility after the commencement of the second riot.

In actual situations, then, there is wide variation in how the issue of level of command is practiced. And there is no generally recommended approach in the literature. Some of the considerations favoring placing authority in the hands of one or another official areas follows.

INFORMATION

In directing the response to a riot, an official needs the military commander's ability to size up the situation in the field, identify the weak points of the opposition, and discern the problems of terrain. What is the layout of the facility? If an assault is necessary, what sorts of obstacles (e.g., locked gates, barricaded stairways) would be encountered by an assault force? How dangerous are the particular inmates who are holding hostages? What are the standing orders in the facility's riot response plan, and can the correctional officers on duty be expected to execute them?

Because these matters of detail vary from one facility to the next, one unit to the next, and one shift to the next, authority over the resolution may best remain in the hands of the warden. The temptation to manage with tighter reins from the top should be weighed against the benefits to be derived from permitting the warden more latitude.

BREADTH OF EXPERIENCE AND RESPONSIBILITY

Top-level corrections officials may have a broader perspective than those assigned to specific institutions. They are more likely to be concerned about the effects of the disturbance on the entire department or even corrections as a whole than officials whose primary identification may be with a particular facility. These are arguments for placing decision-making authority in the hands of the director or commissioner.

EFFECTS ON THE CHAIN OF COMMAND

To many corrections officials, the most compelling argument for keeping the resolution in the hands of the warden concerns the aftermath. Taking the warden's authority from him or her in the course of the disturbance, it is argued, will undermine his or her authority after the riot is over. Middle-level managers, correctional officers, and inmates alike will view the central office, not the warden, as the real authority. In contrast, allowing the warden to remain in command for the riot's duration reaffirms the commitment of the central office to his or her leadership.

Correspondence between Responsibility and Authority

Some in corrections argue that, since the commissioner bears ultimate responsibility for the resolution, direct decision-making authority should reside in his or her hands.

Administrative Framework

Another point of view is that who among the commissioner, regional director, and warden should take command depends on the existing practices. The premise is that prison officials should take advantage of the stable existing framework. In those departments where the decision-making power tends to be concentrated in the central office, it is advantageous for the commissioner to take direct charge of the resolution. This describes, for example, the New York State Department of Correctional Services and the course taken by its commissioner in resolving the Coxsackie riot.

In contrast, in decentralized departments in which wardens have greater latitude to develop their own programs, it may be advantageous for the warden to remain in command. This practice describes the Oklahoma Department of Corrections at the time of the Mack Alford riot and the approach taken to resolve that disturbance.

Location of Command

Somewhat independent of unity of command and level of command is location of command: if decision makers are off site, will they go to the facility or remain in their central or regional headquarters? For example, soon after the Mack Alford riot started, the director, deputy director, and others arrived at the central office in Oklahoma City and continued to exercise their oversight responsibilities from there over a three-day period. In contrast, soon after the start of Coxsackie riot, the commissioner and three other central-office officials were on their way to the facility and, once there, established a command post in the superintendent's office.

As with level of command, there are several competing considerations in this decision.

Existing Administrative and Logistic Resources

It takes time to establish and staff a command post in the field, and the quickly mobilized resources (e.g., communication networks and office equipment) may be inadequate. If decision makers operate from an existing off-site facility, either their own offices or a preestablished emergency operations center, the time and effort needed to establish the field command post may be focused instead on the incident itself. Snags may also be less likely.

INFORMATION

As already noted, it is difficult for top-level corrections officials to have full and detailed knowledge of the line personnel at each facility, the inmates involved in the disturbance, the facility, and the numerous standing orders. Travel to the site will permit the decision maker to see the situation more clearly and rapidly and, as well, more readily take advantage of fleeting opportunities. Details that might not otherwise be reported up the chain of command, perhaps because subordinates want to make a good impression on upper management or simply do not see their significance, may be observed firsthand. Decision makers may be less likely to misinterpret reports if they receive them in person.

LEADERSHIP PRESENCE

Location on site may permit the decision maker to communicate more directly and personally with responding staff. This, in turn, can foster a sense among staff of a connectedness with leadership, a more cohesive sense of mission, and a better understanding of the central task at hand.

Resolution: Strategic Considerations

Strategic choices in the resolution of a riot depend on what sort of riot it is. The feature common to prison riots is that a significant number of inmates use force to take control of a significant portion of the prison for a significant period of time. Beyond this, however, there is great variation among riots in organization, purposes, and scope; the riots in this study illustrate that variation.

Unplanned versus Planned

A riot may begin as an unplanned response to a specific incident or as a planned takeover. The first and second riots at Camp Hill appear to have been examples, respectively, of the former and the latter.[3] Talladega was clearly a planned incident, although it may not have been a planned riot. The detainees may have had other goals in mind, possibly to escape, when they broke out of their enclosed exercise yard. Cimarron appears to have been a spontaneous melee.

Protest Riot, Hostile Outburst, or Intergroup Melee

Atlanta is the purest example of a protest riot. Inmates began the disturbance to advance a specific agenda for policy reform. The Talladega riot started with no reform agenda, but one emerged in the course of the disturbance and was eventually presented to authorities as a list of demands.

At Mack Alford, there was a personal agenda in the sense that the riot leader demanded that he and others not be transferred to a maximum-security facility.

Coxsackie, Kirkland, and ISCI are better characterized as hostile outbursts in that inmates articulated no (substantial) demands. This is not to suggest, however, that the inmates acted without purpose. One objective appears to have been to impose costs on the state, achieved by destroying and burning property, holding hostages, and inflicting casualties on officers. A second purpose may have been the drama of the riot itself. A riot breaks the routine and monotony of prison life, a value that may be particularly important to those accustomed to a life of crime.[4]

At ISCI, several inmates used the opportunity of the riot to kill another inmate, and at Coxsackie one inmate was allegedly raped, but in neither riot did those acts of violence appear to be related to the riot's instigation. Cimarron began as an intergroup melee in that racial and ethnic groups were assaulting one another in what was essentially a large brawl. The melee turned against authorities when they intervened. No officers were taken hostage, even though the opportunity to do so was presented when violence first broke out.

Scope and Geography of the Riot

CELLBLOCK VERSUS MULTIPLE BUILDINGS

The riots at Talladega, ISCI, and Coxsackie were limited to a single cellblock or housing unit; those at Atlanta, Camp Hill, Kirkland, and Mack Alford involved much larger portions of those facilities. The second disturbance at Camp Hill involved even more territory and buildings than the first. The Cimarron riot occurred on the yard and no buildings were seized, although one was vandalized.

SIZE OF PARTICIPATING INMATE GROUP

This can be measured in terms of the number of inmate participants or the proportion of those inmates with an opportunity to join the riot who actually do so. Atlanta and Camp Hill were large in absolute numbers. Talladega and Coxsackie had comparatively few participants measured by the first criterion, but many by the second. ISCI was small in both regards.

Still, in most riots there will be some inmates who actively participate, some who deliberately avoid the disturbance, and a large group in the middle. The latter will include inmates who, while unwilling to incur the costs of being observed actively participating in the riot, will enjoy the freedoms afforded by the disturbance. Further, the number of participants may increase or decrease over the course of the disturbance. At Mack Alford inmates defected throughout the riot so that by its end only a small number of inmates remained on the yard. At Cimarron, the riot expanded in its middle stage as additional inmates joined the initial brawl.

Number of Hostages and Their Treatment

At Cimarron and ISCI, no hostages were taken. At Cimarron, inmates had the opportunity to take hostages when the riot first broke out; however, at this stage, it was primarily an intergroup conflict and seizing hostages was not a priority. At ISCI, correctional officers exited the housing unit's control quickly enough to deny inmates the opportunity to take hostages.

At Atlanta, over 100 hostages were seized, and at Talladega, 11; these hostages and the ones taken at Mack Alford were not physically attacked. At Coxsackie five hostages were taken and were beaten both during the initial takeover and later during the incident; at Camp Hill 24 staff members were taken hostage and were also physically abused. At Kirkland, 22 correctional officers were either taken hostage or trapped. The most serious threat to their safety, the attack on Unit D, was thwarted.

Distance from Central Office to Riot Site

In four prison systems (Pennsylvania, South Carolina, Idaho, and New York) this distance was short and in three (Oklahoma, Arizona, and the Federal Bureau of Prisons) the distance was comparatively long. Both Atlanta and Talladega were distant from the central office, but Atlanta was adjacent to the Bureau's southeast regional office.

These variations contributed to the creation of different problems faced by correctional officials in resolving the disturbances under study.

Choice of Strategy

As noted at the outset, prison riots end in three ways: Prison officials may use force to end the disturbance; the riot may end through negotiations; or the riot may end because inmates tire or simply do not want to riot any longer. Prison officials must compare the benefits and risks of the use of force with those of restraint, negotiation, and possible concessions. Often it is a mix of strategies that leads to resolution.

Under its current leadership, the BOP is committed to using negotiations as its principal method of responding to hostage situations. Most corrections agencies now share a similar commitment, but this has changed over time and may change again.

A minority in corrections continues to advocate a fixed policy of not negotiating.[5] The idea is that if corrections officials declare that they will not negotiate with criminal kidnappers, making that declaration as irrevocable as they can, then inmates will be less likely to seize hostages in the future. Entering into negotiations is itself a concession in that it grants a measure of legitimacy to hostage takers, at least in their eyes and those of other inmates. By this line of reasoning, the immediate costs of not yielding will be more than offset by the benefits of fewer prison riots in the future.

One way to frame the debate is to ask if prison riots are more akin to the hostage taking conducted in the course of international terrorism or to the hostage situations that police departments routinely handle. The U.S. government policy since 1972 has been that, while the government will "talk" with terrorists holding hostages, they will not negotiate in the sense of offering concessions. This policy is generally seen as effective in reducing international terrorism.

On the other hand, over the same 20-year period, police have learned that the hostage incidents they face are better resolved through negotiation than force. Police hostage negotiators maintain that (a) negotiations have been successful in securing the release of hostages in most instances; (b) a hard line would have little deterrent effect, since hostage takers do not calculate the costs and benefits of taking hostages; and (c) the use of force may even encourage future hostage taking, since hostage takers may feel vindicated when the state must "resort" to force.

In principle, these arguments could be applied to and tested against prison riots, but no one has collected the data necessary. Perhaps the least plausible of the above arguments is that the use of force (in the prison context) encourages future hostage taking. It may be noted, however, that the force used to terminate the 1971 Attica riot resulted in more deaths (39) than in any other riot in U.S. history. It was also, without doubt, the most publicized riot. Yet the next year, 1972, had more prison riots than any other year in U.S. history.[6]

Use of Force

In general, the administration can terminate a riot at any time if it is willing to use overwhelming force. This may be a costly choice, however. Inmates may retaliate against hostages if the assault is not swift enough to prevent it. Shots fired can injure or kill hostages as well as inmates (as happened at Attica). The greatest danger comes if inmates are able to overwhelm the assault force and capture their weapons. As a consequence, prison officials can not merely "apply" force but must develop strategies so as to minimize casualties to the hostages, the assault forces, and the inmates, as well as to ensure that the assault force is invincible.

Three types of force were observed in the riots under study. (Excluded from this discussion is the use of force for specific tactical purposes, such as the firing of shots from towers to stop assaults on officers.)

IMMEDIATE FORCE

Force may be used as a first response to a disturbance. Armed personnel may be rushed in to defend or retake specific areas, without waiting for the riot to expand to its potential territorial limit. The key element in achieving the desired result is the speed of mobilizing and equipping a contingent in sufficient numbers.

There are advantages to the early use of force. As noted above, riots may begin without plan or organization. The immediate use of force may preclude inmates from becoming organized, from fashioning weapons, from fortifying their position, and from recruiting additional participants and expanding the territorial limits of the riot. It will also limit the pain and suffering of the hostages already taken.

Further, force used immediately may deny inmates the opportunity to promise to themselves and to authorities that they will harm the hostages unless their demands are met. Once such threats are made, inmates may find it psychologically difficult to back down from them. The Atlanta detainees, for example, consistently promised to kill hostages if an assault were made. Even though they may have realized the dire consequences of killing hostages, their public commitment to this course of action might have psychologically obligated them to make good on it. One of the disadvantages of negotiations, compared to the early use of force, is that inmates are given an opportunity to make threats to which they then may become committed.

No one would deny the advantages of the early use of force. The difficult task is to mobilize the necessary personnel and equipment with sufficient speed. A riot control squad deployed too quickly runs the risk of being overrun and taken hostage. The tension between the opportunities and dangers of an early use of force reached extraordinary proportions at Kirkland. In the riot's opening stages, correctional officers in a housing unit reported to the control center that armed inmates were breaking into the unit that was filling with smoke. Officers were arriving at the facility, but their numbers were insufficient to deploy a squad to rescue the trapped officers. When the number reached 35 (command had wanted at least 100), an assault force was dispatched to rescue the trapped officers. Once this was achieved, momentum was behind the riot squad and they began to clear the yard of inmates.

At Talladega, in contrast, the decision was made not to deploy immediate force. Once the detainees had seized the A side of Alpha Unit, a crucial decision had to be made concerning whether to hold the B side of the unit or evacuate it. Keeping control of B side would have greatly strengthened the government's position, both tactically and psychologically. Also, at this point, B-side detainees were still in their cells, so retaining that wing would have halved the number of detainees who could participate in the disturbance. These advantages notwithstanding, the acting warden decided to evacuate the B side because he felt that the forces present were not sufficient to withstand an inmate assault and more hostages might be taken. The decision was made under the extreme pressures of the moment with still sketchy information, and it is not (in our opinion) the sort of decision that can be usefully second-guessed.

The commission that investigated the Camp Hill disturbance concluded that an immediate show of force might have prevented the first riot from expanding:

> [T]he unarmed "show of force" by a dozen correctional officers in the 30 to 40 minutes after the confrontation was inadequate. An immediate armed contingent of corrections staff and available police would, in all probability, have prevented the retreat by these officers, contained the disturbance and, thereby, avoided the escalation of the disturbance into a riot.[7]

The problem is that the commission does not explain in any detail how this force could have been assembled given the resources at hand, nor does it specify the additional resources that should have been available.

At Coxsackie, prison officials had a compelling reason to use force immediately because they could see inmates assaulting correctional officers. Still, no immediate action was taken. The officers who had assembled at the special housing unit door were insufficient in number. If they had opened that door and then been overwhelmed, not only would more hostages be taken, but the riot might have expanded to other parts of the prison. By not risking the use of force, officers ensured that the riot would be limited to one unit.

PLANNED TACTICAL STRIKE

The essence of the tactical strike is the maximization of the element of surprise. Prison officials attempt to release the hostages and retake the facility before inmates can react. The forces appear suddenly and in overwhelming number, hoping to shock and confuse inmates and, thus, render them temporarily defenseless. Explosive devices (employing light, sound, or chemical agents) may be used to temporarily blind, deafen, or debilitate hostage holders.

The assault at Talladega was of this general nature. Its key elements were these:

- There was a continuous effort to gather intelligence.
- Rehearsals were conducted that accurately simulated the planned mission. This was accomplished by running drills in a nearby housing unit that was similar in design and construction to Alpha Unit. Tactics, ideas, and estimates were proven, and the time necessary to make the forced entry reduced.
- The assault was timed to occur when there was a maximum opportunity of success: in the predawn hours when inmates were asleep or otherwise at a low mental and physical state. The cover of night was used to conceal the team's entry.
- No warnings or ultimata were issued. A meal was served to make inmates feel successful and lower their alertness.
- Unity of command by the assault force was at a maximum. One assault force, the FBI's Hostage Rescue Team, assumed sole responsibility for regaining the building. Special Operations Response Teams from the FBI and BOP were used in support roles.
- Special weapons, including stun grenades, were used to confuse and disorient the detainees.

- The attack was executed with great speed. Explosives were used to breach the entryway doors, with minimal injury to those inside. Taking advantage of intelligence, the hostages were quickly located and freed.

At Mack Alford, a tactical assault was planned and, on several occasions, was moments away from implementation. The plan had been for Mack Alford's tactical squad to retake the building in which hostages were being held. A second tactical squad from the highway patrol was to retake another building being held by inmates, and a tactical squad from another facility was to back up the first two squads. Two other tactical squads from other facilities were to secure the inmates on the yard as they evacuated the buildings.

The disadvantages of the tactical strike are twofold. First, it might be unnecessary. Negotiations may resolve the incident. Even if they do not, inmates given an ultimatum may surrender without the use of force. Second, the costs of a tactical strike may be too high, depending upon the strategic conditions and the intentions and vigilance of the hostage holders. At Atlanta, over 100 hostages were spread among several buildings. Detainees had pledged to kill hostages if an assault were launched against them. They may or may not have acted on their threat, although few (including the FBI) doubted that they would have had the opportunity.[8]

At Mack Alford, inmates also told the hostages that they would be killed if an assault were made. Most of the time the hostages were kept in the prison's secure and difficult-to-reach detention unit. Inmates had used barricades to make it even less accessible. In addition, the hostages had been dressed in inmate uniforms (making them difficult to identify if sniper fire were used) and from time to time a hostage was moved to a different building. Thus, as at Atlanta, an assault would have cost lives unless inmates had chosen to back down from their threats, and there was no reason to believe they would have.

RIOT SQUAD FORMATIONS

A third type of force is akin to that used by police to quell an ongoing urban riot. Riot control squads move in unified groups to force clusters of inmates to move in one direction or to disperse. The American Correctional Association manual describes several of the basic maneuvers: the wedge (inmates are forced to move to the left and the right); echelon left (inmates are forced to move to the right); echelon right (inmates are forced to move to the left); the diamond (correctional officers are protected from all directions); line (inmates are forced to move away from a particular location).[9] The essence of this type of force is reliance on the size, discipline, and firepower of an assembled force to overwhelm inmates and force them to back down. Unlike the tactical strike, where the assault force's presence is concealed as long as possible, a riot squad's presence is deliberately emphasized. Batons and shotguns may be carried not only as weapons but also for "psychological purposes,"[10] that is, to convince inmates that resistance is futile.

The force used to end the second riot at Camp Hill had some elements of a tactical strike, but it was primarily a riot squad movement. Its key elements included the following:

- One column of state police officers began shouting to draw the attention of inmates, so as to create a diversion.
- Two other columns of state police formed riot lines on either side of the inmates, forcing them to move toward their housing units.
- Inmates resisted by throwing debris but, after warning shots from the state police, retreated into housing units. An inmate spokesman threatened to kill a hostage if the assault continued but did not act on the threat.
- Inmates complied with an order to leave the housing units and to surrender on the yard.

The Cimarron riot was resolved with a similar use of force. Its essential elements were these:

- Correctional officers arriving on the yard formed small defensive lines and groups. Their initial goal was to separate inmates fighting along racial/ethnic lines.
- Inmates redirected their hostility toward the riot squads, hurling rocks and shouting at them. Inmates began to advance on officers. Officers became concerned that they might be encircled and their weapons taken.
- As a defensive measure, tear gas was discharged and shotguns loaded with birdshot were fired.

Negotiations

The term "hostage negotiations" here refers to a dialogue between inmates and authorities focused on achieving an end to the incident. Four of the riots under study ended through negotiations: Camp Hill (the first riot), Atlanta, Mack Alford, and Coxsackie. Negotiations were conducted at Talladega and (briefly) at Kirkland and, for each, later abandoned in favor of other approaches. The negotiations observed can be divided into three types, although the distinctions are a matter of degree and emphasis.

NEGOTIATION AS BARGAINING

The dialogue between inmates and prison authorities may be primarily an exercise in bargaining. Inmates believe they have put themselves in a position to bargain with the state. They may see their hostages and the portion of the facility they occupy as "chips." They want to trade those chips for publicity, amnesty, improved conditions, or other benefits. The government may respond to inmates' demands with counterdemands. The resolution comes with the striking of the right bargain. At Atlanta, this was the release of the hostages in return for a new review process and a promise not to prosecute. At Camp Hill (the first riot), inmates released the hostages after the superintendent promised to meet with them the next day to discuss their grievances and to issue a press release announcing that meeting.

NEGOTIATION AS PROBLEM SOLVING

Negotiation may be an attempt to get inmates to surrender by meeting their psychological needs. The negotiations thus may have more in common with the hostage situations commonly resolved by police rather than, say, a labor–management bargaining session. Over the years, law enforcement hostage negotiators have learned that it is usually best to respond as if the hostage holder's demands were authentic, however odd or seemingly disconnected from the situation, and never to dismiss them as trivial.[11]

Thus, for example, the inmates at the Coxsackie riot did not bring forth demands over which negotiations (as a form of bargaining) could take place. Inmate leaders issued personal demands that seemed disproportionate to the means used. The principal demand was that the riot leader be allowed to speak to his stepfather over the phone. (A request that, made outside the context of a riot, might have been granted easily.) Apparently, none of the other inmate participants felt compelled to challenge this demand or add demands of their own. The inmates did, however, seek reassurances that correctional officers would not retaliate for the beatings they inflicted on their hostages or for the riot itself.

Prison officials arranged for the inmate leader to talk on the phone with his stepfather. Also, a government negotiator spent much of his time trying to calm the inmates and reassure them that they would not be injured when they gave up. A video camera was put in place to record the surrender. These concessions were sufficient to end the disturbance. The participants received additional sentences of 2–20 years.

NEGOTIATION AS SITUATION MANAGEMENT

State authorities may use negotiations primarily as a means to manage the situation. The measure of success is not whether an agreement is reached (either through bargaining or by meeting inmates' personal needs), but whether other goals are achieved: stabilizing the situation, obtaining information about the conditions inside the unit, and/or lowering inmates' vigilance against an assault.

At Talladega, negotiations aimed at bargaining reached a dead end after several days.[12] After that, negotiations became primarily an instrument to manage the situation. Bureau of Prison and FBI negotiators tried to calm the detainees and thereby reduce the threat to the hostages. In the riot's last stages, the negotiations were used primarily to support a tactical operation. Negotiations were used to collect information and try to make inmates less vigilant against an assault.

The distinction among negotiation as bargaining, as problem solving, and as situation management should not be overdrawn. The first sees resolution as being achieved by bringing together the interests of the agency and the inmates; the second views resolution as being achieved by meeting the immediate (especially, emotional) needs of the inmates as they articulate them; and the third see negotiations as a means to stabilize the situation and, if necessary, to prepare for a tactical assault. Negotiations always involve all three components. It is a matter of emphasis.

In general, prison officials faced these problems in the negotiation process.

INMATE NEGOTIATING GROUP

In approaching negotiations, prison officials may assume that they are pitted against a single, unified group of inmates when, in fact, there may be schisms among the inmates or no organization whatsoever. Over time, inmates may fuse into one coherent group, fractionate into competing groups, or dissolve into small, antagonistic pockets.[13]

Yet, for progress in negotiations to take place, there must be an inmate or group of inmates to whom officials can talk with a measure of continuity, and who exercises a significant measure of influence over the rioting inmates as a whole. This was true at Mack Alford and the first Camp Hill riot. At Mack Alford, the inmates who initiated the disturbance continued to exercise control over the disturbance and negotiated with prison officials. At Camp Hill (the first riot), a group of inmates emerged as leaders with whom prison authorities could negotiate.

If there is no stable or authoritative inmate leadership, or if it loses sway over the rioters, seeking an agreement to end the riot is of little value. At Coxsackie, one inmate took responsibility for negotiating, but toward the end of the disturbance he seemed to be losing control over the other inmates.

In the early stages of the Atlanta disturbance, no inmate group provided leadership with whom officials could negotiate. On the first day of the Atlanta riot, four inmates presented government negotiators with a list of demands, claiming that they represented the detainees as a whole. Soon other inmates contacted government negotiators asserting their authority. Moreover, at this stage, none of the groups seemed genuinely interested in reaching a settlement.[14]

The absence of leadership took government negotiators by surprise. Several of the government negotiators later wrote:

> After negotiators had spoken to at least 30 different Cuban inmates, all of whom said that they were "in control," federal negotiators were forced to accept a frightening conclusion: no one actually was in control.[15]

Eventually, a loose coalition of inmates formed and bargained with government officials in better faith. By the 11th day of rioting, the coalition had sufficient leverage to effect the release of the hostages after signing an agreement.

The problem of inmate leadership was more grave at Talladega. The detainees were fighting among themselves from the beginning. Prison officials attempted to create a leadership group among the detainees. In one instance, they acceded to a demand made by a relatively moderate detainee, in the hope that he would gain stature in the eyes of the other detainees. A moderate leadership never coalesced and the detainees and government remained far apart on the issues.

GOVERNMENT NEGOTIATORS

The theory behind hostage negotiation teams is now well established. A small group of officials is given specialized training in hostage negotiations. They are carefully chosen based on intelligence, levelheadedness, verbal skills, ability to think on their feet, and overall demeanor. During a disturbance, their job is to negotiate a settlement. Those with command (decision-making authority) must refrain from directly talking to inmates.

The separation between command and negotiation is said to have several advantages: (a) The decisionmaker can make decisions under less stressful conditions; (b) the negotiator can stall for time by referring requests and demands to a higher authority; (c) negotiators may become overinvolved in the process, lose objectivity, or experience high levels of stress, and command personnel can observe and correct this; (d) there may be information that the negotiators should not have (e.g., that an assault is imminent), but to which the person in command would be privy; and (e) the division between command and negotiation may allow negotiators to develop greater rapport with the hostage holder. The government negotiator can appear to the hostage holder to be taking his side in gaining concessions from command.[16]

This theory was followed at both Atlanta and Talladega. At Atlanta, several hours after the riot began, a BOP lieutenant made the first contact with a detainee and arranged for a face-to-face negotiation session. He was soon joined by FBI negotiators, who then assumed control over the negotiations for the duration of the event. At Talladega, a counselor assigned to the unit made the initial contact with the detainees and started negotiations. Later that evening, he withdrew from the negotiations and trained negotiators from the prison, the FBI, and BOP took over.

Coxsackie and Mack Alford passed through a different sequence. At Coxsackie, the first conversations occurred between the inmates and the department's trained negotiators, as well as the deputy superintendent. About five hours into the disturbance, the assistant commissioner began to talk to the inmates in response to the inmates' demand that they speak to an official "from Albany," that is, someone with authority from the central office. From that point on, the assistant commissioner became the lead negotiator, although he worked closely with the department negotiator and the deputy superintendent.

At Mack Alford, two trained department negotiators were brought to the prison. After about an hour, however, the inmates broke off the conversation with them, claiming the negotiators had lied to them. They then insisted that they would speak only with a particular captain, whom they trusted. The captain remained the chief negotiator throughout the disturbance.

Thus, the Coxsackie and Mack Alford negotiations did not follow the standard model. In both cases, however, important principles were preserved. Neither the assistant commissioner at Coxsackie nor the captain at Mack Alford exercised authority in the situation. The advantages that come with splitting command and negotiation functions were not forfeited. The advantage gained was the increased credibility of the negotiators in the inmates' eyes.

CYCLES OF NEGOTIATIONS

Studies of negotiations in other domains, especially labor–management bargaining, have found that they tend to follow a common cycle. Initially, both parties make exaggerated demands. This is followed by a period of withdrawal and a return to negotiations with more moderate demands. When parties try to circumvent this ritual, negotiations tend to break down.[17] Douglas points out that even concessions made too early in the negotiation process can be counterproductive:

> Concessions ahead of schedule benefit no one, not even the receiving party. Not only does a party tantalize and mislead the opponent if it relaxes its firmness too quickly, but the parties also need the opportunity to experience exhaustion of their demands before they can be satisfied that they had drained what was there to be had. Premature movement robs them of this experience.[18]

This pattern seems to have occurred at Atlanta. Soon after the Atlanta riot started, the attorney general offered a moratorium on deportations and a fairer, more rapid review process. About this, one of the FBI negotiators later observed:

> It became apparent to the negotiators that the inmates had been offered "too much, too soon" . . . Apparently, the situation had to "mature" to allow inmates to vent their emotions.[19]

Indeed, during the first several days, government negotiators perceived the detainees as not interested in making progress in the negotiations. The detainees used negotiation sessions as an "opportunity to express their long-standing frustrations"[20] rather than achieve a settlement.

On the other hand, a similar cycle did not develop at Talladega. The Talladega detainees and the government were as far, if not farther, apart at the end of the disturbance than at the start. Likewise, at Coxsackie (described above as least like a labor–management bargaining process), inmates seemed more anxious and hostile as the incident progressed. Coxsackie was shorter in duration than Atlanta and Oakdale and might have followed the identified cycle if it had been given time to mature. We doubt it, however, because the benefits inmates sought in the riot were linked more to acts of defiance than to specific demands that could have been moderated.

Third-Party Involvement

Third parties were used in the negotiations at Atlanta, Mack Alford, and Talladega. They played several roles:

- *As initiators of conversation.* At Mack Alford, two inmate leaders were recruited during the opening stages of the riot to initiate conversation with the rioting inmates, who (at that point) refused to talk to prison officials.
- *As guarantors to the promise that inmates would not be mistreated after surrendering.* At Mack Alford, three state legislators were present at the surrender.
- *As guarantors that an agreement is authentic and in the inmates' interest.* At Atlanta, Bishop Roman made an audio tape stating that he supported the agreement. To overcome a last-minute snag in the negotiations, Bishop Roman assured the detainees that the government officials who signed the agreement had the authority to make a binding commitment.
- *As mediators searching for a middle ground.* At Atlanta, a legal service attorney seemed to work genuinely toward developing a middle ground that was acceptable to both sides. He raised substantive issues with the government and the government responded in a written memo clarifying its position. At the same time, the negotiator helped persuade detainees to accept the agreement without a clause declaring that deportations would cease.
- *As government bargaining chips.* At Talladega, government officials allowed a reporter to talk to the detainees and report their story in return for the release of a hostage. At Coxsackie, prison officials allowed the inmate leader a two-minute telephone conversation with his stepfather.

In all of these instances, the third-party involvement seemed to advance the negotiation process. The BOP's report on Atlanta emphasizes that third-party negotiators must be carefully screened and agree not to raise new issues or to act as advocates for inmates.[21] To this we would add that the purpose of third-party involvement must be kept clearly in mind and that decisions about third-party involvement be made in reference to that purpose rather than other criteria, such as political prominence or a request by inmates per se. This was followed closely at Atlanta.

A device that has been shown to be helpful in other contexts is known (among negotiation specialists) as a "Single Negotiation Text," or SNT.[22] The idea is that the third party, after listening carefully to both sides, drafts a proposed agreement. The text receives criticism from both sides, is modified accordingly, and the process is repeated again and again until the text becomes acceptable to both sides. The advantages of an SNT are twofold. First, an SNT helps parties move away from entrenched positions and toward a common one. Second, when the parties to the negotiations are not well specified—diffuse, poorly organized, changing—an SNT can help bring structure to the process.[23]

The negotiations at Atlanta involved features of the SNT process, with the Atlanta attorney playing a key role. The starting text was the detainees' list of seven demands. The Department of Justice responded to those demands point by point. The Atlanta attorney asked for clarification of the department response, again point by point, and suggested possible solutions where points of contention were still in evidence. For example, the department said that the detainees would receive "full, fair, and equitable reviews." In response, the attorney suggested that a special panel of federal judges could design the process. The attorney general agreed to appoint a "special panel" to design a new review process, a panel that would include the "input" of the attorney and Bishop Roman. This was acceptable to the detainees.

FORCE ULTIMATA

The idea of a force ultimatum is that inmates, given a clear choice between surrender and an armed assault, will choose the former. While ultimata may be necessary to signal the state's resolve, they should delivered carefully so as to avoid inmate panic. Clarity of expression is critical.

Among the riots we studied, force ultimata were issued in the second Camp Hill riot and at Kirkland. At Camp Hill, state police declared over a public address system that inmates were to release the hostages and surrender by exiting the cellblocks and lying face down on the yard. One block at a time was then called. At Kirkland, the warden announced over the public address system that the riot squad had been deployed, that it was instructed to use force if necessary, and that the inmates should lie face down on the ground. In both instances there were no retaliatory actions against hostages, and the riots ended shortly thereafter.

The ultimatum delivered at Kirkland is especially instructive. The ultimatum had two sorts of statements. A prefatory statement attested to the warden's resolve. The language used was clear and strong, leaving no inmate to wonder about the warden's commitment. ("I am not playing games. I am dead serious.")

Useful in discussing the body of the ultimatum (which told inmates what to do) is a distinction negotiation analysts make between a warning and a threat.[24] A "warning" is a statement of fact that informs someone that negative consequences will follow unless a course of action is undertaken. A "threat" also gives advance notice of impending danger, but emphasizes that the person making the threat is the one responsible for the negative consequences. A warning can be delivered by a person friendly to the party at risk, but a threat can not. It is psychologically easier to back down to a warning than a threat. One is bending to necessity; the other connotes capitulation.

The body of the Kirkland ultimatum was presented more as a warning than a threat. Its grammar can be usefully compared to the grammar of the prefatory statement. The prefatory statement, expressing the warden's commitment, is in the active voice (as above, "I am not playing games . . ."). The subject of the sentence is explicit, the warden. The actual warning/threat is in the passive voice:

> The riot squad has been deployed with shotguns. They have been instructed to use all necessary force to quell this disturbance, to include deadly force. Lie down on the ground where you are.[25]

The warden could have emphasized that he personally had deployed the riot squad but, wisely, he did not. The statement as it stands implies a sense of impersonal inevitability. The tone conveyed is that, at this juncture, the outcome is in the hands of the inmates. The inmates and the warden have a common interest in getting the incident resolved.

ISSUE ULTIMATA

The idea of issue ultimata is that inmates, once told that some or all of their demands will not be met, will stop making those demands and focus on matters than can be negotiated. Police hostage negotiators generally discourage the use of issue ultimata: "No matter how unreasonable, exorbitant, or weird a demand, never tell the subject 'no'."[26] Instead, the negotiators should try to recast the demand that can not be met in way that it can, or at least implies no immediate threat.[27]

This advice seems reasonable for prison riots. An exception, though, was observed at Atlanta. As described in chapter 2, during the first six days at Atlanta, the detainees had held fast to the position that the deportation of the detainees to Cuba should be terminated. The government did not tell the detainees that this was not negotiable because they feared the detainees might retaliate. The detainees refused to drop the issue, however, and the negotiations reached an impasse. Finally, a government negotiator told the inmates that their demand would not be met under any conditions. This broke the impasse without provoking retaliation against hostages, allowing the negotiations to go forward.

A related issue concerns the transition from negotiation to force. The literature on police hostage situations debates whether the government negotiator should be alerted that an assault will occur. Many say no because he or she might inadvertently reveal the plan. Others point to possible advantages: The negotiator might be able to distract the subject at the start of the assault, provide reassurances that would lower his defenses, or position him for a sniper shot.[28] None of these advantages was believed to be obtainable at Talladega, and the regional director decided not to inform the negotiators.

Waiting

A third strategy for handling a disturbance is to wait it out. In law enforcement, "stalling for time is a universal tactic among hostage negotiators."[29] The theory is that hostage takers tend to develop sympathy for
the hostages, develop a rapport with police negotiators, or just get tired
of doing what they are doing. In light of this, police hostage teams are
encouraged to avoid the temptation to "get it over with" and to patiently
wait out the situation unless forced to by a material threat to a hostage's
safety.

For prison riots, the evidence for the elements of this argument is
mixed. The hostages in two of the riots, Camp Hill and Coxsackie, were
treated brutally. At Mack Alford, Atlanta, and Talladega, none of the
hostages was physically attacked, but they were subjected to extreme
psychological stress. From the point of view of the hostages, lengthening
the duration of the disturbance came at considerable cost. At Talladega,
additional waiting might have endangered the hostages because hostility
among the detainees was increasing.

Negotiations formally ended the disturbance at Mack Alford, but in
large measure the riot succumbed to massive defection and inmate exhaus-
tion. After three days of rioting, only a fraction of the original participants remained on the yard.

While a strategy of waiting may imply passivity on the part of the
government, usually the opposite is the case. Research on police hostage
negotiations,[30] as well as negotiations in other contexts,[31] emphasizes the
importance of active listening: paying careful attention to what is said,
asking the speaker to clarify what she or he meant, and communicating
back to the speaker that she or he had been understood. Active listening
can be extraordinarily demanding. The regional director in charge of
Talladega's resolution reported that throughout the disturbance, officials
at the scene were continually trying to discern what the detainees wanted,
what they were trying to do, and what their tactical situation was. This
occurred almost 24 hours a day.

A strategy of waiting can also employ tactics that will, by increasing
inmates' discomfort, (a) directly motivate them to end the incident more
quickly or (b) create needs that prison officials can then use to effect a
bargain. At Atlanta, helicopter overflights, plus the cutting off of water
and heat, put pressure on inmates. At Talladega, food, which was in short
supply to begin with, was denied. At Coxsackie and Mack Alford, the
electricity was turned off. Each of these deprivations became a negotiating point for the government.

One problem with this tactic is that the hostages have to endure the
same deprivations as the inmates. Committed hostage holders, such as
those at Talladega, may have much higher thresholds of pain than the state
is willing to inflict on the hostages. At Talladega, both detainees and hostages went 10 days with very little food. The detainees were given food

on the last day, in part to lower their defenses, but also so that it would reach the hostages.

A second problem is that situational stress may impel some inmates to surrender but, for others, only stiffen opposition or increase interinmate hostility. Police facing hostage situations are advised to "increas[e] situational stress if the subject is too comfortable or decreas[e] stress if the subject is very anxious."[32] Yet situational stress is not something that, like a thermostat, can be turned up and down with predictable results. At Atlanta, helicopter overflights, in particular, seemed to anger detainees and stiffen their resolve, without moving them toward surrender. At one point, the detainees held knives to the hostages' throats when helicopters flew above them.[33] The overflights were discontinued, but it took time to regain the trust that had been lost.

Media Management

The media may have an impact on the resolution of riots in four ways. One is that the media coverage may become a bargaining chip. Inmates may, as they did at Mack Alford and Talladega, demand access to media representatives. Prison officials must decide whether, and under what conditions, to trade that concession. At Mack Alford, the warden initially judged its cost as being too high. Acceding to the demand, he believed, would provide an incentive to inmates to riot in the future. As the disturbance wore on, this position was reversed because the inmates held fast to their demand and the resolution proved otherwise difficult to achieve. At Talladega, BOP officials offered detainees the opportunity to speak with a reporter from a Spanish-language publication, but only if they met specific counterdemands. Moves and countermoves by each side followed, resulting in the release of one hostage.

Second, the media may affect the tactical situation. This was most pronounced at Atlanta, where media coverage was intense and the facility's location on a public street allowed television cameras to broadcast live images of the events on the perimeter, including the movement of tactical forces. Bureau of Prisons officials had to take this into account in any decision involving the movement of tactical forces. At Talladega, the media were kept at a much greater distance from the facility, but even with this precaution the media were able to train powerful lenses on parts of the facility.

Third, the media's physical presence may pose a management problem. Large numbers of media personnel can clog facilities and persistent demands for information can add to the pressures of the situation. At Atlanta, the media intruded upon the families of the hostages, and several reporters used deceit to try to obtain interviews.

Finally, a prison riot is very likely to shine the media's spotlight on the agency. Management personnel may be profiled and issues may be raised that go beyond the riot itself. Under certain, limited circumstances, top-level prison officials may be well advised to become directly involved in media relations. A top-level official, as compared to a media specialist, can credibly articulate the values and mission that guide the organization. He or she can show that leadership is acting professionally and effectively. This message must be subtly conveyed and it must not appear to be boosterism. The intended audience may include employees elsewhere in the agency who must continue to deliver services and who may feel uncertain and anxious about the unfolding events, as well as government officials with oversight responsibility for the agency and the public at large.

During the Atlanta/Oakdale disturbances, BOP Director J. Michael Quinlan presided over regular press conferences. He had been in office five months and had never previously been the focus of media attention or held a news conference, yet he was able to convey the BOP's foremost commitment to the safety of the hostages and the deliberateness of the effort. His phrase "my patience is endless" became a symbol of this.

At the same time, the media's audience will often include inmates inside the institution. News releases meant to reassure the public may antagonize inmates holding hostages. After the first riot at Camp Hill, for example, the superintendent announced that none of the inmates' demands would be met. This helped precipitate the second riot.

12

After the Riot

The tasks to be accomplished in the aftermath of a riot, properly considered, may involve a period of years. They consist not only of the short-term task of resecuring the prison, but also of repairing the damage, returning staff to work, and in the long-term restoring or changing the structure of the institution or department.

The Short Term

After the inmates have surrendered, prison officials must search for contraband, move inmates to secure units, assess damage, and clear the count. Medical care must be provided to hostages and inmates as needed. Evidence must be collected for future prosecutions. If outside staff or law enforcement personnel were requested, they must be released from duty as the danger recedes.

At Camp Hill, some of the essential postriot tasks were not completed. Weapons and other debris were left in the hallways of the blocks and the locking mechanisms operating cell doors had been compromised. The prison administration was eager to return the prison to normal and geared its action toward that goal rather than first ensuring that the facility was really secure.

In the other prisons under study, these tasks were handled without major problems. At Cimarron, a pressing need in the immediate aftermath was the provision of medical care to the inmates who had been injured. One was evacuated by helicopter for emergency surgery, and 10 others were transported to hospitals by ambulance. The remainder of the inmates were searched and locked in their cells, and a count was taken. The inmates identified as being most active in the riot were placed in the facility's detention unit. The entire prison was searched for weapons, but no buildup of weapons was found.

At Coxsackie, the immediate aftermath was handled with an especially high level of control and certainty of results. The inmates not requiring immediate medical attention were moved to the gymnasium. They were separated by 20 feet, instructed not to talk, and supervised by one and then two correctional officers per inmate. Each inmate was examined by medical staff and then extensively interviewed. Five hours after the riot, they were transferred in small numbers to other facilities.

At Atlanta, the immediate postriot task involved transferring the detainee population to other facilities. Over a 24-hour period, detainees were escorted out of the compound one at a time. The BOP staff searched each detainee, placed him in restraints, and then put the detainee on a bus for transfer to another facility.

The Medium Term

In the medium term, prison officials must repair the facility, assist employees in coping with their experience, return employees to their work routines, and undertake the administrative follow-up associated with the disturbance.

One of the immediate responsibilities of the agency is to help employees overcome the trauma of the disturbance. In some departments, such as the one in South Carolina, professional and peer-counselling programs are mandatory for officers who have experienced traumatic episodes, such as being held hostage. In Oklahoma, the department established teams to assist staff and their families in dealing with the stress and trauma of the aftermath of a disturbance. (Inmates were also able to request such assistance.) At Mack Alford, these teams went to work as smoke was literally still rising from the burned buildings. The teams were composed of staff psychologists, case managers, and senior staff. In general, the prison officials and officers we interviewed stated that such debriefing sessions were useful.

It would be a mistake, however, to relegate these duties in their entirety to mental health professionals or peer counseling. Effective communication is important within the agency, to address concerns about the riot itself (what happened and why; explain controversial decisions) and the future (how will the riot affect individual careers; plans to rebuild the facility; changes in the facility's mission). Also, a collective public expression of the sacrifices made by hostages, as well as appreciation of the exemplary action of staff during the riot, may be important in reintegrating the corrections community.

Along these lines, public recognition ceremonies were held by the Oklahoma state legislature (for Mack Alford), the South Carolina state legislature (for Kirkland), the Bureau of Prisons (for Atlanta/Oakdale), and the New York Department of Correctional Services (for Coxsackie). Following Talladega, the acting attorney general commented that he felt "grateful beyond words and proud beyond measure." After the Mack Alford disturbance, the central office took the unprecedented step of including Mack Alford staff in the planning of the reconstruction of the prison. This was deeply appreciated by staff, implicitly giving recognition to their contribution.

At Camp Hill, few such efforts were made, which, while understandable given the turmoil that followed the disturbance, was still noticed by staff. Four months after the disturbance, a Camp Hill staff member observed that the prison's staff

> have gone through the worst riot in history. They've seen their colleagues beaten ... There were acts of courage, there were acts of heroism on the part of staff. [But] there's been no ceremonies, no awards, no grateful letters from the commissioner ... There's nothing being done to heal the psychological devastation in there.[1]

Indeed, when the new commissioner assumed office several months later, he found the agency to be near paralysis.

In some riots, though not all, inmates damage the structural integrity of the facility. Surprisingly, the Talladega detainees did comparatively little serious damage to their unit. Employees were able to ready the unit for reopening just a few days after the disturbance. At Coxsackie, in contrast, the inmates destroyed the control center of the special housing unit such that they could not be immediately returned there. In the largest, most destructive riots, such as the ones at Atlanta and Camp Hill, major reconstruction was needed.

Also during the medium term, a report may be commissioned to find out why the incident happened. The report may help frame, for corrections officials, policy makers, and the public, what the riot meant, thereby helping to establish a long-term policy agenda. Are major systemwide changes needed or only minor adjustments of particular policies? The investigation may be conducted by department of corrections staff, by another executive agency, by a specially appointed commission, or by a legislative committee. In some riots, two or more investigations may be undertaken. At Camp Hill, for example, in addition to the department of correction's internal report, reports were issued by a blue-ribbon commission appointed by the Governor, and by judiciary committees of both the state senate and the state house of representatives.

Another aspect of the medium term is the prosecution of the inmates responsible for the disturbance. Arguably, the best deterrent against future riots is not a hard-line approach during the crisis, but determined, effective prosecution after the riot is over.

Successful prosecutions were achieved at Coxsackie (17 convicted, sentences ranging from 2 to 20 years), Idaho (five convicted, one sentenced to life imprisonment), and Kirkland (32 convicted, sentences ranging from 6 months to 15 years). At Cimarron, the department assigned a unit attached to the central office (Intelligence and Investigations) to find and preserve evidence and to debrief staff and inmates to help identify perpetrators for prosecution. The Talladega detainees were deported to Cuba.

Atlanta may (or may not) be an instructive exception. Following both the 1984 and 1987 disturbances, prosecutions were either not pursued or not successfully realized. The jury acquitted the detainees charged with the 1984 riot and the attorney general provided the 1987 detainees amnesty. If one believes in the deterrent effect of prosecution, a plausible argument could be made that the absence of effective prosecution (in 1984 and 1987) contributed to later disturbances (in 1987 and 1991). On the other hand, a conjuncture of circumstances led to the 1987 Atlanta and 1991 Talladega riots. Earlier nonprosecutions may have been an element in that conjuncture, but we know of no proof for it.

Long-Term Solutions

As noted at the outset, a prison riot can be both a tragedy and an opportunity. It is an opportunity if correctional leaders listen carefully, think clearly about the events, and develop policy to reflect what they have learned. A prison riot, by definition, means that prison officials have lost control over the situation for a period of time. A corrections department can become stronger, less likely to lose control, and more effective in resolving disturbances when the following are achieved:[2]

- Gains are made in the ability to forecast a disturbance and the flow of information is improved. The agency, having seen a disturbance, may be more aware of and better able to interpret future warning signs.
- Previously unrecognized problems are addressed. Inmate grievances may be remedied. Riots may reveal weaknesses in facilities, operating procedures, or the organization. When the approach taken is asking how the problems can be resolved, rather than arguing over whether they did or did not contribute to the onset of the riot, progress will be made.
- The outcome of innovations made during the disturbance is reviewed, and successful innovations are incorporated in future riot plans. During the Atlanta disturbance, for example, the BOP developed the idea of a center for hostage families. The success of this effort led the BOP to make this a standard feature of its response.
- Relationships with other agencies are improved. During the riot, new relationships among agencies may emerge or the need for them may be demonstrated, as at Camp Hill. After the disturbance, gains should be consolidated and relationships strengthened.

- Innovations may be made in the reconstruction process. The postriot period can be used to restore what existed prior to the disturbance or to depart from tradition. For example, after the Mack Alford disturbance, prison employees, including correction officers, case managers, and maintenance workers, became involved in developing plans to reconstruct the prison. A delegation was sent to several prisons in another state to develop ideas about architectural design. This break with tradition (previously architectural planning was conducted only in the central office) helped create a sense of ownership among Mack Alford staff.

A riot is unlikely to leave a department's morale untouched. Much depends upon the response during the riot and the outcome. If the resolution went well, if employees perceive that the department faced the crisis squarely and with adequate resources and preparation, and if the responses of the political community and media were positive, then the disturbance may actually enhance the prison staff's sense of mission, loyalty, and confidence in the department. Where these factors are absent, morale may plummet.

One measure of morale is turnover and absenteeism. At the positive extreme, one year after the Kirkland riot, only one of the 22 employees who were trapped or taken hostage had resigned from the department. This was a lower turnover rate than that of the department as a whole. In contrast, at Camp Hill, where 24 hostages were taken, 123 staff members (including 70 correctional officers) were initially placed on disability. Eight months after the riot, about 50 staff members had still not returned to work. Of course, there were many more staff members injured at Camp Hill than at Kirkland. This can account for much of the difference, but not all of it.

If Camp Hill is taken as exemplary of the most serious problems facing prison officials in a riot's wake, it also must be seen as an example of where those challenges were most fully met. A new director was hired. He reorganized the central office, secured a grant to revamp the department's system for emergency preparedness, and improved relationships with other state agencies involved in emergency planning. At Camp Hill, a new warden was hired, who helped direct the rebuilding of the facility.

Historical Analogies and Correctional Administration

The first and second sections of this book recount the events, decisions, and actions that occurred in eight prison disturbances. In this third section, we have compared the separate chronological accounts, in order to distinguish strategies that seemed to have worked from those that led to additional problems. The comparisons have also allowed us to discuss riot causation, as well as (from time to time) general features of correctional administration; still, our central concern has been the strategy of disturbance prevention, response, and recovery.

Specific policy recommendations related to tactics, rules of conduct, or even an overall philosophy of handling disturbances must be left to particular decision makers facing specific situations. There are too many contingencies to permit anything more than flimsy general statements. Still, the chronologies and comparisons developed in this study can be used by decision makers to help provide perspective: to think comprehensively about all that must be done, to separate the important from the unimportant, and to relate different parts of the situation to each other and to the whole. At the most concrete level, the chronologies suggest that specific mistakes made in the past should not be made again.

For example, a prison official, having just resolved a prison disturbance, might be well served by recalling the Camp Hill experience. If so, he or she would naturally take steps to ensure that the information flowing up the chain of command is accurate and complete, that sufficient numbers of staff and other law enforcement personnel are present, that the physical security of the facility has not been compromised by the riot, and that pivotal tasks take precedence over those that can wait. The greater the similarity between the decision maker's situation and Camp Hill, the more useful the comparison.

By the same token, overstated or otherwise inexact comparisons— analogies that group together instances whose causal patterns, complexities, and elements are not comparable—can mislead and misdirect. More careful consideration of the evidence is then needed to reverse the incorrect assessment, if opportunities are not to be missed.

We observed this at Atlanta, when policy makers (in the State Department) extrapolated from the 1984 situation at Atlanta to the one in 1987. The extrapolation falsely suggested that there was little danger in the situation, which in turn precluded Atlanta officials from considering possible preventive measures. Likewise, in the immediate aftermath of the first Camp Hill riot, officials sought to apply the lessons from earlier violent incidents at the facility in which, allegedly, officers retaliated against inmates. The paramount lesson of the earlier incidents was restraint, whereas the 1989 situation called for assertive actions to resecure the facility.

Also, if state authorities publicly state that inmates can be expected to behave in a certain way, based on the "lessons of history," such statements, themselves, may change the situation. This was tragically observed in a 1993 riot at the Southern Ohio Correctional Facility in Lucasville, in which 12 hostages were being held. An agency spokesperson, responding to a media question on the fifth day of the riot, dismissed inmate threats to kill the hostages as the "language of negotiations."[3] However, the inmates were now facing a different kind of situation: Their threats were being brushed off as merely rhetoric. Shortly after this, the inmates murdered a hostage. The extent to which the press statement directly prompted the murder is subject to debate but cannot be ignored.

It should be further noted that inmates, in their own way, may learn (or mislearn) from previous events. The Talladega inmates seemed to have inferred from the Atlanta riot that government officials would not order an assault, regardless of circumstances. Because of this misperception, they did not take the tactical precautions that they had at Atlanta, to the great benefit of the hostages.

Thus, the more general point is that seemingly fixed patterns may dissolve if the situation is altered. Patterns reoccur across time because of the similarity of (a) the cognitive and emotional content of people's minds (what they are thinking about, how they are feeling) and (b) the material circumstance; change either and expect different patterns. Even the mere statement that such patterns exist may change the situation.

The examples discussed thus far are primarily negative ones, misapplied strategies and errors of judgment whose study will assist decision makers to avoid repeating them. While the examination of past events can be used to improve future efforts, history can not be undone. Nothing can bring back lives that were lost, if any, or purge from memory the pain and suffering that has been endured.

On the other side of the coin are positive examples. How may they be taken advantage of? A suggestive analog is the corporate strategy of "benchmarking," in which a firm assembles data on the best practices in each aspect of the business and ensures that it meets or surpasses those standards.[4] (Xerox, for example, used benchmarking to curb its loss of market shares to the Japanese in the 1980s.[5]) Similarly, correctional agencies would be well advised to collect data on the "best practices" in riot planning and preparation, in order to emulate and even improve on them. South Carolina's training program in crisis management, which uses real-time exercises, suggests itself. Other examples from the eight case studies come quickly to mind, although the more important point is the need to collect and collate additional information. In this way, each agency would have external points of reference to judge their effort, with corrections-wide standards ratcheting upward.

In the final analysis, riot planning and preparation can only do so much. How a prison operates under normal circumstances will shape how, and how well, it restores order in a disturbance. The same problems that may have helped give rise to the disturbance (e.g., a divided administration; inaccurate, untimely, or misinterpreted intelligence), will likely appear in the resolution efforts. By the same token, a well-managed agency can use its capacities to achieve an efficient resolution.

Moreover, no riot plan and no amount of field training can compensate for the broader leadership skills that a riot situation requires: prudence; an ability to shift among concerns rapidly and efficiently; patience and equanimity; an eye to the options that inhere in the situation and the humility not to overstate them. Ultimately, riot prevention, control, and resolution depend upon these qualities being embodied in the correctional staff.

Notes

Chapter 1. *Introduction*

1. Carl von Clausewitz, *On War*, eds. and trans. Michael Howard and Peter Paret (Princeton: Princeton University Press, 1976 [1833]), 119. Also useful here is Edward N. Luttwak, *Strategy: The Logic of War and Peace* (Cambridge, Mass.: Harvard University Press, 1987).

2. Actually, short-term tasks can take as much as a week to be fully completed.

3. A note on sampling: We asked every state department of corrections, the District of Columbia Department of Corrections, and the Federal Bureau of Prisons to provide a thumbnail sketch of the disturbances that occurred in their agency during the previous two years. The survey yielded brief accounts of 49 riots. From this list, we selected five riots for study based on (a) their occurrence in an agency known to be innovative in emergency planning and strategy; (b) the advent of exceptional problems in resolution; and (c) variation in riot type and regional location.

The disturbance at Talladega occurred during the course of our fieldwork, and we added it because of its recency and because it met the second criterion above. The disturbance at the U.S. Penitentiary, Atlanta, was studied because of its magnitude and the complicated negotiations that were required for its resolution. The disturbance at Kirkland Correctional Institution was included because of the innovative features of the emergency response program developed by the South Carolina Department of Corrections.

Chapter 2. *United States Penitentiary, Atlanta*

1. The primary source for this chapter is the BOP's report on the riots: U.S. Department of Justice, Federal Bureau of Prisons, *A Report to the Attorney*

General on the Disturbances at the Federal Detention Center, Oakdale, Louisiana, and the U.S. Penitentiary, Atlanta, Georgia, February 1, 1988 (Washington, D.C.: Federal Bureau of Prisons). In addition, we conducted a round of interviews in the BOP's central office. The descriptions of events are from the *Report*, unless noted otherwise.

2. Robert L. Bach, "Cubans," in *Refugees in the United States: A Reference Handbook*, ed. David W. Haines (Westport, Conn.: Greenwood Press, 1985).

3. Testimony of Michael G. Kozak, principal deputy legal advisor, Department of State, House Committee on the Judiciary, Subcommittee on Courts, Civil Liberties, and the Administration of Justice, *Hearing on Mariel Cuban Detainees: Events Preceding and Following the November 1987 Riots*, 100th Cong., 2nd sess., February 4, 1988, 32.

4. Bach, "Cubans."

5. Loren Karacki, "Violence in the Federal Prison System: A Historical Analysis" (Washington, D.C.: Office of Research and Evaluation, Federal Bureau of Prisons, photocopy, April, 1990), 84.

6. Testimony of Warden Jack A. Hanberry, House Committee on Judiciary, Subcommittee on Courts, Civil Liberties, and the Administration of Justice, *Atlanta Federal Penitentiary: Report of the Subcommittee on Courts, Civil Liberties, and the Administration of Justice of the Committee of the Judiciary, U.S. House of Representatives*, 99th Cong., 2nd sess., April, 1986, 24.

7. "Prisons Chief Announces Investigation," *Hartford* (Conn.) *Courant*, 27 November 1987.

8. Kozak testimony, House Committee, *Hearing on the November 1987 Riots*, 49.

9. Ibid.

10. Bureau of Prisons, *Report to the Attorney General*, Atlanta-7 [hereinafter page numbers abbreviated: A-].

11. Ibid., A-7, A-8.

12. "Secret Report Says Cubans' Conditions Poor," *Atlanta Journal*, 3 February 1982.

13. Karacki, "Violence in the Federal Prison System," 87.

14. House Committee on Judiciary, *Atlanta Federal Penitentiary*, iii.

15. Ibid., 5.

16. Bureau of Prisons, *Report to the Attorney General*, Introduction-2.

17. Ibid., A-80.

18. This and the following paragraph draw on Peter L. Nacci, "The Oakdale-Atlanta Prison Disturbances: The Events, the Results," *Federal Probation* 52 (December, 1988), 3–12.

19. "Fort Chaffee Repairs Could Cost $8 Million, Army Officials Think," *Arkansas Gazette* (Little Rock), 30 January 1982.

20. Nacci, "Oakdale-Atlanta Prison Disturbances," 3.

21. "Cuban Detainees Persist in Continuing Hunger Strike," *Atlanta Journal*, 18 November 1983.

22. "Inmates Locked in Cells after Protest," *Atlanta Journal*, 15 October 1984.

23. "Cuban Inmates Escalate Protest," *Atlanta Journal*, 18 October 1984; "Cubans Go on Rampage at U.S. Pen," *Atlanta Journal*, 2 November 1984; "For

Inmate-Defendants, Riot Trial Holds Little Meaning," *Miami Herald*, 16 January 1986.

24. "14 Guards and 12 Inmates Injured in Fight in Brooklyn," *New York Times*, 7 July 1985.

25. "'Powder Keg' Pops: Cubans Ruin Prison," *Arizona Republic* (Phoenix), 23 August 1985.

26. Bert Useem and Peter A. Kimball, *States of Siege: U.S. Prison Riots, 1971–1986* (New York: Oxford University Press, 1989).

27. Ibid.

28. Ibid.; Larry Solomon, "Riots in the U.S. Jails and Prisons 1968–1982" (Washington, D.C.: National Institute of Corrections, photocopy, n.d.).

29. For example, Mark D. Kemple, "Legal Fictions Mask Human Suffering: The Detention of the Mariel Cubans: Constitutional, Statutory, International Law, and Human Considerations," 62, no. 6 (1989) *University of Southern California Law Review*. 1733–1805

30. Congressman John Lewis of Georgia speaking on "A Mocking Memory," April 27, 1987, reprinted in House Committee, *Hearing on the November 1987 Riots*, 12.

31. Letter from Congressman John Lewis and 12 other congressmen to Commissioner Alan Nelson, Immigration and Naturalization Service, July 1, 1987, reprinted in House Committee, *Hearing on the November 1987 Riots*, 16–18.

32. Kozak testimony, House Committee, *Hearing on the November 1987 Riots*, 40.

33. Testimony by Marvin Shoob, U.S. district judge for the northern district of Georgia, House Committee, *Hearing on the November 1987 Riots*, 125.

34. Ibid.; also, "For Inmate-Defendants, Riot Trial Holds Little Meaning," *Miami Herald*, 16 January 1986.

35. Bureau of Prisons, *Report to the Attorney General*, A-48.

36. Ibid., A-47.

37. Ibid., A-49.

38. Ibid., A-53.

39. Ibid., A-48

40. Ibid.

41. Ibid., A-49; testimony of Calvin Whaley, correctional supervisor, House Committee, *Hearing on the November 1987 Riots*, 154.

42. Bureau of Prisons, *Report to the Attorney General*, A-10–A-13, A-49–A-51.

43. Ibid., A-12.

44. "Behind the Prison Riot: Precautions Not Taken," *New York Times*, 6 December 1987.

45. Riot warnings are from Bureau of Prisons, *Report to the Attorney General*, A-49–A-51.

46. "For 11 Days, Cuban Unrest Boiled Over Inside the Pen," *Atlanta Journal*, 6 December 1987.

47. Bureau of Prisons, *Report to the Attorney General*, A-50.

48. Nacci, "Oakdale-Atlanta Prison Disturbances," 5.

49. Bureau of Prisons, *Report to the Attorney General*, A-49.

50. Ibid., A-50.

51. Ibid., A-13.

52. Ibid., A-14.

53. Ibid., A-49.

54. Whaley testimony, House Committee, *Hearing on the November 1987 Riots*, 150.

55. Bureau of Prisons, *Report to the Attorney General*, A-53.

56. Ibid., A-52.

57. Whaley testimony, House Committee, *Hearing on the November 1987 Riots*, 154.

58. "For 11 Days, Cuban Unrest Boiled Over Inside the Pen," *Atlanta Journal*, 6 December 1987.

59. "Prison Swept for Weapons and Traps," *New York Times*, 6 December 1987; "Cuban Rioters Turned into Efficient Jailers," *Chicago Tribune*, 16 December 1987.

60. Bureau of Prisons, *Report to the Attorney General*, Oakdale-27.

61. Memo from Attorney General Edwin Meese III to the Cuban detainees at the Oakdale Federal Detention Center, House Committee, *Hearing on the November 1987 Riots*, 175.

62. "Meese Offers to Delay Cuban Deportations," *Washington Post*, 24 November 1987; "Cuban Inmates Riot in a Second Prison over Immigrant Pact," *New York Times*, 24 November 1987.

63. "Cuban Inmates Riot in a Second Prison over Immigrant Pact," *New York Times*, 24 November 1987.

64. Roger A. Bell, Frederick J. Lanceley, Theodore B. Feldmann, Timothy H. Worley, Dwayne Fuselier, and Clinton Van Zandt, "Hostage Negotiations and Mental Health: Experiences from the Atlanta Prison Riot," *American Journal of Preventive Psychiatry and Neurology*, 3, no. 2 (Fall, 1991), 8–11.

65. "The Atlanta Riot," *Times-Picayune* (New Orleans), 25 November 1987.

66. "Army Advisers Dispatched to Pen from Fort Bragg," *Atlanta Journal*, 26 November 1987; "Talks with Cubans at a 'Standstill' at Atlanta Jail," *New York Times*, 25 November 1987.

67. Letter from Thomas M. Boyd, acting assistant attorney general, to Congressman Robert W. Kastenmeier, April 29, 1988, House Committee, *Hearing on the November 1987 Riots*, 259.

68. Ibid., 258; Bureau of Prisons, *Report to the Attorney General*, A-57.

69. Bureau of Prisons, *Report to the Attorney General*, A-58; Boyd letter to Kastenmeier, April 29, 1988, House Committee, *Hearing on the November 1987 Riots*, 262.

70. Bell et al., "Hostage Negotiations."

71. Ibid., 7.

72. Bureau of Prisons, *Report to the Attorney General*, A-59.

73. Ibid., A-69.

74. "Prison Uprising Transforms Street into 'Mini-City,'" *Atlanta Journal*, 28 November 1987.

75. Bureau of Prisons, *Report to the Attorney General*, A-73.

76. Ibid., A-70.

77. Ibid., Executive Summary-viii.

78. Ibid., A-62.

79. G. Dwayne Fuselier, Clinton Van Zandt, and Frederick Lanceley, "Negotiating the Protracted Incident: The Oakdale and Atlanta Prison Sieges," *FBI Law Enforcement Bulletin*, 58, no. 7 (July, 1989), 3.

80. "Inmates Free Six, Still Hold a Total of 94," *Atlanta Journal*, 25 November 1987.

81. Bureau of Prisons, *Report to the Attorney General*, A-65.

82. "Military Hostage Specialist Sent to Help F.B.I. at Atlanta Prison," *New York Times*, 26 November 1987.

83. Bureau of Prisons, *Report to the Attorney General*, A-24.

84. "As Talks Remain Deadlocked, Feds Shut Off Water and Heat," *Atlanta Journal*, 29 November 1987.

85. "Behind the Prison Riots," *New York Times*, 6 December 1987.

86. Testimony of Congressman John L. Lewis, House Committee, *Hearing on the November 1987 Riots*, 8–9; also, "Outside the Prison, Sobbing Wives," *New York Times*, 24 November 1987.

87. "Three Exiles Standoff Negotiators," *New York Times*, 27 November 1987.

88. "Behind the Prison Riots,"*New York Times*, 6 December 1987.

89. "Document of Disclosure and Requirements Concerning the Cuban Concessions and Final Decisions," House Committee, *Hearing on the November 1987 Riots*, 177.

90. Ibid.

91. Ibid., 177–178.

92. Ibid., 179.

93. Ibid.

94. "Response to 7 'Requirements' From Atlanta Detainees," House Committee, *Hearing on the November 1987 Riots*, 180.

95. Bureau of Prisons, *Report to the Attorney General,* Oakdale-40; Clinton Van Zandt and G. Dwayne Fuselier, "Nine Days of Crisis Negotiations: The Oakdale Siege," *Corrections Today* 51, no. 4 (July, 1989): 20, 22.

96. "Bishop Roman: A Near-Legendary Priest of the Old School," *Atlanta Journal*, 4 December 1987.

97. "Gary Leshaw's Request for Clarification from DOJ—Made before Atlanta Agreement Signed," House Committee, *Hearing on the November 1987 Riots*, 182.

98. "Despair, Anger, Joy: Pen Talks Ran Gamut, Top FBI Agent Recalls," *Atlanta Journal*, 8 December 1987.

99. Bureau of Prisons, *Report to the Attorney General*, A-41.

100. Lewis testimony, House Committee, *Hearing on the November 1987 Riots*, 8–9.

101. Comments by Representative Robert W. Kastenmeier, House Committee, *Hearing on the November 1987 Riots*, 1–2.

102. Testimony by Representative Clyde C. Holloway, House Committee, *Hearing on the November 1987 Riots*, 67.

103. Quoted in "Justice Department to Review Its Handling of Riots by Cubans," *Criminal Justice Newsletter*, 18, no. 24 (December 15, 1987).

Chapter 3. Federal Correctional Institution, Talladega, Alabama

1. The primary source for this chapter is a round of interviews conducted by the authors with the staff at the Talladega facility on December 22 and 23, 1991. A second key source is the BOP's report on the disturbance: U.S. Department of

Justice, Federal Bureau of Prisons, *A Report to the Attorney General: Hostage Situation, Federal Correctional Institution, Talladega, Alabama, August 21–30, 1991* (Washington, D.C.: Federal Bureau of Prisons, November 8, 1991) [hereinafter Report, 1991]. Information not otherwise cited is from the authors' interviews.

2. Bureau of Prisons, *Report, 1991*, 4.

3. Ibid.; letter (with attachments) from Rex J. Ford, associate deputy attorney general, U.S. Department of Justice, to Congressman William J. Hughes, December 11, 1991, House Subcommittee, *Hearing on Cuban Detainees and the Disturbance at the Talladega Federal Prison*, 102nd Cong., 1st sess., October 10, 1991, 268–276.

4. Testimony of J. Michael Quinlan, director of Federal Bureau of Prisons, House Subcommittee on Intellectual Property and Judicial Administration of the Committee on the Judiciary, *Hearing on Cuban Detainees and the Disturbance at the Talladega Federal Prison*, 102nd Cong., 1st sess., October 10, 1991, 268–276; Bureau of Prisons, *Report, 1991*, 21.

5. Bureau of Prisons, *Report, 1991*, 7.

6. Ibid., 5–6.

7. Ibid., 5,

8. Ibid., 7.

9. Ibid.

10. Richard Phillips, "Crisis in Talladega," *Corrections Today*, 53 no. 6 (December, 1991), 132.

11. Bureau of Prisons, *Report, 1991*, 7.

12. Ibid.

13. Ibid.

14. The number of detainees on the yard is an estimate made by staff after the riot. The record on this was destroyed in the disturbance. Bureau of Prisons, *Report, 1991*, 8.

15. Ibid.

16. Ibid., 9.

17. Ibid., 10.

18. Ibid., 11.

19. Ibid., 127.

20. Ibid.

21. Phillips, "Crisis in Talladega," 127.

22. Ibid.; Bureau of Prisons, *Report, 1991*, 30.

23. Bureau of Prisons, *Report, 1991*, 32.

24. Authors' interview.

25. Bureau of Prisons, *Report, 1991*, 17, 31.

26. "Cuban Inmates Seize Prison Wing," *New York Times*, 22 August 1991.

27. Thomas J. Fagan and Clinton R. Van Zandt, "Even in 'Non-Negotiable' Situations, Negotiation Plays an Important Role," *Corrections Today 55*, no. 8 (April, 1993), 137.

28. Ibid.

29. "1987 Cuban Riots Taught Both Sides," *New York Times*, 27 August 1991.

30. Bureau of Prisons, *Report, 1991*, 12.

31. Ibid., 13.

32. Ibid., 12.

33. Ibid., 15.

34. "No Progress Seen in Siege at Prison," *New York Times*, 25 August 1991.

35. Bureau of Prisons, *Report, 1991*, 15.

36. "1987 Cuban Riots Taught Both Sides," *New York Times*, 27 August 1991.

37. Bureau of Prisons, *Report, 1991*, 17.

38. Ibid., 21.

39. Ibid., 23.

40. Ibid., Appendix C.

41. Ibid., 129.

42. "U.S. Agents Storm Prison in Alabama, Freeing 9 Hostages," *New York Times*, 31 August 1991.

43. Bureau of Prisons, *Report, 1991*, iii, 25; Phillips, "Crisis in Talladega," 131.

44. "F.B.I. Rescue Team's Baptism of Fire," *New York Times*, 31 August 1991.

45. "U.S. Agents Storm Prison in Alabama, Freeing 9 Hostages," *New York Times,* 31 August 1991.

46. Ibid.

Chapter 4. *Pennsylvania State Correctional Institution at Camp Hill*

1. Arlin M. Adams, George M. Leader, and Leroy Irvis, "The Final Report of the Governor's Commission to Investigate Disturbances at Camp Hill Correctional Institution" (Harrisburg, Pa., photocopy, December 21, 1989), 4.

2. Ibid, 50; Commonwealth of Pennsylvania, Senate Judiciary Committee, *Public Hearings on Recent Incidents at Pennsylvania State Correctional Institution*, January 10, 1990, 59.

3. Senate Judiciary Committee, *Public Hearings*, January 10, 1990, 75.

4. Quoted from testimony of the superintendent, Commonwealth of Pennsylvania, Senate Judiciary Committee, *Public Hearings on Recent Incidents at Pennsylvania State Correctional Institution*, February 16, 1990, 10. This phrase (or a similar one), however, was used by many others.

5. Commonwealth of Pennsylvania, House Judiciary Committee, "A Report on the 1989 Prison Disturbances and Riots at State Correctional Institution at Grateford, Huntingdon, Rockview, and Camp Hill" (Harrisburg, Pa., photocopy, November 19, 1990), 10.

6. Senate Judiciary Committee, *Public Hearings*, January 10, 1990, 74, 231.

7. Senate Judiciary Committee, *Public Hearings*, February 16, 1990, 12.

8. Senate Judiciary Committee, *Public Hearings*, January 10, 1990, 11.

9. This section is based on John H. Kramer, "The Evolution of Pennsylvania's Sentencing Guidelines," *Overcrowded Times: Solving the Prison Problem*, 4, no. 2 (August, 1992), 6–9; and Commonwealth of Pennsylvania, House of Representatives Committee on Judiciary, *Prison Disturbances at State Correctional Institution at Camp Hill*, March 7, 1990, 176–190.

10. Sentencing guidelines prescribe a relatively narrow range of sentences for an offender based on the gravity of his or her crime and criminal record.

11. Senate Judiciary Committee, *Public Hearings*, February 16, 1990, 74; Commonwealth of Pennsylvania, House of Representatives Committee on Judi-

ciary, *Prison Disturbances at State Correctional Institution at Camp Hill*, January 16, 1990, 81.

12. Senate Judiciary Committee, *Public Hearings*, February 16, 1990, 10.

13. Adams et al., *The Final Report*, 9.

14. Senate Judiciary Committee, *Public Hearings*, January 10, 1990, 174 .

15. House of Representatives Committee on Judiciary, *Prison Disturbances*, January 16, 1990, 10; Commonwealth of Pennsylvania, House of Representatives Committee on Judiciary, *Prison Disturbances at State Correctional Institution at Camp Hill*, January 17, 1990, 141.

16. George Camp and Camille Camp, *Management of Crowded Prisons* (Washington, D.C.: National Institute of Corrections, 1989); Gerald G. Gaes, "Challenging Beliefs about Prison Crowding," *Federal Prisons Journal* 2, no. 3 (Summer, 1991), 22–23.

17. Senate Judiciary Committee, *Public Hearings*, February 16, 1990, 22.

18. Senate Judiciary Committee, *Public Hearings*, January 10, 1990, 18.

19. Senate Judiciary Committee, *Public Hearings*, February 16, 1990, 124.

20. Senate Judiciary Committee, *Public Hearings*, January 10, 1990, 117.

21. Ibid., 16.

22. Senate Judiciary Committee, *Public Hearings*, February 16, 1990, 124.

23. Ibid., 126.

24. Ibid.

25. House of Representatives Committee on Judiciary, *Prison Disturbances*, January 17, 1990, 120.

26. Senate Judiciary Committee, *Public Hearings*, January 10, 1990, 171.

27. Philip Selznick, *Leadership in Administration: A Sociological Interpretation* (New York: Harper and Row, 1957).

28. Senate Judiciary Committee, *Public Hearings*, January 10, 1990, 67, 134; authors' interviews.

29. Commonwealth of Pennsylvania, Senate Judiciary Committee, *Public Hearings on Recent Incidents at Pennsylvania State Correctional Institution*, February 21, 1990, 99.

30. Senate Judiciary Committee, *Public Hearings*, February 16, 1990, 51

31. Commonwealth of Pennsylvania, Senate Judiciary Committee, *Public Hearings on Recent Incidents at Pennsylvania State Correctional Institution*, February 1, 1990, 127.

32. In testimony, a nurse stated that, over a several-year period, the number of doses of medication that they dispensed to inmates rose from 75,000 per month to 179,000 per month, with no increase in nursing staff. Senate Judiciary Committee, *Public Hearings*, February 21, 1990, 98.

33. Ibid., 99.

34. After the policy was implemented, the Camp Hill administration decided that the policy change did require the approval of the central office. The process of securing this approval was just underway when the riot began. Senate Judiciary Committee, *Public Hearings*, January 10, 1990, 48.

35. Ibid.

36. Commonwealth of Pennsylvania, Senate Judiciary Committee, *Public Hearings on Recent Incidents at Pennsylvania State Correctional Institution*, November 27, 1989, 45, 134.

37. Ibid., 46.

38. Senate Judiciary Committee, *Public Hearings*, February 21, 1990, 103.

39. Senate Judiciary Committee, *Public Hearings*, February 16, 1990, 141.

40. Senate Judiciary Committee, *Public Hearings*, February 21, 1990, 84; House of Representatives Committee on Judiciary, *Prison Disturbances*, January 17, 1990, 86.

41. Adams et al., *The Final Report*, 12.

42. Commonwealth of Pennsylvania, Senate Judiciary Committee, *Public Hearings on Recent Incidents at Pennsylvania State Correctional Institution*, February 9, 1990, 3.

43. Senate Judiciary Committee, *Public Hearings*, February 21, 1990, 82.

44. Adams et al., *The Final Report*, 12.

45. Senate Judiciary Committee, *Public Hearings*, February 16, 1990, 53.

46. Adams et al., *The Final Report*, 13.

47. Senate Judiciary Committee, *Public Hearings*, November 27, 1989, 71.

48. Commonwealth of Pennsylvania, Senate Judiciary Committee, *Public Hearings on Recent Disturbance at the Huntingdon State Correctional Institution*, December 18, 1989, 14, 17.

49. Estimates from Senate Judiciary Committee, *Public Hearings*, November 27, 1989, 17; also, Adams et al., *The Final Report*, 13.

50. Based primarily on the testimony of the sergeant on the scene (Senate Judiciary Committee, *Public Hearings*, November 27, 1989, 4), and corroborated by other testimony.

51. Commonwealth of Pennsylvania, Senate Judiciary Committee, *Public Hearings on Recent Incidents at Pennsylvania State Correctional Institution*, October 31, 1989, 34; Adams et al., *The Final Report*, 14.

52. Senate Judiciary Committee, *Public Hearings*, November 27, 1989, 4; House of Representatives Committee on Judiciary, *Prison Disturbances*, January 17, 1990, 78.

53. The Adams report puts the number at 300 (Adams et al., *The Final Report*, 13). Camp Hill's internal report on the incident puts the figure at between 150 and 200, ("Report of Extraordinary Occurrence, Commonwealth of Pennsylvania: October 25–26, 1989 Disturbances," [State Correctional Institution, Camp Hill, January 1, 1990, photocopy], 1).

54. House of Representatives Committee on Judiciary, *Prison Disturbances*, January 17, 1990, 78–79.

55. Authors' interview with staff.

56. "Report of Extraordinary Occurrence, October 25–26, 1989," 1.

57. Ibid., 2.

58. Adams et al., *The Final Report*, 42.

59. "Report of Extraordinary Occurrence, October 25–26, 1989," 1; authors' interview with staff.

60. Adams et al., *The Final Report*, 15.

61. Ibid.

62. "Report of Extraordinary Occurrence, October 25–26, 1989," 2; House of Representatives Committee on Judiciary, *Prison Disturbances*, January 16, 1990, 30.

63. Senate Judiciary Committee, *Public Hearings*, January 10, 1990, 48.

64. "Report of Extraordinary Occurrence, October 25–26, 1989," 2.

65. Adams et al., *The Final Report*, 17.

66. House of Representatives Committee on Judiciary, *Prison Disturbances*, January 16, 1990, 122.

67. Ibid.
68. Senate Judiciary Committee, *Public Hearings*, February 16, 1990, 131.
69. Ibid., 111.
70. Ibid., 131.
71. Ibid., 19.
72. Ibid.
73. House of Representatives Committee on Judiciary, *Prison Disturbances*, January 16, 1990, 12.
74. Senate Judiciary Committee, *Public Hearings*, February 16, 1990, 18.
75. Ibid.
76. Ibid.
77. Ibid., 17.
78. Ibid.
79. Ibid., 21.
80. House of Representatives Committee on Judiciary, *Prison Disturbances*, January 16, 1990, 14.
81. Senate Judiciary Committee, *Public Hearings*, February 16, 1990, 20, 22.
82. House of Representatives Committee on Judiciary, *Prison Disturbances*, March 7, 1990, 60.
83. Senate Judiciary Committee, *Public Hearings*, February 16, 1990, 15.
84. House of Representatives Committee on Judiciary, *Prison Disturbances*, January 16, 1990, 178.
85. Senate Judiciary Committee, *Public Hearings*, November 27, 1989, 10.
86. Ibid., 17; House of Representatives Committee on Judiciary, *Prison Disturbances*, January 16, 1990, 107.
87. Senate Judiciary Committee, *Public Hearings*, November 27, 1989, 52.
88. House of Representatives Committee on Judiciary, *Prison Disturbances*, March 7, 1990, 61.
89. Senate Judiciary Committee, *Public Hearings*, February 16, 1990, 18.
90. "Report of Extraordinary Occurrence, October 25–26, 1989," 5.
91. House of Representatives Committee on Judiciary, *Prison Disturbances*, January 16, 1990, 107.
92. Ibid., 100.
93. Ibid., 102.
94. Adams et al., *The Final Report*, 28–29.
95. Ibid., 28.
96. Ibid., 29.
97. Senate Judiciary Committee, *Public Hearings*, January 10, 1990, 68.
98. House of Representatives Committee on Judiciary, *Prison Disturbances*, March 7, 1990, 105.
99. Senate Judiciary Committee, *Public Hearings*, November 27, 1989, 28, 40.
100. Ibid., 8.
101. Ibid., 115.
102. Ibid., 10.
103. House of Representatives Committee on Judiciary, *Prison Disturbances*, January 16, 1990, 105.
104. Ibid., 117.

105. Senate Judiciary Committee, Public Hearings; January 10, 1990, 69, 70.

106. "Report of Extraordinary Occurrence, October 25–26, 1989," 5.

107. Ibid., 6.

108. Ibid.

109. Senate Judiciary Committee, *Public Hearings*, November 27, 1989, 17.

110. Adams et al., *The Final Report*, 30.

111. Senate Judiciary Committee, *Public Hearings*, February 16, 1990, 25.

112. Adams et al., *The Final Report*, 31.

113. Senate Judiciary Committee, *Public Hearings*, January 10, 1990, 157.

114. Senate Judiciary Committee, *Public Hearings*, November 27, 1989, 13; Adams et al., *The Final Report*, 31.

115. Senate Judiciary Committee, *Public Hearings*, February 1, 1990, 124.

116. Senate Judiciary Committee, *Public Hearings*, November 27, 1989, 14.

117. "Report of Extraordinary Occurrence, October 25–26, 1989," 7.

118. Senate Judiciary Committee, *Public Hearings*, February 1, 1990, 90; Senate Judiciary Committee, *Public Hearings*, February 16, 1990, 127.

119. "Report of Extraordinary Occurrence, October 25–26, 1989," 7.

120. Senate Judiciary Committee, *Public Hearings*, February 1, 1990, 10; Adams et al., *The Final Report*, 43.

121. Senate Judiciary Committee, *Public Hearings*, February 1, 1990, 11.

122. House of Representatives Committee on Judiciary, *Prison Disturbances*, January 16, 1990, 55.

123. Senate Judiciary Committee, *Public Hearings*, February 16, 1990, 49.

124. Ibid., 27.

125. Ibid.

126. House of Representatives Committee on Judiciary, *Prison Disturbances*, January 17, 1990, 35; Senate Judiciary Committee, *Public Hearings*, February 16, 1990, 47; House of Representatives Committee on Judiciary, *Prison Disturbances*, January 16, 1990, 20.

127. House of Representatives Committee on Judiciary, *Prison Disturbances*, January 17, 1990, 35.

128. House of Representatives Committee on Judiciary, *Prison Disturbances*, January 16, 1990, 67.

129. Ibid., 32.

130. Senate Judiciary Committee, *Public Hearings*, January 10, 1990, 160.

131. House of Representatives Committee on Judiciary, *Prison Disturbances*, January 16, 1990, 107.

132. Adams et al., *The Final Report*, 33.

133. House of Representatives Committee on Judiciary, *Prison Disturbances*, January 16, 1990, 33.

134. "Report of Extraordinary Occurrence, October 25–26, 1989," 2.

135. Senate Judiciary Committee, *Public Hearings*, February 16, 1990, 137.

136. Adams et al., *The Final Report*, 34.

137. Senate Judiciary Committee, *Public Hearings*, October 31, 1989, 57.

138. Ibid.

139. Senate Judiciary Committee, *Public Hearings*, February 16, 1990, 138.

140. Ibid.

141. Ibid., 5.

142. "Report of Extraordinary Occurrence, October 25–26, 1989," 8; House of Representatives Committee on Judiciary, *Prison Disturbances*, January 16, 1990, 84.

143. Senate Judiciary Committee, *Public Hearings*, February 16, 1990, 139.

144. Adams et al., *The Final Report*, 35.

145. Senate Judiciary Committee, *Public Hearings*, February 16, 1990, 138.

146. Adams et al., *The Final Report*, 36.

147. House of Representatives Committee on Judiciary, *Prison Disturbances*, March 7, 1990, 27.

148. Senate Judiciary Committee, *Public Hearings*, October 31, 1989, 12.

149. Ibid., 12, 13.

150. "1,280 Inmates Remain Manacled," *Harrisburg Patriot*, 2, November 1989.

151. Senate Judiciary Committee, *Public Hearings*, January 10, 1990, 13; authors' interviews.

152. "Report of Extraordinary Occurrence, October 25–26, 1989," 8.

153. Ibid., 9.

154. "Casey to Form Riot-Probe Panel," *Harrisburg Patriot*, 29 October 1989.

155. Senate Judiciary Committee, *Public Hearings*, February 16, 1990, 78–79.

156. Senate Judiciary Committee, *Public Hearings*, January 10, 1990, 23.

157. Senate Judiciary Committee, *Public Hearings*, February 16, 1990, 156.

158. House Judiciary Committee, *A Report on the 1989 Prison Disturbances and Riots*, 6.

159. "Prison Chief Resigns," *Post Gazette* (Harrisburg, Pa.) 21 February 1990.

160. Senate Judiciary Committee, *Public Hearings*, February 16, 1990, 117.

161. Authors' interview with staff, August 4, 1993.

162. Ibid.

163. Based on both the authors' observation of the facility and testimony before the state legislature. The testimony includes this statement by a captain: "I feel safe going in there now, because what I experienced was a total turn around with . . . [the new] Superintendent." Senate Judiciary Committee, *Public Hearings*, January 10, 1990, 65.

164. Authors' interview with staff, August 4, 1993.

Chapter 5.   *Mack Alford Correctional Institution, Oklahoma*

1. This chapter is based on two sources of information. First, in March 1991, we conducted a set of interviews with (a) senior officials in the central office in Oklahoma City, including the director and his executive staff, and (b) Mack Alford staff at all ranks, including the former hostages. Second, the department provided us with its report on the riot, as well as the material on which the report was based. The latter included transcripts of interviews of 31 inmates (including the riot leaders) and 104 staff members at all ranks.

2. A Mack Alford policy paper, "Hostage Situations," dated June 1987, states: "Commands considered as being issued by any person held hostage will be considered as being issued while under duress and, irrespective of their position, shall be disregarded."

Chapter 6. Coxsackie Correctional Facility, New York

1. William A. Gamson, *The Strategy of Social Protest*, 2nd ed. (Homewood, Ill.: Dorsey, 1990), 139.

2. Charles Tilly, Louise Tilly, and Richard Tilly, *The Rebellious Century: 1830–1930* (Cambridge, Mass.: Harvard University Press, 1975), 293.

3. This chapter relies on a number of sources, in addition to the authors' interviews conducted both in the New York State Department of Correctional Services' headquarters in Albany and at the Coxsackie facility. One is a report by the New York State Commission of Correction, an independent agency within the executive branch that oversees the operation of all state correctional institutions and local jails. Commission staff members were on site as observers for most of the incident. New York State Commission of Correction, "Investigation of Incident at Coxsackie Correctional Facility Special Housing Unit August 1, 1988" (Albany, N.Y., photocopy, January, 1989).

Information regarding the facility, including that on capacity, population, and programming, is taken from a report prepared for a standards compliance audit of the institution, which was conducted on February 5–7, 1990, by the American Correctional Association. Coxsackie Correctional Facility, Commission for Corrections, "Standards Compliance Audit: Coxsackie Correctional Facility, February 5, 6, and 7, 1990" (photocopy, n.d.).

Finally, much of the chronological information is culled from several internal reports. They include Superintendent J. Twomey, "Unusual Incident Report," August 1, 1988; Inspector General's Office, New York State Department of Correctional Services, "Investigation at the Coxsackie Correctional Facility on August 1, 1988. Preliminary Report, August 28, 1988"; and memo by Richard Roy [director, crisis intervention unit] to Inspector General's Office, "Chronological Log," August 10, 1988.

4. Authors' interviews with staff.

5. "Prison Siege Is Described as Unplanned," *New York Times*, 3 August 1988.

6. Commission of Correction, "Investigation of Incident," 33.

7. Ibid., 34–35.

8. Ibid., 35.

9. Ibid.

10. Memo by Roy, "Chronological Log," 1.

11. "Reasoning Ended Prison Revolt," *Daily News* (New York), 3 August 1988.

12. The record is not clear about when the electricity was turned back on. A log kept by a central office official on the scene reports that electricity was restored at 11:45 A.M. In the same log, entries around noon indicate that the Central Office was told that the electricity in the unit had not been turned on and that inmates were upset about that. In any event, the power was restored not later than 12:20 P.M. Memo by Roy, "Chronological Log," 1, 2.

13. Ibid., 6.

14. Commission of Correction, "Investigation of Incident," 20.

15. Ibid., 7–11.

16. Ibid., 12.

17. "Coxsackie Crisis, '15 Hours of Terror,'" *Albany Times Union*, 3 August 1988.

18. Inspector General's Office, "Investigation at the Coxsackie Correctional Facility," 12.

Chapter 7. *Kirkland Correctional Institution, South Carolina*

1. A note on sources: In the fall of 1990, the authors conducted interviews with staff both at the department's central headquarters in Columbia and at the Kirkland facility. Another source was a report on the riot by William D. Catoe [deputy commissioner for operations] and James L. Harvey [regional administrator], "A Review of the Kirkland Correctional Institution Disturbance on April 1, 1986, A Report for the Board of Corrections and the Commissioner of the South Carolina Department of Corrections" (Columbia: South Carolina Department of Corrections, photocopy, May 20, 1986). A third source is a videotape on the riot prepared by the department for training. Unless otherwise noted, information is from the authors' interviews.
2. Catoe and Harvey, "Kirkland Correctional Institution Disturbance," 24.
3. Ibid., 19.
4. Ibid., 6.
5. Ibid., 7.
6. Ibid., 14. A detailed description of this counseling program is in Lawrence H. Bergmann and Timothy R. Queen, "The Aftermath: Treating Traumatic Stress Is Crucial," *Corrections Today*, 49 (August, 1987), 100–104; and Anonymous, "Correctional Employees Receive Debriefing after Prison Riot," *Counseling and Readjustment Services Update*, 1, no. 2 (Columbia: State of South Carolina, October, 1986), 1–2.

Chapter 8. *Arizona State Prison Complex, Cimarron Unit*

1. Note on sources: The authors conducted interviews with department staff (in Phoenix) and Cimarron staff (in Tucson) from February 13 through 17, 1991. Information not otherwise cited is from these interviews.
2. "Guards' Gunfire Injures 15 Inmates in Big Brawl," *Arizona Daily Star*, 22 June 1990.
3. "Buckshot Injures 15 in Inmate Uprising," *Scottsdale* (Arizona) *Daily Progress*, 22 June 1990.
4. "Prison-Riot Probe to Focus on Guard's Shooting at Inmates," *Arizona Republic*, 23 June 1990.
5. "Prison Officials Clean Up, Investigate Causes of Racially Divided Fight," *Arizona Daily Star*, 23 June 1990.
6. "Report: Guard Justified in Shooting at Inmates," *Phoenix Gazette*, 11 August 1990.
7. "Prison Officials Clean Up," *Arizona Daily Star*, 23 June 1990.
8. Arizona Department of Corrections, Criminal Investigation Bureau, "Supplemental Report" (Phoenix: Department of Corrections, photocopy, July 27, 1990), 7–8.
9. Paul K. Nixon, Arizona Department of Public Safety, "Investigative Report, Department of Corrections Riot/Incident, Cimarron North Prison Complex" (Phoenix: Department of Corrections, photocopy, August 1, 1990), 5.
10. Ibid., 6.
11. "Cimarron Unit Quiet after Lockdown," *Tucson Citizen*, 23 June 1990.

12. Ibid.; Nixon, Arizona Department of Public Safety, "Investigative Report," 6.

13. "Prison Brawl Injures 24 Men," *Tucson Citizen*, 22 June 1990; "Cimarron Unit Quiet," *Tucson Citizen*, 23 June 1990.

14. Nixon, Arizona Department of Public Safety, "Investigative Report," 7.

15. Ibid.; "Prison Riot Injures 21 Inmates, Six Guards at Tucson Facility," *Casa Grande Dispatch*, 22 June 1990.

16. Nixon, Arizona Department of Public Safety, "Investigative Report," 8.

17. This section is from the authors' interviews with staff, especially the warden. Information is also drawn from Criminal Investigation Bureau, "Supplemental Report"; and "Prison Officials Clean Up," *Arizona Daily Star*, 23 June 1990.

Chapter 9.   Idaho State Correctional Institution

1. The events described are from information gathered through the authors' interviews both at the central office and at the facility. A second source is a report prepared by a four-person panel, Bona Miller (deputy director of administration, Idaho Department of Corrections), chair, "Serious Incident Review Report, Unit 9 Riot, September 25, 1988" (Boise: Department of Corrections, photocopy, October 24, 1988).

Chapter 10.   Before the Riot

1. U.S. Department of Justice, Federal Bureau of Prisons, *A Report to the Attorney General: Hostage Situation, Federal Correctional Institution, Talladega, Alabama, August 21–30, 1991* (Washington, D.C.: Federal Bureau of Prisons, November 8, 1991), 37.

2. American Correctional Association, *Causes, Preventive Measures, and Methods of Controlling Riots and Disturbances in Correctional Institutions*, 3rd ed. (Laurel, Md.: American Correctional Association, 1990) [hereinafter *Riots and Disturbances*, 1990] 74. This publication, while issued by the American Correctional Association, is not a policy statement voted on by their governing body.

3. Jonathan M. House provides an excellent discussion of the problems of intelligence. *Military Intelligence, 1870–1991* (Westport, Conn.: Greenwood Press, 1993), 1–27.

4. U.S. Department of Justice, Federal Bureau of Prisons, *A Report to the Attorney General on the Disturbances at the Federal Detention Center, Oakdale, Louisiana, and the U.S. Penitentiary, Atlanta, Georgia, February 1, 1988*, (Washington, D.C.: Federal Bureau of Prisons), Atlanta-50 [hereinafter *Report, 1988*].

5. *Report, 1988*, Atlanta-50–Atlanta-52.

6. Ibid., Atlanta-49.

7. Ibid.

8. Ibid., Atlanta-48.

9. Ibid.

10. Philip Selznick, *Leadership in Administration: A Sociological Interpretation* (New York: Harper and Row, 1957), 105–106; James Q. Wilson, *Bureaucracy: What Government Agencies Do and Why They Do It* (New York: Basic Books, 1989), 26–27, 109–110; Gerald Garvey, *Facing the Bureaucracy: Living and Dying in a Public Agency* (San Francisco, Jossey-Bass, 1993), 1–10, 219–220.

11. American Correctional Association, *Riots and Disturbances*, 1990, 42.

12. William D. Leeke, "Prevention and Deterrence of Violence in Correctional Institutions—Research Efforts to Date," in U.S. Department of Justice, Law Enforcement Administration, National Institute of Law Enforcement and Criminal Justice, *Prevention of Violence in Correctional Institutions* (Washington, D.C.: Government Printing Office, 1973).

13. South Carolina Department of Corrections, Collective Violence Project, *Collective Violence in Correctional Institutions: A Search for Causes.* (Columbia: South Carolina Department of Corrections, 1973).

14. *Riots and Disturbances*, 1990, 38.

15. Letter from Acting Assistant Attorney Thomas M. Boyd to Congressman Robert W. Kastenmeier, March 18, 1988, reprinted in *Hearing before the Subcommittee on Courts, Civil Liberties, and the Administration of Justice of the Committee on the Judiciary, House of Representatives on Mariel Cuban Detainees: Events Preceding and Following the November 1987 Riots*, 100th Cong., 2nd sess., February 4, 1988 (Washington, D.C.: U.S. Government Printing Office), 213.

16. This point is made in regard to military readiness by Melvin R. Laird and Lawrence J. Korb in *The Problem of Military Readiness* (Washington, D.C.: American Enterprise Institute, 1980), 17.

17. In an analogous context, the problem of coordinating between tactical and negotiation units is illustrated by the FBI's response to the standoff at the Branch Davidian compound, Waco, Texas, February 28–April 19, 1993. According to the Department of Justice's report on the incident, the negotiating and tactical teams often felt at odds with each other, "more often contradictory than complementary" in strategy, tactics, and thinking. *Report to the Deputy Attorney General on the Events at Waco, Texas, February 28 to April 19, 1993* (Washington, D.C.: U.S. Government Printing Office, 1993), 139–142.

18. From the Latin, *si vis pacen, para bellum*. Mentioned and discussed by Edward Luttwak, *Strategy: The Logic of War and Peace"* (Cambridge, Mass.: Harvard University Press, 1987), 33ff.

19. Larry Hirschhorn, "History of Segregation Correctional Center: A Case Study in the Role of Leadership in a Troubled Prison Setting" (Philadelphia: The Program on Correctional Leadership and Innovation, The Wharton Center for Applied Research, photocopy, October, 1986).

Chapter 11.   During the Riot

1. On command more generally, see Jay Shafritz, Todd Shafritz, and David Robertson, *Dictionary of Military Science* (New York: Facts on File, 1989), 96–97; John I. Alger, *Definitions and Doctrine of the Military Art: Past and Present* (West Point: U.S. Military Academy, 1985), 88–89.

2. Shafritz et al., *Military Science*, 364, 380.

3. The evidence for this (as assembled by the Adams commission) allows for no definitive conclusion. The Adams commission infers that the second riot was probably planned "from the swiftness with which the inmates released themselves." Arlin M. Adams, George M. Leader, and Leroy Irvis, "The Final Report of the Governor's Commission to Investigate Disturbances at Camp Hill Correctional Institution" (Harrisburg, Pa.: Commonwealth of Pennsylvania, photocopy, December 21, 1989), 30.

4. One does not need a special psychology to understand why inmates would be attracted to the drama of a riot. Kenneth E. Boulding cites an English historian as having said, "what people really want in the world is trouble, and if they do not have enough of it, they will create it artificially, the institution of sport being the proof" (Kenneth E. Boulding, *Conflict and Defense: A General Theory* [New York: Harper and Row, 1962], 306). Of course, a riot adds more than zest to prison life. Hostages may be taken and, in some case, treated brutally.

More difficult to explain is how, or if, inmates weigh the benefits of a riot (the inherent value of "trouble"; possible concessions) against its costs (lost privileges; additional years of confinement). We still need to learn much more about what a riot looks like from inmates' point of view.

5. The 1981 edition of the American Correctional Association manual on riots quotes a practitioner who states that negotiations should *never* be attempted:

> Prison disturbances occur almost every day, all with the potential of becoming another New Mexico . . . The key is you don't negotiate . . . Hostages are much more likely to be injured or killed if there is a drawn out negotiation process than if quick action is taken. (American Correctional Association, *Riots and Disturbances in Correctional Institutions: A Discussion of Causes, Preventive Measures and Methods of Control* [College Park, Md.: American Correctional Association, 1981], 34)

The success in negotiating the end of the Atlanta/Oakdale disturbances may have further diminished the support for this position. The 1990 edition of the manual, which draws heavily on the Atlanta/Oakdale riots for illustrative material, does not mention the "no negotiation" position.

6. Based on data collected by the authors from the *New York Times*.

7. Adams et al., *The Final Report*, 2.

8. Based, in part, on an author's interview with Frederick Lanceley, one of the FBI negotiators.

9. American Correctional Association, *Riots and Disturbances*, 1990, 42.

10. Ibid.

11. Frank Bolz and E. Hershey, *Hostage Cop* (New York: Rawson, Wade, 1979), 240; John T. Dolan and G. Dwayne Fuselier, "A Guide for First Responders to Hostage Situations," *FBI Law Enforcement Bulletin*, 58, no. 4 (April, 1989), 12.

12. Thomas J. Fagan and Clinton R. Van Zandt, "Lesson from Talladega: Even in 'Non-negotiable' Situations, Negotiation Plays an Important Role," *Corrections Today* 55 (April, 1993), 132, 134, 136–141.

13. This point is made by Howard Raiffa with regard to multiparty negotiations in general in *The Art and Science of Negotiation* (Cambridge, Mass.: Harvard University Press, 1982), 251–255.

14. U.S. Department of Justice, Federal Bureau of Prisons, *A Report to the Attorney General on the Disturbances at the Federal Detention Center, Oakdale, Louisiana, and the U.S. Penitentiary, Atlanta, Georgia, February 1, 1988* (Washington, D.C.: Federal Bureau of Prisons), Atlanta-62 [hereinafter *Report, 1988*].

15. Roger A. Bell, Frederick J. Lanceley, Theodore B. Feldmann, Timothy H. Worley, Dwayne Fuselier, and Clinton Van Zandt, "Hostage Negotiations and Mental Health: Experiences from the Atlanta Prison Riot," *American Journal of Preventive Psychiatry and Neurology*, 3, no. 2 (Fall, 1991), 9.

16. G. Dwayne Fuselier, "What Every Negotiator Would Like His Chief to Know," *FBI Law Enforcement Bulletin* 55, no. 3 (March, 1986), 14; Michael

G. Wargo, "The Chief's Role in a Hostage/Barricade Subject Incident," *The Police Chief* 56 (November, 1989), 59–62.

17. Boulding, *Conflict and Defense*, 319–320; Richard E. Walton and Robert B. McKersie, *A Behavior Theory of Labor Negotiations* (New York: McGraw-Hill, 1965), 111–112; James A. Schellenberg, *The Science of Conflict* (New York: Oxford University Press, 1982), 203–219; Raymond A. Friedman, *Front Stage, Backstage: The Dramatic Structure of Labor Negotiations* (Cambridge, Mass.: MIT Press, 1994), 85–112.

18. Ann Douglas, *Industrial Peacemaking* (New York: Columbia University Press, 1962), 42.

19. G. Dwayne Fuselier, Clinton Van Zandt, and Frederick Lanceley, "Negotiating the Protracted Incident: The Oakdale and Atlanta Prison Sieges," *FBI Law Enforcement Bulletin*, 58, no. 7 (July, 1989), 3.

20. Bell et al., "Hostage Negotiations," 11.

21. *Report, 1988*, Atlanta-62–Atlanta-64.

22. Roger Fisher and William Ury, *Getting to Yes: Negotiating Agreement without Giving In* (New York: Penguin, 1981), 118–122; Roger Fisher, Elizabeth Kopelman, and Andrea K. Schneider, *Beyond Machiavelli: Tools for Coping with Conflict* (Cambridge, Mass.: Harvard University Press, 1994), 128–132; Raiffa, *The Art and Science of Negotiation*, 210–217.

23. Raiffa, *Art and Science of Negotiation*, 254.

24. William Ury, *Getting Past No: Negotiating with Difficult People* (New York: Bantam, 1991).

25. William D. Catoe (Deputy Commissioner for Operations) and James L. Harvey (Regional Administrator), "A Review of the Kirkland Correctional Institution Disturbance on April 1, 1986, A Report for the Board of Corrections and the Commissioner of the South Carolina Department of Corrections" (Columbia: South Carolina Department of Corrections, photocopy, May 20, 1986), 6.

26. Dolan and Fuselier, "First Responders to Hostage Situations," 12.

27. Doland and Fuselier give the example of a hostage holder demanding a car and $100,000 in 30 minutes. A suggested response would be "O.K. I understand you would like some money and transportation, and I'll make sure someone starts working on it as soon as they get here." Ibid.

28. Fuselier, "What Every Negotiator," 15.

29. Frederick J. Lanceley, "The Antisocial Personality as a Hostage-Taker," *Journal of Police Science and Administration*, 9, no. 1 (1981), 32.

30. Dolan and Fuselier, "First Responders to Hostage Situations," 11.

31. Fisher and Ury, *Getting to Yes*, 35–37; Ury, *Getting Past No*, 37–40.

32. Fuselier, "What Every Negotiator," 15.

33. *Report, 1988*, Atlanta-86.

Chapter 12. After the Riot

1. Commonwealth of Pennsylvania, Senate Judiciary Committee, *Public Hearings on Recent Incidents at Pennsylvania State Correctional Institution*, February 16, 1990, 72, 73.

2. Helpful here was Rosabeth Moss Kanter, Barry A. Stein, and Todd D. Jick, *The Challenge of Organizational Change: How Companies Experience It and Leaders Guide It* (New York: Free Press, 1992), 243–247.

3. Ohio Civil Service Employees Association, AFSCME Local 11, "Report and Recommendations Concerning the Ohio Department of Rehabilitative and Correction and the Southern Ohio Correctional Facility, Lucasville, Ohio" (Columbus, photocopy, n.d.), 64; also, Simon Dinitz et al., "Final Report and Recommendations of the Governor's Select Committee on Corrections" (Columbus, photocopy, January, 1994).

4. David A. Garvin, "Building a Learning Organization," *Harvard Business Review*, 71 (July/August, 1993), 78–91; Barbara Ettorre, "Benchmarking: The Next Generation," *Management Review*, 82 (June, 1993), 10–16.

5. Robert C. Camp, *Benchmarking: The Search for Industry Best Practices That Lead to Superior Performance* (Milwaukee, Wis.: ASQC Quality Press, 1989).

Index